Worlds Apart

Worlds Apart: The and the Theater in Anglo-American Thought, 1550–1750

JEAN-CHRISTOPHE AGNEW

*American Studies Program
and Department of History
Yale University*

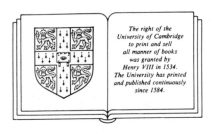

The right of the
University of Cambridge
to print and sell
all manner of books
was granted by
Henry VIII in 1534.
The University has printed
and published continuously
since 1584.

CAMBRIDGE UNIVERSITY PRESS

CAMBRIDGE
NEW YORK   NEW ROCHELLE
MELBOURNE   SYDNEY

Published by the Press Syndicate of the University of Cambridge
The Pitt Building, Trumpington Street, Cambridge CB2 1RP
32 East 57th Street, New York, NY 10022, USA
10 Stamford Road, Oakleigh, Melbourne 3166, Australia

First published 1986
First paperback edition 1988

Printed in the United States of America

Library of Congress Cataloging in Publication Data
Agnew, Jean-Christophe.

Worlds apart.

Bibliography: p.

1. Theater and society – Great Britain – History.
2. Theater – Great Britain – History. 3. Marketing –
Great Britain – History. 4. English literature – Early
modern, 1500–1700 – History and criticism. 5. English
literature – 18th century – History and criticism.
6. Melville, Herman, 1819–1891. Confidence-man.
7. Theater in literature. I. Title.
PN2585.A36 1986 306'.484 85–25457

British Library Cataloguing in Publication Data
Agnew, Jean-Christophe

Worlds apart: the market and the theater in
Anglo-American thought, 1550–1750.

1. Markets – Social aspects – Great Britain –
History   2. Markets – Social aspects – United
States – History   3. Theater and society – Great
Britain – History   4. Theater and society –
United States – History
I. Title
306'.3   HF5474.G7

ISBN 0 521 24322 X hard covers
ISBN 0 521 37910 5 paperback

For my mother and father

Contents

Preface

MARKET AND THEATER. What different meanings these two words evoke. One word summons up ancient images of stalls, scales, and ledger books, of raucous hucksters and sober, black-coated clerks. The other conjures up a magical world of sets, costumes, and greasepaint, of gallant heroes, scheming villains, and clowns in motley. Markets we are accustomed to think of as meeting every sort of material need. Theaters we associate with more symbolic, less tangible human longings. Commerce involves risk and therefore prizes the clear and specific assignment of liability. Comedies, by contrast, glory in their avowed inconsequentiality as they do in the immunities that innocuousness invites. Theatricality is to the serious person of business what commerciality is to the serious person of the theater: a threat to the foundation of trust on which each enterprise stands. From this perspective, the two figures appear to inhabit entirely different, if not wholly contradictory, realms. Reality and fiction. Materialism and symbolism. Necessity and freedom. Work and play. What are these terms but variants of the pairing of market and theater? And how else to think of them except as worlds apart?

One of my purposes in this book is to answer that question. Yet the answer I offer is an admittedly equivocal one in that it both denies and affirms this image of separate worlds. On the one hand, I want to show that the themes of commerciality and theatricality have actually sustained a long, intimate, and complex relationship in Anglo-American thought; on the other hand, I believe that people brought and, in a sense, thought these two themes together precisely because they experienced their markets and their stage as distinct and different universes. Only here I propose that the decisive historical difference lay not so much between the two institutions as between them and the common social world whose needs commerce and comedy were understood to serve. To be thus set against one another, the two institutions had first to be detached from everything else.

It is in this sense, then, that markets and theaters have stood as worlds apart. Owing to the special and often implicit conditions of belief and accountability that operate within their bounds, the two institutions have for long periods of time stood at some remove from the rules and rituals of ordinary social intercourse. And often enough, their bounds have been effectively coexistensive. The theater of late medieval and early modern England, for example, was a theater in and of the marketplace. And though the rules governing credit in the market stalls of those times may have differed in detail from the conventions governing credibility in the adjoining theatrical booths, the fact nonetheless remains that in either instance the customer's will to believe was a stipulated or conditional act, a matter less of faith than of suspended disbelief. What bound the market and theater together, then as now, were the same peculiar experiential properties that set them apart from other kinds of exchange.

Why, then, my interest in the years between 1550 and 1750? If markets and theaters have for so long been linked by virtue of their shared differences from ordinary life, why single out these two centuries for special scrutiny? To that question this study is itself an extended reply. But a short answer might begin by pointing to this epoch as a time when the residual boundaries separating market from other forms of exchange were rapidly dissolving. To be sure, merchants and lawyers of the time contrived a variety of sophisticated commercial instruments, together with a body of equally intricate contractual law, in order to oversee and underwrite the very transactions that an older, ceremonialized marketplace could no longer secure. But such commercial and legal inventions did little to resolve (and much to aggravate) the larger, more refractory questions of personal identity and accountability arising within an increasingly placeless and timeless market process. Such solutions did not indicate, for example, how one's self, one's motives, and one's relations were to be represented in a world where traditional reference points were increasingly subject to the market's overarching rule of full commensurability. Nor did they indicate how or where human acts of representation were to be anchored in the face of such detached and impersonal abstractions as exchange value. These were social and cultural problems and as such were left to the theater (among other institutions) to take up during this period. It is thus in the evolution of the theater and *its* conventions of representation – its theatricality – that I trace a protracted struggle to forge a broader sociocultural accommodation with an expansive system of capital formation and commodity exchange. In these years, the theater became a laboratory of and for the new social relations of agricultural and commercial capitalism.

It is not enough, consequently, to treat the Anglo-American theater as a mere text or register in which to read the cultural consequences of an emerging market economy. The early modern stage did more than reflect relations occurring elsewhere; it modeled and in important respects materialized those relations. Elizabethan and Jacobean theater, as we shall see, did not just hold the mirror up to nature; it brought forth "another nature" – a new world of "artificial persons" – the features of which audiences were just beginning to make out in the similarly new and enigmatic exchange relations then developing outside the theater. Without an appreciation of the theater's constitutive and exploratory powers in this regard, it is correspondingly difficult to understand the violence and antipathy visited on the stage in these years. The theater bestowed an intelligible albeit Protean human shape on the very *form*lessness that money values were introducing into exchange; for such an achievement, spectators were alternately grateful and horrified.

I emphasize the word "form" here because it occupies the foreground of this study. Some readers will no doubt be disappointed to see so little attention given to the immediate and ultimate purposes for which the theaters were built, that is, the plays themselves; others will just as likely wonder at my seeming indifference to the putative object of all markets, namely, the allocation of scarce resources among competing interests. In the pages that follow I as rarely take up the content of a particular play as I do that of a particular trade. But that is because I am concerned above all to chart the changing formal and informal resemblances between commercial and theatrical convention over time. To speak of the market and theater in Anglo-American thought is, in this regard, to speak of the understandings men and women held of the social structuration of their commercial and theatrical experience. It is to speak, in short, of changing definitions of commerciality and theatricality. Studied in sufficient detail, these two themes can illuminate one another as well as some of the broader intellectual traditions in which they were lodged, say, within political theory or moral philosophy. But even more important, these themes can shed light on the historical emergence of a market culture in Britain and America; that is to say, they can reveal how fundamental structures of meaning and feeling came to be framed around the characteristic problems and prospects of an expansive market system.

So while the spine of this study remains, strictly speaking, an intellectual history of two related ideas – market and theater – the body of the narrative resembles something more in the nature of a cultural history: a history of meanings and feelings broadly defined, as embedded in expressive practices widely observed. Obviously, no historian could hope to recover, much less fully consider, the whole range of expressive practices ascribable to either the market or the theater in the years between 1550 and 1750. Fortunately, however, there already exists a considerable body of research and writing on these subjects, from which I have drawn liberally in my efforts to situate the texts that, as intellectual history, lie at the heart of my narrative. I have tried to record my debt to this rich historiography in the footnotes; there I have made an effort to include where relevant more general references, rather than to confine them to a separate bibliographical essay.

Bound up with these contextual "facts," of course, are methods and theories for interpreting them. In this case, the obstacles I encountered in my attempts to interpret practices that had been at once textual and performative, figurative and material, ephemeral and fateful led me to consult a number of writers in other disciplines, notably political economy, economic and symbolic anthropology, philology, and literature. If my argument has been successful, it is in no small part due to insights already familiar within those disciplines but still novel to a historian like myself.

If, on the other hand, I have stumbled, it is not for lack of illumination from others but from my own defects and limits of vision and the special difficulties my subject posed. Commerciality and theatricality are inescapably dialectical ideas – labile, reflexive, deconstructive – and, like the practices of which they are the abstracted properties, they invite the observer to invest too much, to overreach, which is why I have kept to the texts as my anchor.

Still, the reader will almost immediately notice that my "Anglo-American" texts are drawn for the most part from one side of the Atlantic. Despite the book's hyphenated subtitle, the thought and culture examined herein are largely British. In part this is because the most influential texts before 1750 were British and were read on both sides of the ocean. But the predominance of British texts also reflects the fact that before 1750, indeed almost before 1850, few Americans were compelled to create, much less to confront, formal and figurative parallels between commercial and theatrical practice. Yet despite this instance of economic and cultural "lag," I have retained the American side of my subtitle as I have that of my narrative, even if only in the form of an epilogue. I have done so because the trajectory of that narrative is quite deliberately Anglo-American: *from* England *to* America.

Curiously, my initial interest in this project turned on an altogether unexamined assumption that the cultural interplay of commerciality and theatricality in contemporary mass culture was a peculiarly modern and peculiarly American phenomenon, an assumption against which this book itself may stand as refutation. Readers will find in my narrative, I hope, the seeds of questions applicable to our own market culture, for it was these questions that originally pushed this narrative backward in time and outward in reach. Americans' engagement with the predicaments and problematics sketched in this book came later than it did in Britain, and to a certain extent we are still very much engaged and bemused by them. As late as 1870, an actor could still be denied a Christian burial in New York City; today, an actor has become president by claiming allegiance to the very traditions that would have categorically condemned him as a hypocrite a century earlier. To this public change of heart or mind, I plan to devote another volume. If, then, the Anglo-American subtitle still seems to be a case of bait and switch, I can only reply, like Melville, that "something further may follow of this Masquerade."

Acknowledgments

IF THERE IS ONE LESSON I should have brought away from my work on markets, it is that of the ultimate futility of itemizing one's personal, not to mention scholarly, debts. Nevertheless, this book owes much to the wisdom and generosity of many friends and colleagues, and I would like to express my gratitude to them.

This study began some years ago as an introduction to a dissertation on American theater. But, as so often happens to historians, a casual foray into other times and places – to get my bearings, so to speak – eventually developed into a full-scale inquiry of its own. Donald H. Fleming offered indispensable direction during the early states of this inquiry, and I remain deeply appreciative of his forebearance in what could only have seemed at first to be a curious historical digression. The staffs of the Houghton Library at Harvard and the Beinecke Library at Yale were likewise immensely helpful, as was the time afforded me to write by a Morse Fellowship. I am also grateful to Steve Fraser and Frank Smith, my editors at Cambridge University Press, to Mary Nevader, who copyedited my manuscript with singular precision and tact, and to Jim O'Brien, for his careful work on my index. A grant from the Griswold Fund underwrote some of the expenses incurred in the preparation of the manuscript. Portions of Chapter 1 first appeared in slightly different form in the *Radical History Review*, and I thank the journal's editors for their permission to reprint.

I also want to thank John Brewer, Gary Kornblith, Peter Linebaugh, William Parker, Alan Trachtenberg, and Michael Wallace for their comments on various portions of my manuscript. As I have tried to indicate in my endnotes, I have benefited enormously from the close readings, apt suggestions, and scholarly example of David Marshall, who, it was my good fortune to discover, had chosen to follow some of the same curious byways of eighteenth-century theatricality that I had. From him and from the interdisciplinary seminar we taught together at Yale, I've acquired a greater appreciation, if not skill, for rigorous textual analysis. I am equally indebted to my friends and colleagues, Betsy Blackmar, Roy Rosenzweig, and Robert Westbrook, who all took time away from their own work to give to mine. They and David have been at the center of my intellectual and personal support system. Their criticisms and suggestions have thus made this a much better or, at least, more accurate book than it would otherwise have been, though, of course, I remain responsible for any errors of fact or interpretation that remain. It certainly feels as if I had stood on the shoulders of giants; I only hope that I have not ridden roughshod over them as well.

Finally, I want to thank my wife, Leslie, whose patience and faith in this project far exceeded anything I had a right to expect. For this gift, above all, I am most grateful.

Prologue: Commerce and culture

ARKET RELATIONS ARE COMMONPLACE in the
English-speaking world, yet their cultural dimension
remains oddly inaccessible to the historian. The different meanings that Britons and Americans have attached to
their experience of the market over time have yet to be explored
in any depth. An abundance of documentary material exists to
throw light on the surface of commodity exchange, to be sure,
but it is a light that, more often than not, obscures by its brightness the interior of the market transaction. Statistics and equations
dispose us to see the history of the market as a calculable rather
than an interpretable phenomenon; they thereby deflect our vision
away from that ambiguous, subjective terrain where material
necessity, social constraint, and cultural imperative meet as the
fusable and fissionable constituents of all human exchange. Rarely,
if ever, do market relations appear in our cultural chronicle as
they do in our cultural life: as a constant, mediate, and immediate
presence.

Why should this be so? Given the extraordinary array of commodities in the contemporary world, how is it that such items
and the culture underwriting their exchange should remain so
consistently opaque? Why do we lack anything approximating a
phenomenology of market experience? What is it that debars us
from describing in a systematic fashion the fundamental structures of meaning and feeling that have accompanied the different
forms of commodity exchange over time? And, in this connection, why do we encounter such difficulty in our efforts to form
an adequate historical conception of the cultural conditions and
consequences associated with the movement toward fully developed market economies?[1]

Whatever the obstacles to our understanding may be, we can
scarcely surmount them by appealing to current market theory
or, for that matter, by consulting the older tradition of classical
and neoclassical economics. As Bernard Barber has discovered,

1

"The history of economic thought shows a surprisingly small amount of attention given to the idea of market." This is no doubt because economists prefer to regard the market as a timeless, natural arrangement for the satisfaction of human needs.[2] In fact, mainstream economic theory commonly regards the logic of market transactions as immanent in all forms of exchange, regardless of their ritual or ceremonial trappings. Such logic, the theory holds, becomes visible only when demographic, ecological, or technological pressures impel its translation into an autonomous institutional mechanism. An event such as the establishment of the Royal Exchange in London in 1658 is, according to this perspective, but a more complex and sophisticated variation of transactions carried out elsewhere with yams, shells, and salt.[3]

Only when we place economic theory in the historical context of its own development can we appreciate the attractions that such an ahistorical model of the market holds out to it. By reconstructing the circumstances surrounding the emergence of political economy as an independent discipline, it is possible to make some sense of its characteristic inclination to set historical and cultural contingencies aside in its analysis of exchange. We can begin to understand, for example, how the same pressures for market predictability that inspired an institution like the Royal Exchange also registered themselves in sixteenth- and seventeenth-century economic treatises as a new assumption about the uniformity of human motivation in exchange. Indeed, long before the specter of Economic Man stalked the pages of *The Wealth of Nations* (1776), the simplified cash nexus of commerce had begun to supplant the complex human nexus of society and culture in the minds of England's early political economists. As cynosures of public attention, the first banks and exchanges seemed to isolate within their walls the final moments of countless transactions initiated elsewhere, and they did so in much the same manner as contemporary economic thought narrowed its attention to the consummating instant of exchange. As Joyce Appleby has shown, early economic writers focused only on the conclusion of each bargain, "summarized in the impersonal price, the method of whose determination could not be retraced."[4] Prices were not presumed to respond to history so much as history was supposed to wait, like the expectant broker, on news of the market.

The legacy of this reductionism continues to operate as a kind of conceptual entail or constraint on our endeavors to recover the market experience and its meanings. Current economic theory, faithful as it is to these intellectual origins, fails to render an adequate account of the motives at play in the market, because it consistently excludes from consideration the very social, cultural, and historical contexts within which those motives have been variously structured. The prominence that the act of choice occupies in virtually all economic thinking, whether it be a choice of utilities, pleasures, or resources, invariably directs our attention toward the moment of economic "trade-off," toward the outcome of a personal and interpersonal sequence of exchange and away from its process. However embedded that process might be in a particular social and cultural situation, it is consistently recast by theory in the image of its outcome, that is, as an infinitely divisible series of trade-offs consciously or unconsciously entertained by the individual.[5]

Maximization, Jeremy Bentham's ungainly word for gain, furnishes the rule by which this hedonistic calculus of the market is understood to operate. But even in its more sophisticated, if equally awkward, formulations as "Pareto optimality" or "satisficing behavior," gain itself is *not* the distinctive property of market relations. Indeed, as Karl Polanyi has argued, it is the ambiguity of gain that conceals just those features of interaction that distinguish so-called primitive exchange at administered prices from so-called modern exchange at a bargained rate. Both forms of exchange, archaic and modern, involve gain, but it is the latter (exchange at fluctuating prices) that "aims at a gain that can be attained only by an attitude involving a distinctive antagonistic relationship between the partners."[6]

To be sure, a variety of impersonal commercial instruments may develop out of the money medium to diffuse the more visibly personal conflicts of the direct bargain. But, as Georg Simmel notes, money transactions can themselves "erect a barrier between persons, in that only one of the parties to the transaction receives what he *actually* wants, what corresponds to his specific needs, whereas the other party to the transaction, who only receives money, has to search for a third party to satisfy his needs."[7] Economists ordinarily treat this delay (first noted by Aristotle) as an unalloyed advantage, since the money form relieves its owner of the cumbersome "transaction costs" of searching for an appropriate reciprocating partner in barter.[8] By their lights, a fully monetized exchange relation allows the individual to discover his or her demand schedule over time, just as it allows economists to represent that schedule over space through the austere but graceful movements of "indifference curves." But though the term "indifference" is generally intended to evoke the harmonizing or equilibrating function of the pricing mechanism as a barometer of human desire, it also unwittingly captures the potentially disruptive implications that fully negotiable financial instruments can have for the cognitive and affective structures within which societies value their cultural goods. Here, the market antagonism is not so much dispelled as displaced – incorporated within the individual as a sharpened sense of opportunities foregone, or withheld. Once the environment itself assumes the character of a more or less calculable liquidity and becomes, like money, not a source but a store of value, the individual may be said to enter into a perpetual process of internal bargaining.

A pure money form embodies what Simmel calls the promise of "infinite purposiveness" and, as such, endows every undertaking with an aspect of presumptive loss, a loss that is in its own way the dark side of the hedonistic calculus.[9] So although commercial instruments such as bills of exchange may depersonalize market transactions by broadening the range of items exchangeable against one another and by buffering that exchange though a variety of abstract media, they do not necessarily dissolve the anxieties or hostilities that attend the prospect of risk and loss. If anything, they may heighten those tensions by multiplying the number of negotiable items and instances of ordinary life. When freed of ritual, religious, or juridical restraints, a money medium can imbue life itself with a pervasive and ongoing sense of risk, a recurrent anticipation of gain and loss that lends to all social intercourse a pointed, transactional quality.

Political economy merely rationalizes this transactional experience of the world by implanting a trucking and bartering instinct in the individual in such a way as to make the appearance of autonomous market mechanisms in history a logical fulfillment of sociobiological needs. In this respect, theory naturalizes what is in every other respect a radical disruption and restructuration of needs and their mode of gratification via the market. In other words, theory takes as absolute and eternal a particular grammar of motives – the hedonistic calculus – that should rather be seen historically as one of many efforts to render intelligible, acceptable, and controllable the socially and culturally subversive implications of the "free" market.[10]

Two observations can be made here, however provisionally: first, that from the point of view of the cultural historian, the categories and concepts bequeathed to us by political economy are impoverished; second, that they turn the proper understanding of market culture on its head. Whatever their operational usefulness in predicting the behavior of prices in mature market economies, these categories and concepts do little to enrich our view of the specifically social and cultural dimension of that maturation. Political economists insist that societies be understood in terms of their respective allocations of scarce means to alternative ends, despite clear evidence that societies can and have operated with negligible notions of scarcity or opportunity costs.[11] At the same time, economists treat social exchange as a matter of buyers and sellers (or their surrogates) engaging in the pursuit of their self-interests, though evidence again indicates that the very concepts of selves and their interests are historically conditioned ideas.[12] Classical and neoclassical economic theory thus takes as its starting points categories of explanations that are, in fact, the end points of protracted historical struggles and debates. This logical inversion of historical sequence brings me to my second observation.

The conspicuously "economic" concepts and categories that inform our common understanding of the market do more than reduce the complexity of feeling and meaning associated with commodity exchange; they reverse the terms of that association. We are given to believe, for example, that "scarcity" and "interests" are eternal and inescapable problems, for which the market is a timely and spontaneous solution. For the cultural historian, however, it is far less fruitful to regard the "free" market as a practical solution to the material problems posed by these motives than to regard a motivational category like "self-interest" as itself an ideological solution to the cultural confusions produced by the spread of market exchange. "Motives are words," C. Wright Mills has argued and, as such, are used as "answers to questions." In this instance, "self-interest" was but one of a number of answers contrived to cope with the deep and widely displayed anxieties about the coherence of self and society in seventeenth- and eighteenth-century Anglo-American society.[13] As these answers accumulated over time, of course, they began to form an imposing ideological edifice of their own: the nineteenth-century trinity of individualism, utilitarianism, and Common Sense philosophy. But the authority that this structure's design exercised over those High Victorian minds who inhabited it rested in no small part on the new grammar of motives – the new hedonistic terms of placement – into which earlier writers and thinkers were able to fit the peculiar ambiguities of market activity; its authority rested as well on repeated acts of selected inattention to the ways in which those same ambiguities continued to subvert the new categories of explanation.

In view of the characteristic and "ineradicable" antagonism that Polanyi locates at the heart of the market, this inattention is hardly surprising. At the very least, it helps to explain the blank face that the autobiographical record of market experience offers up to the historian. A discrete and retrograde amnesia appears to repeat itself each time experience rediscovers and relives the antagonism of market relations in a form that ideology has yet to resolve. This repression need not be covert; it can advance under the noblest of standards, including that of "civilization" itself. Cultural studies owe their birth, after all, to the concerted efforts of nineteenth-century Anglo-American thinkers to reserve a portion of their collective world of meaning from incorporation within the price system; these writers strained to keep the "priceless" aspects of culture at a safe remove from a symbolic system (money) the operational principles of which they were otherwise content to leave unchallenged.[14] Far from contradicting the claims of political economy, the Victorian champions of Civilization merely consented to operate outside its dominion. Aestheticism and economism effectively cartelized the social world by dividing cultural exchange and market exchange into separate disciplinary jurisdictions. As a consequence, the juncture of these two aspects of life vanished from view, and the deep and unacceptable division *within* market culture reemerged as the deep but eminently acceptable division *between* the market and culture.

Because this book is in the broadest sense a study of the making of an identifiable market culture during the period of the Anglo-American "transition" to capitalism, it rejects this dichotomy. Because it is concerned with structures of meaning and feeling, it sets its sights on just those conjunctures of material and symbolic exchange from which we have been conditioned, in effect, to avert our eyes. Market culture deserves more than the sidelong glance we have been accustomed to accord it. A fully monetized economy is too complex and significant a symbolic system to have its cultural impact adequately summarized by a few casual references to acquisitiveness and time-thrift. To reduce the culture of the market to the hedonistic calculus would be to accept the answers proposed by market apologists (and critics) in place of the questions that the market itself provoked in the societies for which it was becoming a principal mode of organization. Like amnesiacs, we find ourselves retracing our steps to the moment of these first provocations, steps that the doubled vision of economism and aestheticism has missed. Backtracking seems indispensable to our project. For if indeed Mills was correct in suggesting that motives are best thought of as answers to questions, then it is to the peculiar confusions and perplexities occasioned by market relations that we should first turn if we hope to penetrate the culture that arose to relieve them.

This study is divided into two parts. The first half encompasses the years (1550–1650) in which the disruptive and transformative powers of market exchange were first brought home to Britons and, not least of all, to those who saw fit to emigrate. The second half embraces the years (1650–1750) in which Britons and Americans alike began to fashion a culture of the market, a culture that managed to displace and dismiss, without dissolving, those same disruptive and transformative powers.

The years between 1550 and 1650 formed part of what historians have called the "long sixteenth century."[15] For England, as for Europe, these were years of expansion and differentiation of trade, of unprecedented prosperity and depression in the textile industry, of unrelenting inflation, and of the seemingly inexorable commodification of land and labor. The conflicts that these secular trends engendered or sharpened were apparent throughout the society, whether in the brittle relations between city master and suburban journeyman, between rural rack renter and beleaguered leaseholder, between settled yeoman and migratory laborer, between import merchant and local artisan, or between textile middleman and country cottager. Each of these relationships generated its own pattern of bewilderment and conviction over customary entitlements and natural rights, just as each locale created its own arrangements by which these conflicting claims could be held – for a time at least – in a precarious equilibrium.

Historians have christened these socioeconomic arrangements in a number of ways: household mode of production, simple commodity production, and small commodity production. But whatever category we choose, we cannot afford to overlook the perceived volatility and vulnerability of these arrangements before the subversive powers of the market. The number of challenges and complaints these frequently tense and hostile relationships produced would fill this volume; they did, in fact, fill the pages of countless petitions, public remonstrances, and anonymous letters.[16] But when these complaints and protests are taken together, they reveal a shared distress that extends beyond the facts of social antagonism to its form. It may be true that the historical movement away from ritual, kin, and prescriptive bonds and toward contractual, commutable, and convertible forms of compensation multiplied the occasions for exploitation without necessarily (or at first) increasing its measure in absolute terms.[17] Profound and abiding social antagonisms had long preceded the introduction of market mechanisms into the cycles of ordinary life, and these differences had been acknowledged, if not legitimized, in the emblematic division of feudal society into those who worked, those who prayed, and those who fought.[18] But it was precisely the dissolution of this structure of estates – which never, of course, quite existed in the pristine form of the medieval emblem – that led so many Britons to ponder the character of exchange that bound their society together.

This shared sense of the shifting ground of mutuality, dependence, and exploitation gave to the local literature of complaint a commonality that transcended the particular or momentary objects of concern. Conventional metaphors and tropes no longer seemed capable of expressing the labile qualities of money or the social relations that money mediated. The formless, qualityless, characterless nature of the money form became a recurring motif in the prolonged rumination about self and society to which so much Renaissance and Reformation literature contributed. And though this tradition of thought – if we can call it that – rarely hesitated to appropriate pastoral imagery to evoke a harmonious, nonpecuniary past, it was not limited to nostalgic evocations. This tradition also included a considerable fraction of the forward-looking self-help manuals that poured forth from the presses of England's cosmopolitan printers. Whether this literature struck a note of lament or promise, it nonetheless kept to the theme of a newly discovered, Protean social world, one in which the conventional signposts of social and individual identity had become mobile and manipulable reference points. What stands out in the "long-sixteenth-century" inventory of complaints is its groping to envisage a social abstraction – commodity exchange – that was lived rather than thought. Whatever else it was, this litany of lamentation was an attempt to give practical and figurative form to the very principles of liquidity and exchangeability that were dissolving, dividing, and destroying form and that, in doing so, were confounding the character of all exchange.

In the century preceding the English Civil War, then, Britons could be described as feeling their way round a problematic of exchange; that is to say, they were putting forward a coherent and repeated pattern of problems or questions about the nature of social identity, intentionality, accountability, transparency, and reciprocity in commodity transactions – the who, what, when, where, and why of exchange. The answers to such questions form the basis of any ruling class's claim to authority, legitimacy, and justice, and all such classes must continually satisfy their subjects (and themselves) on these counts in order to survive. But for many sixteenth- and seventeenth-century Britons, these counts added up to a broad and ominous indictment of contemporary social, political, and religious representation. The peculiarly shape-shifting character of the target inspired, in its turn, a corresponding impulse to sharpen boundaries, to render meanings more precisely, or in other words to "purify" the terms of all social relations. This struggle to name the cause of social anxieties may strike us at first as a problem of expression, especially since the effort to formulate the issues drew on such profound and conflicting feelings about the obligations and expectations brought to exchange. But since these confusions included serious questions about the character and authority of the "self" on whose behalf these anxieties were to be expressed, it is perhaps more useful to think of these sentiments as having been structured around problems of *representation*.

It seems to have been the case that for every effort to devise instrumentalities that would frame and mediate the new political, commercial, and religious relations of Tudor–Stuart society, there appeared a parallel pressure to find emblematic forms that could capture the elusive character of those relations. The practical problem of how individuals were to represent themselves to one another in the protocontractual relationships of parliamentary politics, mercantile trade, capitalist agriculture, and Protestant orthodoxy brought with it the less immediate but certainly no less obdurate problem of how they were to represent these relationships to themselves.

These questions were as stubbornly abstract as the lived abstractions they sought to clarify. What conventions, after all, could convey the experience of conventionality, the sensed hollowness of ritual that the liquidity and impersonality of the money form conferred on the customary frameworks of exchange? What rhetorical devices or forms of address could accommodate the new and unsettling confusion over personal distance and intimacy that perplexed those brought together in commodity transactions? What image of the individual could take adequate measure of a self no longer, or at least not fully, authorized within the traditional religious, familial, or class frame? And if such conventions, devices, and imagery were indeed available, where might they develop freely enough to coalesce into an intelligible, formal analogue of the increasingly fugitive and abstract social relations of a burgeoning market society?

Where else, we might ask, but the theater?

The theater of the Tudor–Stuart epoch was many things – a curious amalgam of religious drama, morality play, bawdy interlude, courtly masque, classical comedy, and civic processional. Yet despite these many roots, or perhaps because of them, the theater of this period was an experimental medium, one in which ancient meanings and associations mingled with current allusions and passing topicality. Narrative structures, rhetorical practices, visual and gestural emblems appropriated from ritual drama and classical oratory blended imperceptibly with an almost reportorial sense of history and society drawn from the hurly-burly of London's streets. The theater not only mimed new social relations within the visible framework of the old; it improvised – as a matter of its own constitutive conventions – a new social contract between itself and its audience, a new set of conditions for the suspension of disbelief that became over time the preconditions of most modern drama. And it did all these things within a special cultural enclave, a protected social sphere that its actors had created for themselves, though with some important collaboration from patrons and audiences. For the brief moment of Elizabethan and Jacobean rule, English theater enjoyed a deliberate, if delicate, extraterritorial status: a marginal existence in which the potent possibilities of marginality were explored in unprecedented depth and with extraordinary imagination.

These experimental, exploratory, and extraterritorial qualities, I believe, allowed the theater of that epoch to operate as a proxy form of the new and but partly fathomable relations of a nascent market society. The professional theater of the English Renaissance became in effect a "physiognomic metaphor" for the mobile and polymorphous features of the market.[19] But it did not merely represent those features; at its most venturesome, it thematized representation and misrepresentation as the pivotal problems of its drama. For the first time, perhaps, theater made what Anne Righter has called the "idea of the play" its cardinal concern and, by thus confronting the conditions of its own performance, it invoked the same problematic of exchange – the same questions of authenticity, accountability, and intentionality – at issue in the "idea of [the] market."[20] The complex and mutually illuminating relation between these two ideas – between the practical liquidity of the commodity form and the imaginative liquidity of the theatrical form – is the subject of this study.

What follows is an effort to reconstruct some of the cultural conditions and consequences of market development during the transition to capitalism, as those conditions and consequences were understood or misunderstood at the time. To recover those understandings and misunderstandings, we need to know how the market was made meaningful at the very moment that meaning itself was becoming marketable. We need to know how Renaissance and Reformation thinkers went about formulating relations whose polyvalent and polymorphous properties subverted form itself. We need to know, in short, how culture was married to a form of exchange – the measured equivalence of incommensurable qualities – that promised only promiscuity. And in knowing these things, we shall see more clearly how market relations are culturally reproduced and how, in that process, individuals come to see themselves in the likeness of commodities.

As I have already indicated, my argument falls into two parts. In the first, I endeavor to show how the English stage developed formal, narrative, and thematic conventions that effectively reproduced the representational strategies and difficulties of the marketplace; how the stage then furnished its urban audience with a laboratory and an idiom within which these difficulties and contradictions could be acted out; how, in the course of these enactments, the deepened resonance between commerciality and theatricality transformed the ancient Stoic and Christian metaphor of the *theatrum mundi* from a simple, otherworldly statement on human vanity into a complex, secular commentary on the commodity world; and finally, how the theater became sufficiently threatening in these respects to bring on its own repression in the mid–seventeenth century, both as an institution and as a figure of thought.

The cultural crisis signaled by the suppression of the English stage in 1642 formed part of what historians have called the "general crisis of the seventeenth century" – a simultaneous collapse of agriculture, trade, industry, and political authority.[21] Out of the rubble of this collapse, one in which many remnants of feudal rule were swept away, arose the socioeconomic structure of commercial and industrial capitalism and, with it, the three-tiered ideological framework of individualism, political economy, and Common Sense philosophy. Within this framework, the antagonisms of the market came to be seen as its impetus rather than its incubus, so that by the early years of the nineteenth century, the "free" market and its hedonistic calculus were securely enthroned in Anglo-American ideology.

Yet, as the second half of this study attempts to show, the theatrical perspective, in which so many of the riddles of the market had been inscribed, likewise underwent a rebirth during the eighteenth century. On the broadest plane, the theatrical perspective entered into the ideological mainstream as an amusing gloss on the literate ideal of the detached and impartial observer of life, the discriminating consumer of the urban spectacle. More controversially, it became, at the hands of Adam Smith, a startlingly novel, wholly secular, and decidedly functionalist social psychology of market society. Some writers (Smith included) went so far as to extract out of the hedonistic calculus, with all of its complacent assurances about the maximization of human satisfactions, the kernel of a histrionic calculus in which the arithmetic of material interest subordinated itself to the exigencies of social performance.

Historians have long noted the renascent theatricality of Restoration and Hanoverian England, but its sources remain obscure. On the one hand, I attempt to link this exuberant exhibitionism to the maneuvers of class and faction in the wake of the Revolution settlement, to the new relation of the state to speculative capital, and to the emergence of a distinctively urban, consumer culture. On the other hand, I try to show how these developments encouraged some thinkers, at least, to reconsider the notion – first broached by Hobbes – of a commodity self: a mercurial exchange value or "bubble" floating on the tides of what attention others were disposed to invest.[22] Given the individualistic presuppositions of prevailing ideology, this disturbingly weightless image of the self remained as suspect as the figure of the actor with whom it was most closely identified, but nonetheless it remained. And from that vantage point, a number of writers (not all of them English but many influenced by the Scottish Enlightenment) continued to use the vernacular of the stage to suggest possibilities of personal and cultural detachment and alienation that challenged the Common Sense world itself. From Rousseau (1758) to Melville (1857), the theatrical perspective continued to furnish a far more sensitive cultural barometer of the transatlantic consequences of commodity exchange than the fluctuations of the price index.

Whatever relation these ideas may have had to the mainstream of Anglo-American thought, however, the course they ran no longer passed through the theater. Once the English stage divested itself of its sociologically heterodox audience, as it did after the Restoration, the source of the theatrical perspective shifted from the public experience of the stage to the private experience of the novel, a new cultural commodity that deliberately borrowed theatrical language and conventions to frame the question of its own authenticity, intentionality, and transparency in the eyes of an anonymous reading public.[23] It is in the fiction of this period, though not always in its most popular examples, that we see spelled out both the affirmative and subversive implications of a commodity exchange that was gradually becoming the constitutive relation of Anglo-American society and culture. There, in the novel, we find the adumbration of what Robert Jay Lifton has called "Protean Man" – the plastic, polymorphous, performative figure that is both the ideal and the nightmare of modernity. But it is only as part of the history of the theatrical perspective – the view of the world as a stage – that such fiction allows us to see this figure for what it is: the collective dream work of commodity culture.

Although this book is in the broadest sense a cultural history of market relations, it is in a narrower sense an intellectual history of one of the most durable metaphors left to us from antiquity: the metaphor of the world as a stage. In the fifteen hundred years between its formulation by the Greeks and its revival by Renaissance Neoplatonists, the meaning of the figure or "topic" of the *theatrum mundi* (or *scaena vitae*) remained relatively fixed.[24] Whether the texts were preSocratic or patristic, there was a virtually uniform reliance on the theatrical metaphor to remind people of the vanity of human achievements. Individuals were to be understood as the mere playthings or puppets of God; God was the stage manager and spectator of His own divine comedy.

In the hands of the Stoics, it is true, the metaphor acquired a hard edge it had not displayed before, a more fully developed sense of the futility and fatedness of things. And this sentiment, in turn, entered into the admonitory tradition of the Christian writers. Saint Augustine, for example, first used the theatrical metaphor to describe the ages of man twelve centuries before Shakespeare's Jaques. John Chrysostom, whose pulpit eloquence was equaled only by his contempt for players, was the first to link the image of the theater and the dream, a favored analogy of Renaissance writers.[25]

The point of the theatrical emblem was, quite simply, the pointlessness of secular aspiration, and it was on this point that the church fathers honed their sharpest warnings against worldly temptations. Chrysostom was but one of many religious thinkers to use the contrast between the lowly player and his kingly roles as a homily on the utter uselessness of man's envious and acquisitive impulses. When John of Salisbury resuscitated the trope in his influential *Policraticus* (1159), he may well have widened its reference – the stage was now the cosmos, a true theater of the world – but the Stoical element of worldly critique remained unchanged.[26] By the close of the Middle Ages, the theatrical metaphor had joined other popular images, such as the Wheel of Fortune, the Dance of Death, and the Ship of Fools, in representing the irreality of the secular world when juxtaposed to that which lay beyond. The obvious inconsequentiality of stage deeds bespoke the leveling presence of Death, thus making of the theater and of its metaphor a ritualized reminder of man's proper place in the scheme of things.[27]

From this ancient homiletic tradition, then, Renaissance writers and dramatists inherited a metaphor that comprised, on the one hand, an almost architectonic analogy between the stage and the cosmos and, on the other, an emotionally laden theatrical emblem of otherworldliness. The world was merely a stage. Thus, *theatrum mundi* could only mean *contemptus mundi*.[28] But if, by the time of the English Renaissance, this deeply ascetic concept of worldly theatricality no longer suited the sensibilities of the secular world it condemned, still the emblem survived. More than that, it prevailed over the other medieval tropes of otherworldliness with which it had once been associated. The images of

Death, Fortune, and Madness presupposed a superreal or supernatural sphere that redeemed, even as it reinforced, the illusive
character of the here and now. Only the emblem of the *theatrum
mundi,* as it happened, could continue to conjure up a comparable
sense of irreality without the corresponding appeal to the divine.

It is my aim to show how the same theatrical metaphor that had
for so long served churchmen to wean the faithful from their attachments to the secular world became over time a symbolic representation of attachments and moorings *already lost,* and lost not through
some putatively divine intervention *in* the world or some voluntary,
personal withdrawal *from* the world, but rather through the radically
defamiliarizing effects of commodity exchange. What made the theatrical metaphor so resilient was no doubt its capacity to evoke the
sense of a lived abstraction of distinctively human contrivance, a
"second nature" whose facticity was best represented by a theater that
was itself increasingly detached from any ritual relation to God. Thus,
although the outward scaffolding and inward sentiment of the theatrical analogy persisted into the seventeenth century, its meanings
changed – changed in response to the transformation of both the
theater and the world.

It is, of course, possible to treat the *theatrum mundi* not just as an
observation about the world but as a comment on the duality or
reflexivity of consciousness, the inherent capacity of the human
mind to take itself as object, to become its own spectator. Still, a
capacity is distinguishable from a disposition, an inclination, or a
compulsion, so that the moments when this perceived duality
changes from a passing conceit to a pressing social and cultural
concern must be understood as historically conditioned.[29] Few
commonplaces can boast a genealogy as ancient as the idea of the
world as stage; yet it is, for all that, a genealogy, a history. The
place, however common, that the metaphor occupied in the minds
of such figures as Pythagoras and Democritus is in fact quite different from the place it occupies in our own thoughts. The meaning of the theatrical perspective is neither as timeless as its principal
metaphor nor as timely as its current sociological embodiment in
role theory.[30] The chapters that follow constitute an effort to lo-
cate at least one specific time and place where the meaning of the
metaphor began to change and, in situating that change, to his-
toricize yet another timeless abstraction: the market.

1. The threshold of exchange

Pythagoras said, that this world was like a Stage
Whereon many play their partes: the lookers on the sage
Phylosophers are said he, whose parte is to learne
The manners of all Nations, and the good from the
bad to discerne.

> Richard Edwardes, *The Excellent*
> *Comedie of the two most faithfullest*
> *Freendes, Damon and Pithias* (1565)

[Pythagoras] sayde that this worlde was nothing but
a very mercate, where there meete three sortes of men,
the one to buy, the other to sell, and the thirde to
looke on, who (he sayde) were the Philosophers, whom
hee counted the happiest of them all.

> Stephen Guazzo, *The Civile*
> *Conversation* (1581)

WHAT IS A MARKET? Is it a place? a process? a principle? a power? History yields no definitive answers to these questions, partly because the motives of exchange are almost always overdetermined and partly because the earliest markets have left so few records behind them. To be sure, the absence of documentation is scarcely a deterrent for those who prefer to think of markets as the institutional expression of a natural human propensity to truck and barter. If anything, the seemingly magical appearance of markets in the landscape of antiquity tends to confirm this view of trade as a kind of socio-biological tropism, suggesting, as it does, a spontaneous gravitational pull toward commodity exchange encoded deep within the cellular structure of primitive societies. To those economic geographers for whom trade is always an indigenous (or endogenous) development, the map of human settlement invariably resembles a honeycomb grid of marketing areas. Seen though the spectacles of "central-place theory," an otherwise featureless terrain can be made to reveal an intricate hivelike pattern of polygonal trading zones in which the size of each cell is determined by the diminishing "travel willingness" and "price willingness" of consumers as one moves outward toward the cell's periphery from its nucleus: the central marketplace.[1] From this perspective, the very obscurity of market origins – so much like that of life itself – merely strengthens the organismic image of commodity exchange as an inherently expansive or meta-static process, invading and reorganizing all social space in its path.

Yet what we do know of early trade suggests that this view of the market as an engulfing phenomenon is largely metaphorical: more trope than tropism. That the view should enjoy such popularity among economic geographers more directly reflects our current predicament, wherein the felt boundaries separating commodity from other sorts of exchange have all but vanished. In this respect, it is misleading to speak, as I have hitherto, of *the* market. What historical and anthropological sources record is the evolution not of *the* market or *a* market but of many different markets, the first of which came into being as the products of earlier spatial arrangements within and between societies. These arrangements, in turn, may be said to have placed, framed, or contained the occasion of commodity exchange as a peculiarly equivocal instance of reciprocity when transactions appeared pregnant with possibilities for mutuality or antagonism. As we shall have occasion to see, early markets did not so much control space as they were controlled by spatial arrangements growing out of the organization of other kinds of social exchange, including gift and tributary practices. These markets were, in every possible sense of the term, *situated* phenomena; that is to say, they were assigned to precise sites – in space and time – in societies where the particularities of place and season were intricately linked to the dominant patterns of meaning and feeling and where the configuration of the landscape was itself used as a mnemonic repository of collective myth, memory, and practical wisdom.[2]

I

A market was emphatically a *place* in antiquity. The Greeks had no word for and certainly no conception of a specifically market process. What we commonly refer to as the "economy" has only the most distant connection to the Greek word from which it is derived. *Oikonomia* referred not to the abstract and self-regulating process of resource allocation through the price mechanism but rather to the concrete task of household *(oikos)* management, a task that was conceived, at least in Aristotelian terms, as no more than a means to the civic ideal of full participation in the life of the *polis*.[3] The earlier, Homeric world had no word for "merchant" and no room for markets or fairs; gain at the expense of another (which was the only way in which market exchange was understood) was explicitly excluded from the common practice of gift exchange and confined to the predatory sphere, where the options of "raiding or trading" remained evenly balanced. Poetry occasionally recorded the presuppositions of economic practice, as, for example, when Odysseus was made to recoil at the insinuation that he was a trader who preferred a quick profit to the prospect of honor and glory. For Homeric audiences, only the heroic ideals to which Odysseus devoted himself could redeem the obvious guile with which he pursued them.[4] Gift exchange, of course, was not entirely divorced from commerce. It could be used to initiate trading partnerships by overcoming the ordinary diffidence between strangers; and like the tradition of games and athletic contests to which it was, in form, related, giving could display distinct elements of rivalry and antagonism. Indeed, our own word "gift" derives from the German word for poison.[5]

Still, the exchange of gifts in antiquity was above all a discrete and idiosyncratic symbolic gesture aimed at binding the participants together through the mutual ascription of social identity via the gift. Framed within an elaborate etiquette of rank, gifts were vehicles for imputing, imposing, or endorsing a particular social status and for controlling the corresponding fears of envy. They were presentations whose object it was to represent; their attributes served, etymologically and functionally, as tributes. In sum, the practice of gift exchange clarified the grounds and bounds of all exchange; it threw into relief the same boundaries of self and social grouping that the "protean character . . . of trade" obscured.[6] Unlike commerce, gift exchange remained firmly situated within the individual and civic household, whose formal traditions of hospitality, liberality, and guest-friendship endured well into the later Middle Ages.

By contrast, in Greece early trade developed at the outskirts of the household economy. Embryonic markets first materialized at the periphery of settlement, in neutral zones or marches lying between villages, tribes, and societies. Their neutrality was secured by a variety of magical or religious rites associated with the crossing of boundaries. In retrospect, these ritual safeguards appear to have been both propitiatory gestures toward the unknown and practical displays of intention in ambiguous settings – ambiguous because such neutral zones were the sites alternatively of trade and warfare.[7]

Like the amulet worn against the Evil Eye of neighborly envy, the phallic boundary stone, or *herm,* marked off the ancient place of exchange as sacred ground, protecting it by its prominence from the appropriative inclinations of strangers. Situated within a domestic mode of production, where the redistribution of goods was structured largely within and among households, such inland exchange as occurred among early Greek communities frequently took the form of a mutually sanctioned theft – a "silent trade" between persons who never saw one another but merely left and retrieved their goods at a sacred boundary stone or its analogues. By the standards of modern economics, the transaction costs of this trade were extremely high; periodic rural markets had yet to appear in rural Greece as late as the fifth century B.C.[8]

This sporadic and secretive inland trade operated not only under a ritual protection but under a mythic aegis as well. Appropriately, it was Hermes, god of the boundary stone, who became the Greek patron of trade, embodying as he did the suspicion and apprehension toward strangers common to most household economies. Hermes shared with Proteus the image of duplicity, if not of multiplicity. He was known as both trickster and thief, the two being difficult to distinguish, as Norman O. Brown has remarked, in a setting where no clear juridical concept of private property or contractual alienation had taken hold.[9] As a god, Hermes was a marginal figure known for his "skill at the oath," that is to say, his ability to manipulate the literalism that others brought to transactions bound by kinship or familial honor. Thus, the only vulnerable point in Odysseus's genealogy was, as M. I.

Finley notes, his maternal grandfather Autolycus, who was thought to be Hermes's son and who " 'surpassed all men in thievishness and the oath, for that was a gift from the god Hermes.' "[10] Hermes himself came into being as a rustic deity but was gradually urbanized when the locus of trade shifted from the countryside to the *agora* – the main political, religious, and military assembly point of the Greek city-state. There the messenger god became the patron of craftsman and trader, who, in concert with the unskilled laborer, formed the "Third Estate of Greek social history."[11]

Although cities, coinage, and central markets all made their appearance in Greece before the sixth century B.C., they did not thereby introduce an autonomous commercial economy. The quickening of market activity during this epoch depended in great measure on the mobile wealth amassed on behalf of the householding oligarchy of the city-state.[12] Still, the entry of commodity exchange into the ritual and deliberative confines of the *agora* stirred several authors to ponder the relation of commerce and citizenship, perhaps for the first time. Xenophon pointedly observed that the Persians had excluded hucksters from their public space, and Herodotus recorded an incident in which Cyrus, the Persian emperor, was warned not to attack the Greek city-states. "I have never yet feared men of this kind," Cyrus was said to have replied, "who set up a place in the center of the city where they assemble and cheat each other with oaths."[13] The higgling-haggling of the marketplace was for classical thinkers a mere caricature of the collaborative ideal of the *oikos* and the deliberative ideal of the *polis*. Moreover, market exchange and, in particular, usury struck writers like Aristotle as a radical distortion of the relation between means and ends. Exchange for the sake of exchange, which Aristotle labeled "chrematistic exchange," threatened to transform the *nomos* of *oikonomos* from the householder's obligation of hospitality and liberality into a narrow calculus of cost and benefit; it diverted goods from their natural uses and limits to a sphere of intermediaries, where circulation and accumulation could accelerate and expand without purpose and, more important, without limit.[14]

According to S. C. Humphreys, "Attic texts of the fourth century B.C. show clearly that trading and exchange carried out by professional merchants for profit were regarded not merely as degrading occupations but as a threat to social norms and cohesion."[15] Plato's and Aristotle's efforts to distinguish an idealized civic sphere to which all else was but mere provision can be seen, in part, as a response to this perceived encroachment of means and middlemen within the household and the *agora*. As J. G. A. Pocock has observed, "every theory of corruption," from the ancient philosophers through Marx and Hannah Arendt, "is a theory of how intermediaries substitute their own good and profit for that of their supposed principals."[16] Yet linked to this vision has been a more general concern to keep a form of exchange understood as marginal from supplanting other forms of exchange (political, religious, social) regarded as central. The rare pronouncements on market relations that do appear in antiquity suggest a conscious desire to confine the instrumental fictions and representations of exchange to their original purposes and within their original boundaries.

The difficulty that exchange in and for the market presented was that it necessarily involved the crossing of boundaries; there was then a pointed logic in the appropriation of Hermes as a patronal deity by the merchants, or "professional boundary crossers," of antiquity. The marginality of the original marketplace found its complement in the marginality of those who conducted its affairs, once those affairs were removed from the periphery of the city-state and installed at its core. Trade was restricted to a large group of resident aliens to whom the rights of property ownership and citizenship were systematically denied.[17] These strictures placed formidable obstacles in the way of the monetization and capitalization of land, just as they effectively deprived the owners of mobile wealth of direct access to political power. Equally important, these prohibitions isolated and dramatized the abstract mobility of market exchange as a distinctive social and cultural phenomenon by assigning or attributing it to a class. Alien merchants were called *metics,* a title derived from the root word for intermediary and, generally, for change.[18] The merchants' ambivalent social status corresponded precisely to the kind of socially constructed space that had been interiorized with the incorporation of the marketplace into the civic center. This was an interstitial space, a space "between" inhabited by "go-betweens"; it preserved the affective and cognitive associations of a boundary, a border, a frontier, or a limit. But it was at the same time a culturally inscribed limit that, by its very ritual and mythological associations, was identified with, if not defined by, its own transgression. The ancient marketplace was, as the etymology of "limitation" suggests, a *limen,* a threshold.

As a threshold, the early marketplace was assigned a symbolic space defined by the movement of people and commodities and, even more important, by the permanent possibility of their movement. Because the actual movement between one status and another in antiquity commonly required a ritual rehearsal and because such preenactments frequently appropriated the form of an actual journey or pilgrimage, it is not surprising that the Greeks should have attached the symbolic meanings and immunities associated with such passages to the movement of merchants and their goods. The rights of passage conferred on the *metics* were secured by rites of passage; the culture of antiquity was far more likely to resort to symbol than to statute in placing or domesticating the mercurial figure of the market intermediary.

The image of domestication is especially apt since anthropologists have likened the symbolic ordering of maturational, educational, and spiritual passages in precapitalist societies to the movement between the rooms of a house. So far as is known, the earliest rites of passage originated as journeys to the margins of settlement but eventually telescoped themselves, in time and space, into the ordinary threshold ceremonies of the domestic and civic household. The taboos against treading the door sill, the worship of Limentinus (the threshold god) or of Janus (the gate god), and the triumphal arches designed for military entrances and departures all sprang from the same social anxieties as our lingering, twentieth-century impulse to avoid cracks in the sidewalk. Each rite sought to condense and counteract the risks and dangers associated with life's transitional or liminal moments by symbolically confining them to designated places and occasions.[19]

Threshold rituals thus developed as ceremonial metaphors straddling the uncharted realm between the physical and the symbolic, the secular and the sacred, the past and the future. They ordered the passage from one stage of life to another, one state of mind to another, one household to another. Recalling that from Homer onward, only one god – Hermes – inhabited both Olympus and the underworld, we may say that all such rituals of passage were characteristically Hermetic. They bridged the abyss between different social worlds, underwriting the wish not so much to act as to transact. They protected transactions and transitions alike from the consequences of formlessness and pollution that the experience of change and exchange implied and that the corresponding threat of placelessness inspired.[20]

The anthropologist Victor Turner has referred to those immersed in the transitional moment of ritual passage as "liminaries" – figures of or at the threshold – and has noted how frequently such initiates are presented as masked, androgynous, and anonymous travesties of the surrounding social structure. In their momentarily marginal relationship to that structure, liminaries are pronounced ritually "dead to the world." They become, in effect, formless, propertyless beings, wrenched out of time and place and "ground down into a sort of homogeneous social matter," out of which their new, resituated selves may then emerge.[21] Regarded from this perspective, ancient ritual thus condoned – as a temporary instrument of social reclassification – what ancient philosophy condemned: the personal transgression of social boundaries and the multiplication of identities. Plato associated these transgressions with the actor, but conventional wisdom assigned them to the *metic*.[22]

Once the place of the ancient centralized market is understood as a threshold phenomenon, a liminal space located "betwixt and between" the householding autarchies of antiquity, then the rites, ceremonies, and festivities attached to the periodic market can be seen as purifying it by a form of symbolic segregation. Indeed, to enter the *agora,* one was expected to perform a rite of purification at the boundary stone. With the displacement of rural trade to the city *agora,* the power of the Hermetic myth and ritual associated with peripheral exchange was turned to the creation of a distinctive market "peace" or "freedom" at the core. For years silent trade had maintained good relations, in Marshall Sahlins's words, "by preventing any relations." Now the application to the early marketplace of the traditional threshold covenant, with its automatic obligation of hospitality to strangers, furnished the pretext for exchange in a domestic economy where all gain remained suspect and where windfall surpluses were routinely concealed from the acquisitive gazes of neighbors and tax collectors alike.[23]

From a functionalist perspective, the centralization of the ancient marketplace appears to have been an implosive, integrative response to the economic and political insularity of household production. By making visibility the distinguishing feature of commodity exchange, the architecturally and ritually confined *agora* provided an economic convenience to its inhabitants and tolltakers. In this respect, the removal of commodity exchange from the boundaries of settlement to preestablished assembly points within the city-state seems little more than an effort to ease the task of information gathering and, hence, to quicken the responsiveness of prices to the actual fluctuations of supply and demand.[24]

Yet what may appear retrospectively to have been a spontaneous affirmation of economic rationality may well have reflected a desire to suppress rather than to liberate the price-*making* possibilities of free and open commodity exchange. By assigning an extraterritorial status to commodity transactions and by circumscribing those same transactions with a variety of ceremonial and festive practices, city leaders sought to turn the market's explosive aspect to creative and controlled account. The Greeks' insistence on oaths, witnesses, and/or visible tokens, or *symbola,* for all contracts attests to their concern to frame the market within the governing structure of authority and power. A *horkus,* or oath, was itself etymologically derived from the word for fence or enclosure. Here, as elsewhere, the point was to set clear bounds upon trade's mysterious capacity to bring incommensurable qualities, meanings, and values into equivalence through (what Plato and Aristotle considered) the purely fictive convention of the money form and, by thus setting such limits, to harness that power on behalf of a stratified society and an honorific culture.[25]

The early market was a place, then, but a place created as much by culture as by convenience. As a threshold of exchange, the market drew on earlier rituals of passage to distance itself from the many worlds that were indiscriminately mixed within it. With the passage of time, of course, this distance became increasingly a matter of sensibility rather than of space, at least of physical space. Because the market's legitimacy sprang from its embrace of a public presence (as opposed to the seclusion and privacy common to most rites of passage), its polyvalent, promiscuous, and peripheral associations continued to press against the fragile restraining wall of ritual and ceremony separating commodity transactions from other sorts of social exchange. By the middle of the fifth century B.C., as Humphreys observes, migration to the city "meant permanent adoption of the economic behavior associated with traders and markets – which had developed as an independent sphere with its own rules just *because* it had been kept at the margin of social life."[26]

We need not accept so sharp or so early a division between country and city to appreciate how far the ambiguities specific to threshold rituals had been multiplied and extended by the periodic city market. For the forty thousand citizens of Plato's Athens, the intense but occasional *liminal* moment of a communal rite of passage threatened to become the diluted but recurrent *liminoid* experience of commodity exchange; for the ten thousand *metics,* that experience had already become a way of life.[27] So too for the medieval tradesmen. The customary location of marketplaces near places of worship, the seasonal cycle of festive celebration, and the eventual development of religious processional, civic pageantry, and guild ceremony are all testimony, of course, to the importance of ceremonial and redistributive gestures to the legitimation of class power and authority. But these practices bear witness as well to the felt powers of that social and spatial construction which required such expansive and expensive rites to contain it: the market.

Economic and cultural costs are rarely commensurable. The same commercial instrumentalities that promise an economy, clarity, and congruity of information on the one hand may produce a multiplicity, obscurity, and incongruity of meanings on the other – so much so, in fact, that a "perfect knowledge" of the commodity world tends to be taken as an assumption rather than a consequence of market analysis.[28] Ultimately, however, it is the structure of meanings and feelings that determines what is to count as "information," and these structures change far more slowly than the data they organize. As long as commodity exchange inhabited cultural systems anterior and exterior to it, the quest for such informational economies and instrumentalities (of which the money medium is perhaps the most critical) continued to be constrained by other cognitive and affective priorities.[29] In antiquity as in the nearly two millennia of Western society that followed, it was society and culture that put the market in its place.

II

What held true for the marketplace in antiquity held true, in great measure, for England during the Middle Ages. There, markets and market fairs appeared in the twelfth and thirteenth centuries, often at crossroads or at the borders between villages. The "advantages of trade," as one nineteenth-century historian observed, were so clearly felt that such boundaries came to be treated "as a neutral territory where men might occasionally meet for their mutual benefit, if not on friendly terms, at least without hostility." The boundary stone was "the predecessor of the market cross, and the neutral zone around it the market-place."[30] A similarly centripetal movement of outlying marketplaces occurred after the Norman Conquest, so that by the early seventeenth century, nearly all English towns displayed at least one market cross, often within sight of the church or chantry that once held its charter. By that time, in fact, there were more than eight hundred such towns in England and Wales, a number estimated to be but a third of the total existing before the Black Death. When to this figure we add the thousand periodic fairs in more than three hundred important fair towns across England, we have some measure of commodity exchange during the transition from feudalism to capitalism.[31]

It is tempting to situate this elaborate pattern of markets within the wider context of the "commercial revolution" of the Middle Ages, but to the extent that this revolution fed on external rather than internal trade, the connection is misleading. What these numbers measure above all is the *intensity* of circulation, both in the sense of its frequency and in the sense of its predominant localism.[32] Compared with a modern market economy, the otherwise remarkable sixteenth-century network of local marketplaces appears at first glance to have been a cumbersome vestige of early trade, particularly considering the numerous restrictions as to time, place, personnel, and standards with which the public market was hedged. When these constraints are taken together with the execution (1278) and expulsion (1290) of the Jews, the riots against the Italian merchants of London's Cheapside in the mid–fourteenth century, and the persistent battle between townsmen and husbandmen over market rights, an unpleasant picture of a stagnant, xenophobic, backward-looking society emerges – a picture quite at odds with the mature, well-articulated pattern of commerce that a market map of the period would at first suggest and that a number of historians have endorsed.[33] Despite the grant of some twenty-eight hundred market charters by the crown in the years between 1198 and 1583, "no real economic growth" had occurred by the end of the English Middle Ages, according to J. L. Bolton.[34]

The truth, predictably, is more complex than either of these images. To look at the marketing arrangements of the fifteenth and sixteenth centuries as either the backbone of a future capitalism or the backwater of an earlier feudalism is to miss the peculiar meanings and motives such arrangements held out to the society of that epoch. It is possible to see the late medieval market*place,* in contradistinction to the more general and abstract market *process,* as at least a temporary locus of peasant resistance to the importunities of manorialism on the one hand and of entrepreneurialism on the other.

Aspects of the ancient marketplace survived well into the Middle Ages. Public marketing held fast to its semireligious protections through the Tudor accession and, in some instances, beyond. The market cross at Cheapside, for example, became the site at which transactions could be witnessed, proclamations read, executions performed, and condemned documents publicly destroyed. Rebuilt and relocated during the late fourteenth century, the cross survived intact until its royal provenance and Catholic imagery brought about its eventual destruction in 1643.[35] But for the better part of the Middle Ages, the church provided an occasion and an authority in the presence of which oaths and pledges could be taken on commodity transactions. Before the Conquest, Saxon laws had prohibited any exchange over fourpence "except in privileged places and in the presence, and under the sanction, of the chief local official." To be excommunicated was to be barred from dealing in the marketplace. Similar prohibitions persisted through the sixteenth century.[36]

The presence of such statutes reflected the importance of market tolls (from which priories, manors, and boroughs drew considerable revenue) and the power of local guilds to control the "freedom" or franchise of their cities. But the insistence on witnesses also reflected a lingering distrust of written documents in comparison with oral testimony under oath. In England as in most of Europe, written charters and conveyances were little more than symbolic moments – and subsidiary ones at that – in public ceremonies composed of the parties to a transaction, their witnesses, and a notary. Only after the twelfth century did sealed instruments of dated transactions begin to rise in legal and mercantile estimation. Even then, contracting parties continued to insist on witnesses as well as on physical symbols of their covenant. Knives, rings, and bound copies of the Gospels served in place of the Saxon *wed* and the Greek *symbolon*. Like the "gods-pennies" that were given to servants at hiring fairs, these relics were intended not as down payments but as tokens of the solemnity of the occasion.[37] The scholastic writer John of Salisbury was among the first to claim that a written conveyance could represent the terms rather than the mere fact of an agreement. Written words, he concluded, "speak voicelessly the utterances of the absent."[38] Yet it was not until the seventeenth century that such representations became sufficiently detached from their ceremonial and personal origins to become, like the negotiable sight note, fully autonomous and creditable commercial instruments.[39] Until then, written conveyances of whatever kind retained a subordinate, often subterranean, economic status – suspiciously obscure and counterfeitable in the eyes of those for whom the paraphernalia of seals, iconic emblems, and performative utterances remained the true signs of authority and authenticity. Such diffidence was not altogether surprising in a society where forgery was rife and where, according to at least one historian, "financial dealings were accompanied wherever plausible by unblushing perjury."[40]

To the many who, like Montaigne, deemed the bargains of

the marketplace a matter of mutually exclusive gains, security lay in the visible forms of clerical and juridical authority; it resided as well in the more exhibitionist forms of personal honor whereby a person's body and the honor of his kin were symbolically offered in pledge. For all such bonds, the church provided a convenient and convincing point of reference. Countless marketing assemblies grew out of Sabbath meetings, and though the trend was to move away from ecclesiastical sites and toward secular, city markets, the successive but never quite successful edicts and statutes against churchyard markets and fairs from the tenth to the seventeenth centuries indicate how widespread and long-lived was the Sunday-marketing practice.[41]

All these means and measures were intended to preserve the transparency of exchange and the accountability of its participants in a setting where personal identity was formally framed or "subsumed" within a structure of familial or household relations.[42] The church, the guilds, and the magistrates of the Middle Ages prized the visibility of exchange almost as much as they valued the "mysteries" of their respective callings. As the record of litigation and fines reveals, the rules were numerous and enforceable, not just through the common law but through the extensive network of merchant courts. Many of these regulations, of course, served to reinforce the monopoly of a particular guild, staple, or market authority (such as a lord or abbot), but many also aimed at preventing various forms of price gouging, particularly in the provisioning of a city. Victualers, for example, were the most closely watched and most politically powerless of urban tradesmen.[43]

Again, the mercantile rule of thumb held that goods be presented, not represented. Husbandmen and other outlivers were prohibited from selling many of their crops or cloth by sample. Guild masters appointed craft searchers and city magistrates appointed market searchers to inspect the quality of goods displayed, to enforce the assizes of bread, ale, and wine, and to check the operations of forestallers, regraters, and engrossers.[44] With the notable exception of London, markets occurred generally once or twice a week, depending on the size of the city, and were distinguishable from the occasional, private marketing assembly by the tolls charged to country folk not admitted to the "freedom" of the city. A market was, in effect, a privileged point in space and time. With its cross, weighing beam, booths, stalls, pillories, and tumbrils, the market made of its publicity the basis for its claim of utility, security, and equity.

In each of these claims, the public marketplace offered English peasants an alternative to the bonds and protections of the manor. Market jurisdictions generally extended over a seven-mile radius (about a third of a day's journey), and producers (especially those in the south of England) were never more than a few miles from at least one marketplace. Even where market towns thinned out, as along the "commercial boundary" between southwest and northeast England, market fairs tended to group themselves more densely.[45] The presence of so many market towns and fairs in England pointed to the eventual, if partial, accommodation of the town to the country in the form of a provincial or regionally based agricultural capitalism. But the process of this accommodation, marked as it was by the erratic expansion and contraction of market towns, left behind a trail of protest and litigation over the depredations of petty hucksters and urban monopolists.[46]

As early as 1381, insurgent peasants and rural artisans demanded free access to all city and borough markets in England and attacked urban lawyers, manorial clerks, and royal advisors, wherever they could find them. These were targets lodged in the interstices of the three-tiered feudal hierarchy, marginal figures whose predations were judged to have gone quite literally beyond the pale. Yet these violent campaigns against certain classes of intermediaries stemmed not from some collective nostalgia for the "natural economy" of the manor but rather from an exceptional involvement in market production. And it was precisely this involvement that made the remaining marketplace exclusions and monopolies that much more burdensome, inasmuch as their effect was, in some instances, to thrust the peasant back toward an older and unwanted condition of villeinage. The peasants' revolt of 1381, like the Great Rebellion three centuries later, drew some of its greatest support from the more developed areas of southeast England as well as from the disenfranchised poor of London's teeming slums.[47] Only those already bound up, however inequitably, in the complex relations of the market could fully appreciate the political and material significance of its franchise.

As exclusive as the "freedom" of London's Cheapside, Newgate, or Leadenhall markets might have appeared to the individual yeoman or husbandman, once secured through toll or franchise it furnished a resource for his household against the insistent pressures from above to refeudalize. Though the radical priest John Ball warned his followers to "beware of guile in borough," the various statutory, spatial, temporal, and ceremonial restrictions on the medieval marketplace encouraged small producers to cross the threshold of commodity exchange.[48] The effect of this movement was to produce a peasantry (and an urban artisanry) momentarily bound together in cash and credit reciprocities that rubbed obstinately against the vertical grain of manorialism. By fostering a network of mutual indebtedness, the late medieval marketplace came to operate as a vehicle of "lateral connections" among household producers within the larger symbolic household of feudalism.[49]

As a ritually defined threshold within that larger household, the marketplace could inspire the same spontaneous group identity that anthropologists have elsewhere linked to such liminal settings as pilgrimages. Indeed, peasant revolts often took the form of a secular pilgrimage, as historians have observed, which makes it all the more intriguing that a figure like Wat Tyler should have ended his political pilgrimage of 1381 in the vicinity of the Smithfield market. There, outside London, he put to the king the peasants' second set of demands. Two days later, crowds raised the gate on London Bridge, allowing the insurgents to cross from the great "cheaping town" of Southwark into the city of London. The moment of crossing was, to use Turner's term, the moment of *communitas*.[50]

That moment, it should be added, was doubly significant, for Tyler's advance on the City was made during the feast of Corpus Christi, a climactic, communal occasion in the life of most medieval towns. The church had introduced this seasonal and dramatic celebration more than a century earlier as a vehicle for spreading the still novel doctrine of transubstantiation. At that time, religious festivals and liturgical drama were gravitating out of the church and monastic refectories, where their satire and indecorum had begun to offend churchmen, and into the marketplace, where the rising craft guilds and town corporations assumed the task of their funding and administration.[51] Historians of the theater have long singled out the Corpus Christi plays and the mystery cycles in general as the foundation of vernacular drama in England, but it is equally important to see them in their relation to the peculiarly liminal setting of the medieval marketplace.

In their earliest versions, the mystery and miracle plays brought the timeless, placeless, and essentially emblematic characteristics of ritual enactment into a milieu (the marketplace) whose ancient ambiguities had already drawn to it a complex, confining, and controlling body of ceremonial and legal practices. To a space widely conceived of as the epitome of a spatial boundary, the seasonal festivals added the evocation of a temporal boundary: the annual solstice when time, like the sun, was thought to stand still.[52] The result of this symbolic foreshortening of space and time was to make the place where the city provisioned itself the place where it envisioned itself as well. As religious drama gradually extricated itself from the confines of the church, the medieval market square became the site where actors and spectators – the roles were interchangeable – could mime, mum, and mock the hierarchical principles of the surrounding society.[53]

Festive celebration of this kind sought to revive what one folklorist has called the "topocosm," that is, the entire complex of any given locality conceived of as a living organism – hence the enormous investments of time and money by the guilds and corporations.[54] The stately processions, together with the plays that dramatized their principal themes, invited a collective affirmation of group identity and of the social rank by which that identity was structured. According to Glynne Wickham, "no other occasion in the life of that community could compare with them in promoting unity of purpose, self-fulfillment, and egalitarianism in the sight of the Almighty, notwithstanding the obvious distinctions of birth, wealth, education and skill dividing each member of that community from his fellows."[55] York was justly famous for its magisterial cycle of forty-eight miracle plays, and its Corpus Christi fair represented the "annual apogee of the city's economic endeavor." Moreover, the festival also climaxed a six-month period of initiations and promotions inside the city's guild and civic organizations, each of which was carefully indexed to the festive schedule.[56] Urban festivals thus marked boundaries or break points in the seasonal and liturgical calendars, in the social and sexual hierarchies, and in the sacred and profane worlds of medieval cosmology, and they did so, appropriately, within the ambit of that ancient and sacred threshold: the marketplace. Corpus Christi amounted to a communal rite of passage in which everyone could become a liminary. By momentarily embracing that marginal status, one joined others in a lasting appreciation of the whole.[57]

It is worth noting that the efficacy of these rituals as instruments of "mechanical solidarity" depended, paradoxically, on the participants' awareness that such communal feeling was by no means a foregone conclusion. Indeed, the success of festive celebration as a mechanism of social order or of class control hinged to a large extent on the heightened sense of risk with which ordinary people stepped into the extraterritorial world of the marketplace carnival.[58] The anger, grudges, jealousy, and desires that entered into the seasonal celebrations of the Middle Ages ran quite deep, yet at the same time lay close to the surface. Carnival would have offered little more than empty ritual had it not retained the possibility that one – indeed, many more than one – could be carried away by it. For that reason, the ultimate function of these rituals of misrule, whether as calls to arms, safety valves, or sounding boards of social antagonism, was a thing known only and quite literally *post festum*. Carnival's violent, antistructural side lay enfolded within the outer envelope of communal celebration. Carnival effectively projected another reality sitting astride the workaday world of the Middle Ages and, on appointed occasions, turning it upside down and inside out. Retrospect may allow us to see the general effect of this "reversible world" as one in which the dominant ideals of community, order, honor, and otherworldliness were clarified and reaffirmed. But in each instance, this effect remained, like everything else in carnival, open to question until the festivities had ended.[59]

The ritual boundaries of the marketplace festival served to immunize the celebrants to the otherwise threatening consequences of their brief immersion in a world of boundlessness and marginality. The license granted by rite allowed separate and incompatible structures of meaning and memory to be telescoped into a multivalent typology of symbolic renewal. Christian themes of crucifixion and resurrection merged imperceptibly with older seasonal mythologies of death and rebirth to produce entertainments rich in the symbolism of transgression and transfiguration.[60] Feasting, masking, burlesque, and the symbolic inversion of social roles distinguished the Shrove Tuesday, Hocktide, and Midsummer's Eve celebrations. Men dressed as women, and servants as masters; a subdeacon was elected the Abbot of Unreason, and a choirboy became the Boy Bishop. The visible, public boundaries of the self, so scrupulously mapped out in the traditional strictures of sumptuary laws and the newer rules of civility, were systematically manipulated, where they were not altogether erased.[61] Because the human body was periodically subject to the unpleasant regimen of famine and fast, it was engorged with food and distended with drink during carnival. Because the body was also idealized as the symbolic membrane of personal honor, it was deliberately shamed and defiled by means of kettling, ducking, and other rough, symbolic play.[62]

In each of these instances, celebrants acted out the Protean possibilities of carnival in a manner that might forestall or rectify the countless natural and social affronts that flesh and spirit were heir to. Impersonations that would have brought swift punishment under ordinary circumstances brought only laughter in the context of festive ridicule, as anonymity and androgyny were put to the service of merry remonstrance. Although the word "travesty" (borrowed from the Italian and French words for disguise) did not enter the English language until the late seventeenth century, the corrective virtues of burlesque and transvestitism were long familiar to the denizens of the marketplace. To re-dress was, in effect, to redress.[63]

Whether it was the flamboyant misrepresentation of self in burlesque, the mock coinage passed from hand to hand during the rituals of misrule, or the reckless invective hurled at all available targets, the medieval carnival declared itself a creature of the marketplace.[64] That connection is as visible in the lively sixteenth-century panoramas of Pieter Bruegel as in the cautionary tableaux of William Hogarth some two centuries later. And it is the connection drawn by Mikhail Bakhtin in his now classic study of Rabelais's world. In that analysis, Bakhtin puts Rabelais's scholastic and ecclesiastical background to the side and singles out a "second," unofficial folk culture as the immediate inspiration for *Pantagruel* (1533) and *Gargantua* (1534). Both works, he argues, staked out the countercultural terrain of the carnivalesque, where street theater mixed freely and easily with the theater of the streets. Carnival, and the ritual drama with which it was associated, shared the "freedom, frankness, and familiarity" of the marketplace; if anything, they amplified the peculiar inflections of irony and self-mockery already audible in the cries of hucksters and chapmen.[65] The spirit of the Trickster infused the marketplace festival of the Middle Ages in much the same way as it had entered into the Roman Kalends or Saturnalia, as a satirical reminder of the seasonal, regional, social, and personal differences brought together, if not reconciled, at the threshold of exchange. "Men will change their dress so as to cheat others," Rabelais wrote of carnival, "and they will run about in the streets like fools and madmen." The reversible world of festive celebration exaggerated just those functional properties of the marketplace as an "interface" between buyers and sellers that had fostered its characteristic "two-faced Janus" idiom of negotiation – a language punctuated by deeply ambivalent terms of praise and abuse.[66]

Given these ambivalences, it is almost impossible to gauge the depth and permanency of the festive and commercial ties emerging out of the late medieval marketplace. Did cases of mutual indebtedness, Rodney Hilton wonders, "indicate that neighbours were helping each other, or exploiting their needs for a cash profit?" The distinction is not altogether clear, he concludes, "but in the context of the pre-capitalist village community, it might be best to stress the element of mutual help whilst at the same time appreciating that this could imperceptibly develop into a largely commercial relationship."[67] Hilton is understandably circumspect about the motives underpinning particular market relations. After all, rituals of reciprocity may be used by one or another party to conceal a passage from mutual aid to its opposite, fraud and exploitation; they may even provide the pretext by which both partners deceive themselves as to the extent of their propitiatory or predatory calculations.[68] Yet it is at the same time difficult to understand the survival of such marketplace rituals except insofar as they visibly embodied the collective recognition of cross-purposes in exchange.

None of the commercial or juridical regulations of the medieval marketplace had ever entirely eliminated the dickering over goods from its environs, nor had they been intended to. Sharp bargains continued to be driven at the perimeter and in the interstices of the market assembly. Still, this higgling was not so much a forerunner of the "self-regulating market mechanism" as a survival of an older commercial athleticism that put wit, honor, and manliness periodically to the test.[69] What impulses the mercantile and legal restrictions on the marketplace could not, or would not, suppress, the festive and ritual forms of marketplace life thus diffused through a candid acknowledgment and caricature of *all* strategies of unequal exchange, whatever their provenance. And though the city market may have furnished the most appropriate symbolic locale for these entertainments, the tricksterism they celebrated blended equal elements of rural and urban mythology, as instanced in such shrewd country rascals as Mak, Robin Goodfellow, and Tyll Howlglass. With each of these antiheroes, the more aggressive and predatory dimensions of market activity were confronted and converted to comic fables of licit and illicit opportunism between linked pairs of antagonists.

This view of exchange as a paired activity, whether friendly or vindictive, deserves underscoring, for whatever differences there might have been between the official and unofficial voices of medieval moralism, canonists and comedians were in accord in treating market exchange as a distinctively bilateral or reciprocal relationship. To be sure, questions of commutative (or individual) justice overshadowed questions of distributive (or social) justice in ethical and casuistical writing from Aquinas onward, but this was largely because the answers to the distributive questions were already embedded in the rules of access to markets, the prohibitions against hoarding, the provisions for public granaries, and, not least of all, the retributive resources of carnival.[70]

Marketplace rivalry was commonly understood to be a contest

between rather than among individuals, an assumption reflected in the long-standing and widespread diffidence toward speculative investment and fully negotiable commercial instruments. The market was a *place* and the trader was expected to make his ventures within it, not against it. The costly "freedom" that towns and cities offered their merchants and craftsmen was, in many respects, a freedom *from* the hardships of what would now be called unrestricted competition. Indeed, the word "competition," in its ancient and medieval Latin form, was little more than a neutral term used to denote instances of simultaneity, parallelism, coincidence, or agreement; it did not as yet suggest the conflictual or antagonistic associations it would acquire as an Anglicized noun in the late sixteenth century, much less the economically productive and socially liberatory connotations it would gain as a category of late eighteenth-century Physiocratic theory.[71]

Medieval schoolmen and satirists confined themselves to the microprocessual aspects of commodity exchange precisely because for them the aggregate effects of individual preferences were conceptually divorced from the behavior of the market and the society as a whole. Specific price transactions could conceivably deviate *from* the norm, as individual buyers and sellers outwitted one another, but they were not to be treated in any rigorous sense as fluctuating constituents or determinants *of* the norm, except perhaps at just those moments of dearth when authorities (or the populace itself) intervened to set prices. It is true, of course, that the "just price" of the Middle Ages was not an administered price but rather a market price or, more precisely, a "common estimate" *(publica aestimatio)* of value in the absence of force, fraud, or conspiracy.[72] Still, when the intricate pattern of statutory and symbolic expectations surrounding the medieval marketplace is taken into account, that common estimate appears to have been quite as intimately bound up with the shared predispositions of a "moral economy" as with the aggregate calculations of a political economy.

It is worth recalling here that Edward Thompson first introduced the concept of a moral economy in order to explain the cultural, as opposed to the immediately material, context of eighteenth-century crowd actions in the marketplace. By that phrase he meant to indicate the survival in preindustrial England of a "popular consensus" or "traditional view of social norms and obligations, [and] of the proper economic functions of several parties within the community," such as merchants, millers, and bakers. Now, to the degree that this consensus was taken as a sanction for direct, popular intervention to set prices or measures during inflationary times, it could, like carnival, legitimize the expression of a corrective egalitarianism. On such occasions, the ordinary preoccupation with petty tricksterism would give way to a concern over larger (and ordinarily unquestioned) exactions by local notables. But, as Thompson acknowledges, the consensus itself remained unequivocally hierarchical in its outlook on marketplace responsibilities.[73] The "moral" of moral economy refers to the customary imperatives of a paternalist culture, not to the categorical imperatives of a bourgeois ideology.[74]

What Thompson says of the eighteenth-century marketplace applies with even greater force to its medieval forerunner, where the bonds of corporate obligation (that is, of guild, church, or estate) cut far more deeply. In the years extending from the Conquest through the Tudor ascendancy, the market occupied a specially appointed space where local society materially and culturally reproduced itself. It was an island in space and time, a threshold at which the antagonisms, reciprocities, and solidarities of a particular locality could be periodically confined and tempered into the social and cultural matrix of simple or small commodity production.

Regarded in this light, the intensity of commodity circulation in late medieval and early modern England acquires a double aspect: on the one hand, the startling numerical density of market towns and fairs throughout the countryside and, on the other, the remarkable symbolic density of meanings and expectations attached to each marketing assembly. To this twofold intensity of the marketplace we may link, if only conjecturally, the marked though temporary success of rural and urban communes in resisting both the seigneurial pressures toward refeudalization and the countervailing entrepreneurial pressures toward industrial capitalism during the fifteenth and sixteenth centuries.[75] Neither form of resistance survived the English Civil War, but together they provide the most appropriate context in which to situate the complex social and cultural responses to the gradual diffusion or displacement of market exchange during the waning years of the sixteenth century and the early years of the seventeenth. They also help to explain the peculiarly theatrical terms into which the response to that displacement was cast.

III

So closely identified were the institutions of market and theater during the later Middle Ages that few contemporaries ever thought to compare them. It was as if they shared a common anatomy or frame that occasion might dress out differently according to the needs of the ecclesiastical and commercial calendars. Throughout the fifteenth and sixteenth centuries, market crosses and city gates were converted to platforms for spectacular civic pageantry quite as easily as hucksters' stalls were adapted to the more modest demands of booth theater.[76] Both forms of exchange evoked the experience of a threshold; both occupied extraterritorial, extratemporal spaces that served imagination as well as interest, cosmology as well as commerce; and both operated as containers or crucibles of social antagonism. Events repeatedly showed the capacity of ritual drama to reconcile social conflict or, as in the case of Kett's Rebellion (1549), to inflame it.[77] The legitimacy of the marketplace as a social institution was inseparable from its theatricality, for the medieval criteria of authority and authenticity required that both attributes be bodied forth: deliberately displayed, performed, and witnessed. The marketplace of the Middle Ages, like the vernacular theater that had grown up within its bounds, was above all a "place for seeing."[78] Visibility was its indispensable property.

The point warrants emphasis because it was the one on which attitudes toward both theater and market eventually turned during the English Renaissance. As early as the opening decades of the seventeenth century, a significant number of Britons had come to suspect that the visibility of the marketplace had been seriously compromised; by that point, its theatricality no longer served as an unequivocal voucher of the secular world, nor for that matter as a mimetic reminder of the world that lay beyond. Rather, theatricality itself had begun to acquire renewed connotations of invisibility, concealment, and *mis*representation, connotations that were at once intriguing and incriminating. Renaissance writers reenacted the ambivalent response of antiquity to the marketplace, first in their Neoplatonic attraction to "self-fashioning" and then in their equally Platonic revulsion from impersonation.[79] Such changed perceptions and mixed feelings found wide expression throughout the documentary culture of the period, but nowhere were these confusions and misgivings more readily apparent than in the words with which writers chose to resolve them – the popular linguistic coinages that Francis Bacon aptly labeled "idols of the market-place."[80]

The word "market" entered the English language during the twelfth century, at approximately the same time that documents record the first statutory efforts to set aside public places and times for the purchase and sale of provisions and livestock.[81] In its earliest usage, the word referred alternately to the area, the occasion, or the gathering of buyers and sellers assembled within a specified time and place. The medieval "market" suggests a more or less sharply delineated sphere of commerce, an experienced physical and social space. It was, in short, a distinctively situated term.

By the sixteenth century, however, the meanings of "market" had multiplied and grown more abstract, articulating the progressive differentiation of social relations the word had been called upon to express. "Market" now referred to the acts of both buying and selling, regardless of locale, and to the price or exchange value of goods and services. A culturally confined site was no longer the precondition of a market so-called. Rather, the topography of exchange had been made to depend on a market now understood to be the mere presence of marketable items or disposable income. As a matter of customary usage, the process of commodity exchange had spilled over the boundaries that had once defined it. By the end of the eighteenth century, "market" had come to imply, especially in literate circles, a boundless and timeless phenomenon – so much so, in fact, that legal thinkers felt constrained to set off the original, situated meaning·of the term as a "market overt."

By thus revealing the gradual separation of the generality of a market *process* from the particularity of a market *place,* etymology makes its own modest contribution to the critique of political economy; that is, it traces out, as a matter of popular idiom, a critical transformation in the productive and distributive relations of early modern England. In this instance, language records the historical appearance of exchange value as a perceived or half-perceived property of the commodity distinct from and alien to its specifically useful or aesthetic aspects as a human artifact.[82] Like the commodity, the word "market" comes to live a dual existence in language. Within the word, a reference to market-ability appears alongside a reference to the marketplace, subordinating the particular place to the abstract process that has ranged itself around it.

This etymological inversion of the container (marketplace) with the contained (market process) bears a striking resemblance to Marx's classic formulation of the shifting relation between commodities and money: from the centripetal or implosive relations of the precapitalist market to the centrifugal or explosive relations of the capitalist market. According to this version of the transition to capitalism, the more frequently commodities are consumed and thereby removed from an expanding circulation, the farther money, as the durable token of equivalence, seems to move away of its own accord from its point of departure in the marketplace. As a result, what begins as a bounded process of the circulation of commodities through the medium of money (C–M–C) ends as the boundless circulation of money via the medium of commodities (M–C–M). "Circulation," Marx wrote, "sweats money from every pore."[83]

To those caught up in this expanded circulation of commodities of the early modern epoch, the very liquidity of the money form – its apparent capacity to commute specific obligations, utilities, and meanings into general, fungible equivalents – bespoke the same boundless autonomy that Aristotle had once condemned as an unnatural, "chrematistic" form of exchange.[84] As the extent of dealing *outside* the public marketplace widened during the "long sixteenth century," drawing land, labor, and a variety of continental credit innovations into the expanding circle of England's internal trade, fewer and fewer transactions fell into the bilateral mold of traditional exchange. For the "progressive" landowner as for the rising number of middlemen making their way to his door, the ceremonial, periodic, and provincial character of the public marketplace had become a burdensome restraint of trade as early as the sixteenth century. By resisting or evading its rules, they could free themselves to gather information and to enter into contracts without regard to fixed times or places. The conclusion, though not the profit, was foregone: a net reduction in the information costs of capitalist landlord, country jobber, and urban broker.

For the immediate producer or consumer, however, the immediate conveniences of private negotiation were balanced by new information costs, the measure of which now lay concealed behind a mysterious veil of commercial instruments and intermediaries. Once out of sight of the market cross, "professional middlemen and speculative traders" found themselves in an ideal position "to exploit the partial and incomplete distribution of information about commodities" that their presence had occasioned.[85] "Among the upper ranks of society," Joan Thirsk writes, "among the gentry, yeomen, and merchants with an eye for good business, an almost encyclopedic body of knowledge existed by the late sixteenth century about where the best markets were to be found for different types of goods."[86] Thus it was that the same means and measures that reduced the cost of tenants' access *to* commodity markets also raised the marginal cost of success *within* them. As the sixteenth century advanced, the multiplication of intermediaries and the expanded scope of their operation obscured, even as they lubricated, the new "mechanisms" of marketing procedure. The transparency of commodity exchange declined accordingly.[87]

That market relations should grow opaque in tandem with the monetization of the factors and products of production is scarcely surprising. The word "liquidity" itself conveys the paradoxical sense of a pecuniary measure that clarifies and renders indisputable in one instance only to homogenize and render formless in another. Money provides the standard by which values can be assigned in exchange; yet it is also the "liquid" medium that, according to Marx, splits the exchange transaction "into two mutually indifferent acts: exchange of commodities for money, exchange of money for commodities; purchase and sale."[88] "Money is the purest embodiment of liquidity," economists insist, and as such, it "makes it possible to divide the act of exchange of real goods between two dates."[89] By thus extending the moment and the distance of exchange, money undermines the immediate bilateral negotiation of direct barter, while simultaneously underwriting a prolonged, multilateral competition among buyers and sellers. Money thus seems to bear within itself the seed of capitalism. And since money served as a medium of England's public markets throughout their long history, it is but a short step – and one that at least some historians have taken – to suggest the presence of a protocapitalist market in England almost from the moment of the Conquest.[90]

Yet money's capacity to defer or postpone consumption (and hence to expand its role as a source of liquidity) had always been limited during the Middle Ages in several important respects: first, by the custom of England's periodic markets to clear their transactions within the space and span of a day's assembly; second, by the encumbrances imposed on exchange by the market's highly personal, symbolic, and hierarchical character; third, by the commitment of most money income to nonmarket obligations such as rents, fines, tallages, and taxes; and finally, by the persistent disjunction between the use of money as a unit of account and its use as a medium of exchange – a disjuncture not recognized until the late fifteenth century nor fully remedied until the late seventeenth century.[91]

Considered against the background of these constraints, the medieval concept of liquidity is best understood in the restrictive, precautionary sense of a hoard or asset saved to settle, clear, or "liquidate" actual or potential liabilities. Liquidity was a measure by which to establish rather than to expand the "natural limits" of exchange. Money could not beget itself, as it were; nor could it yield to its owner goods or services beyond those procured in a single act of exchange. Money was a "consumptible" in scholastic terminology; it was to be lent out of charity for purposes of consumption, consumed in the process of its use, and replaced without increment.[92] Despite or, perhaps, because of its position as the "indispensable moneylender of the period," the church drew freely on Roman law and on Aristotle's disdainful discussion of chrematistic exchange to paint a picture of money as a "barren metal."[93] Profit was allowed as a return on risk or labor, to be sure, and interest was countenanced under certain stipulated exceptions to the doctrinal prohibitions against usury. And evidence shows that the number of testamentary restitutions for usury began to fall after 1350, suggesting the waning influence of ecclesiastical policy on the private conscience.[94] Still, the general canonical and theological strictures against interest remained relatively unchanged and unchallenged until the mid–fifteenth century, with the result that credit and loan transactions were forced either into the narrow but licit channel of partnership and annuity or, as was more often the case, into the broad but illicit channel of the triple contract *(contractus trina)*, the dead pledge *(vadium mortium)*, the conditional sale, and the interest-bearing traffic in exchange notes. Given such elaborate and circuitous credit mechanisms, it is not surprising that the weight of ecclesiastical reproach tended to fall on the all too visible transactions of the petty pawnbroker rather than on the more discreet ventures of the large-scale investor.[95]

The concealment of large loans protected the church as well as the investor. As long as bills of exchange remained non-negotiable instruments, as they did in England well into the seventeenth century, ecclesiastical authorities did not have to reckon with the practices of a full-blown money market. And, indeed, English tracts against usury did not begin to proliferate until the late sixteenth century, when such a market did in fact begin to materialize. Of course, as long as the church and lay critics held fast to the medieval vision of usury, prospective bankers and merchants found themselves at a distinct and continuing disadvantage. And so it was for England in the later Middle Ages, for on the rare occasions when the most dynamic aspects of liquidity were even acknowledged, it was with the specific purpose, often as not, of proscribing them. English law forbade its citizens from becoming private money-changers, just as it required alien merchants to obtain hosts or sponsors for their trade. Lombards and Jews thus operated (and suffered) as the despised *metics* of medieval England, while native entrepreneurs turned instead to such devices as the sale of rents in order to translate their otherwise fixed capital from "a smaller to a greater liquidity."[96]

During the late fifteenth century, it is true, a debate arose within the church over two controversial titles to interest *(damnum emergens,* or "loss occurring," and *lucrum cessans,* or "profit ceasing"), the consequence of which was to inch the scholastic writers closer to a recognition of money as short-term capital. But it was only within the context of the expanded commerce of the sixteenth and seventeenth centuries that ecclesiastical authors such as Cajetan, Summenhart, and Lessius began to embrace a definition of interest as the opportunity or displacement cost of sums available not just for settlement but for investment. Once this view was broached, the "liquidity preference" itself acquired a speculative connotation to balance its earlier, precautionary associations. Money now appeared to be a source of productive possibilities, not just a protection against them. The desire for liquidity thereby came to mean something more than the thirst for solvency; it suggested a simultaneous readiness and reluctance to transact – a threshold moment of indecision in the cycle of exchange, a moment frozen in the money form itself. Redefined in this way, liquidity thus translated and condensed the liminal associations of the marketplace and the market process into a permanent speculative posture or attitude that subjected the world to a reflexive calculus of returns on capital. And to the degree that liquidity became a principle brought *to* early modern society – a criterion of exchangeability against which that society could itself be measured – it promised to extend the threshold experience out of the residuary, ritual confines of the marketplace and into the midst of everyday life. "He that buyes must sell," Thomas Nashe wrote in 1593; "shrewd Alcumists there are risen vp, that will pick a merchandise out of euery thing, and not spare to set vp theyr shops of buying and selling even in the Temple."[97]

IV

Perhaps the most effective and, in its way, theatrical force behind the gradual erosion of the bounded marketplace was the fair. The fair was, generally speaking, an annual or semiannual institution that figured significantly in the commercial revolution of the Middle Ages (950–1350) and that, historians agree, declined thereafter. But though English fairs did share in the decay that afflicted the great fairs of Champagne and Flanders during the fourteenth century, they expanded once again during the seventeenth century.[98] Their revival during this epoch is impossible to understand apart from the particular economic developments to which they were instrumental: the money market, the labor market, the agricultural trade, and the new "consumer industries" of the sixteenth and seventeenth centuries. In each of these cases, the fair tended to move transactions outside the purview of manorial and municipal authority and thus to bypass the regulative structure of the public market.

Fairs were above all marketing assemblies and, for that reason alone, displayed obvious resemblances to and connections with the traditional marketplace. Indeed, the rights to hold a yearly fair and a weekly market were often granted to the same owner and within the same charter. Like the first manorial markets, early fairs had seigneurial and ecclesiastical sponsors; most of them dated from the twelfth and thirteenth centuries and were associated with specific saint's days, despite some evidence of pre-Christian origins.[99] Bartholomew Fair was but one example. Chartered by the prior of St. Bartholomew in 1133, the fair was held every August 24 outside London's walls in the "liberty" of Smithfield, where the guilds performed their mysteries against the backdrop of an active livestock market. Although the priory was dissolved in 1538, the fair and its market survived well into the nineteenth century, its resilience undoubtedly springing from its capacity to supply meat to the plebian, mead to the publican, meditation to the philosopher, and, as we shall see, metaphor to the playwright.[100]

Fairs were nonetheless distinguishable from the fixed marketplace by their infrequency and informality. Local surplus was disposed of in the weekly markets; wholesale goods found their way to the fair. From the merchant-bankers to the petty chapmen, the entire "mercantile estate," as Marx called them, ventured to the fair, where the usual tolls and prohibitions against "foreigners" and usury were suspended.[101] Because of the fair's slack bookkeeping, peasants and middlemen who sought to avoid the sharp scrutiny of the local market search flocked to its grounds. Though each fair had its lord or corporation, its jurisdictional court of "pie-powder," and its religious associations, its boundaries were considerably more permeable than those of the market hall.

As the structure of rural land tenure in England tipped toward capitalist tenantry during the sixteenth century, and as the extent of private marketing correspondingly expanded, factors, jobbers, brokers, and badgers entered more aggressively into bulk trade by forestalling grain, cereals, and other agricultural goods at or near the point of production in order to resell them by samples at the country fairs.[102] Fairs also served as temporary entrepôts for the flourishing sixteenth- and seventeenth-century trade in low-priced domestic goods and handicrafts. The circulation of these goods in the countryside brought cash to the landless rural craftsmen, for whom these industries were an indispensable by-employment, at the same time that it bound these producers together by means of the multiple ligatures of petty credit trans-actions. In either case, the moving finger of the fair traced and retraced a reticulate pattern of inland commerce whose delicate and mobile filaments eluded the grasp of the guilds' visible hand.[103]

Still, the intricate network of private dealing that emerged in the Tudor countryside was scarcely the design of an invisible hand. The deliberate consolidation of landholding among the gentry and greater yeomanry in the country and of craft and commercial activity among the merchant guilds in the cities left a growing number of landless and masterless producers stranded in the middle. The multiple employments or "livings" to which these producers gravitated in order to survive conformed neither to the feudal division of estates nor to the emerging doctrine of callings nor, for that matter, to Adam Smith's ideal of speciali-zation via the technical division of labor.[104] They fell outside all available schemes of social classification. The itinerant farm la-borer of East Anglia who produced and occasionally peddled the brightly colored new draperies of the early seventeenth century thus foiled the disciplinary intent of the Statute of Artificers (1563) by circumventing its antiquarian categories, just as he escaped the patent dues on his cloth by dealing with chapmen privately, circuitously, and at the fairs.[105] The informal freemasonry of the wayfaring trader in these goods, with its secret tokens and rep-resentations of membership, only strengthened the suspicions already harbored toward freelance marketeers by guildsmen, whose own collusion had always taken the form of an overt and ritually sanctified franchise. Hence, when depression struck the English cloth industry in the 1620s, London drapers did not hesitate to blame "the false and deceitful making, dyeing and dressing of our cloth and stuff" by domestic interlopers in their trade.[106]

Popular suspicion of commercial deception, however, ran deeper than the dye. Of the many tracts on trade that appeared in the early seventeenth century, the majority fretted less about the adulteration of cloth than about the debasement of money.[107] Here again, the target was a money market that had originated in the credit arrangements Italian merchants had introduced at the thirteenth-century fairs of Europe. Although earlier fairs had followed the common practice of settling all accounts at the end of each fair's activities, later fairs came to mark quarterly solstices in a new fiscal and financial calendar whereby longer-term, interregional debts were liquidated or reassigned. English merchants, for example, collected on their king's purchases at the four great fairs of Northampton, St. Ives, Boston, and Winchester, and English wool factors settled their accounts with Dutch and Flemish clothiers at the four seasonal "marts" of the Netherlands.[108] There, in the exchange fairs, the personal and ceremonial apparatus of the marketplace gradually gave way to the relatively impersonal framework of a money and credit market; and there, under the successive auspices of Genoese, Flemish, and English merchants, the commercial bill of exchange moved steadily toward the ideal of unlimited and unrestricted endorsement. All along the sixteenth-century "commercial axis" that linked the Antwerp and London exchanges, new forms of liquidity were developing that overflowed, where they did not burst, the mold of medieval commerce.[109]

It was not that public marketplaces had somehow ceased to exist in the sixteenth and seventeenth centuries; it was rather that they had yielded primacy of place to a marketing network – a "counter market" in Braudel's phrase – that had grown up around them. London cutlers, for example, had once been prohibited from working "within any Aley, Chambre, Garet" or elsewhere than "in open Schoppe by the Strete side," and armorers and brasiers had been repeatedly warned not to make their sales "in innes and privy places."[110] By the early seventeenth century, however, middlemen were purchasing a significant and ever growing proportion of agricultural and industrial commodities at the point of production only to resell them at the inns and shops ringing the market squares. At the same time, London's own hucksters were invading the city's public markets, thereby displacing the country folk who had come to sell their wares. True, producers, retailers, and consumers had always carried on some measure of private dealing in country and city alike, but the practice broadened and accelerated considerably during this epoch. Unlicensed rural artificers established themselves at "the boundaries of parishes, hundreds, or counties, where jurisdiction was disputed," while their urban counterparts thronged to the "liberties" around London.[111] Because economic and legal jurisdiction over this expansive suburban corridor had been mooted by the dissolution of its religious houses, thousands of weavers, winders, tanners, glovers, brewers, and beggars streamed to the hastily constructed tenements of Southwark, Stepney, and St. Giles in order to enjoy the districts' residual immunities.[112] So it transpired that in the early seventeenth century, a new extraterritorial zone of production and exchange sprang up outside London's ancient marketplaces and thus out of reach of their juridical, ceremonial, and talismanic protections – and restrictions. Carried along on a tide of commercial paper that spoke "voicelessly the utterances of the absent," commerce now seemed to fill the intervals between fairs and the interstices between markets. For those guildsmen who still clung to traditional principles and prerogatives, the foe had become a new and boundless silent trade.

Boundlessness was not without its benefits, to be sure. The centrifugal expansion of commodity circulation reduced provincial disparities in prices and buffered the regional impact of shortage and surplus, especially following the lean decades of the 1620s and 1630s. Yet if England was to become less "harvest sensitive" by the mid–seventeenth century, it had already become far more price sensitive than it had ever been before. The blessings of productivity were secured only at the cost of new price fluctuations, which fell with variable force on the different social classes and which, in doing so, further undermined the regulatory features of the public market.[113]

As the circle of guild authority steadily shrank during these years, it fell to the state to urge local enforcement of a moral economy that recurring depressions and their companions – theft, profiteering, and riot – threatened to shatter. By the turn of the century, commercial evasions of the public market were bringing swift and often violent retaliation by angry crowds. When unemployed rural artisans and their wives rose up in the marketplaces and docksides of western England's manufacturing towns and ports, for example, they made no effort to set "just" or customary compensation for the merchants and shipmasters whose foodstuffs they had seized and distributed among themselves. And on these grounds, Buchanan Sharp has described such riots less as examples of popular justice than as desperate petitions for immediate relief.[114] But if we are to regard these late-sixteenth and early-seventeenth-century disorders as "representations" of collective grievances, then we must see them as ones in which the expressive aims of popular assembly had given way to the instantaneous rewards and revenge of direct expropriation.

Although these collective confiscations sprang out of an overwhelming sense of despair and resignation, they were nonetheless overt acts of power. And, as such, they threatened to overthrow the very rules of representation and authority within which class negotiations had theretofore operated. Only a tempered response by the crown (itself increasingly beleaguered) seemed capable of reclaiming for these popular interventions in the marketplace their original status as demonstrative gestures within an encompassing paternalist dialogue. Rioters were thus met with a mixture of terror and mercy calculated to deflect the insurrectionary potential of disorder by depriving it of its immediate material rewards while, at the same time, recognizing its expressive legitimacy. Ringleaders were executed in deliberately public displays, but equally public measures were taken to enforce communal sanctions on commercial middlemen.[115] In 1587 Elizabeth's Privy Council issued a *Book of Orders,* instructing local justices as to the measures required to counteract grain exports and price gouging in time of scarcity and unemployment. Revisions of this code were reissued with every crisis thereafter, and though the evidence of the orders' immediate economic efficacy remains thin, their symbolic authority may well have reduced the incidence of popular disturbance over profiteering. If the flood tides of civil war may be said to have washed away this "highwater mark of Elizabethan paternalism," they yet failed to remove the sediment of popular memory.[116] The eighteenth century, not the seventeenth, became the age of the food riot as an instrument of *taxation populaire*.[117]

By that time, of course, the ground of commodity exchange had shifted considerably. From the dissolution of the monasteries to the Restoration, between a quarter and a third of England's total landed area entered the private market, with sales peaking by the second decade of the seventeenth century. Capitalist tenantry likewise increased as more and more rural families grasped at that precarious lease on life: the copyhold.[118] Those unable to own or rent land joined the swelling ranks of wage labor on the road or at the hiring fairs. And as wages changed from a supplementary to a single source of income for rural families, the status of wage work correspondingly plummeted to a point unknown since antiquity. By the beginning of the seventeenth century, wages had fallen to their lowest level in three centuries, while geographic mobility had surged to what was perhaps its highest point.[119] "We see here," Marx wrote of such phenomena, "how the exchange of commodities breaks through all local and personal bounds inseparable from direct barter, and develops the circulation of the products of social labour; and on the other hand, how it develops a whole network of social relations spontaneous in their growth and entirely beyond the control of the actors." For no one was this observation more accurate than for the sixteenth century's itinerant laborers. Half peasant, half proletarian, they found themselves "ground down into a sort of homogeneous social matter," liminaries poised forever on the threshold of their own exchange.[120]

If a larger theory of these vast transformations eluded most contemporary observers, as the documentary record suggests it did, the experience of such changes nonetheless left its legible imprint on ordinary language. Thus, to the question What is a market?, we have seen etymology supply a rough yet illuminating chronology of definitions, with each successive meaning supplementing and altering the sense of the original. In a way, the word "market" has served as a convenient palimpsest on which each age has inscribed its understanding of exchange without wholly effacing the record of those that went before. In fact, the earliest definition of the word as a market*place* has never entirely faded

from view. Rather, within the word, the sense of place was made
to surrender its peculiarly liminal and extraterritorial associations
to a transactional *process* that had sprung up around it. Close upon
this redefinition came yet another, for the process of exchange
yielded, in its turn, a *principle* of exchange value or liquidity that
abstracted still further from the original meaning.

This tangled trail of definitions discloses a double movement
over time. On the one hand, linguistic usage indicates that exchange had moved outward, as the expanded circulation of commodities; on the other, it suggests that exchange had moved
inward, as a subjective standard of commensurability against
which the world itself could be judged. Whereas the classical and
medieval definitions of the market implied a society that placed
exchange at the threshold, seventeenth-century usage intimated
an exchange that put society at the threshold, translating the
infinitely various contents of that society into a rich and readily
transactionable stock. "Such is the world," one English observer
concluded, "which is nothing but a shop of all change."[121]

Mercurial and Protean imagery was, of course, a commonplace
of the English Renaissance, one that Marx himself did not hesitate
to appropriate when describing money as the "god among commodities" and the "fraternization of impossibilities."[122] The vivid
metaphors that poets and projectors employed to capture the
effects of liquidity revealed a more or less inchoate view of the
market as something more than a generative principle, something
closer, in fact, to a transformative *power*.

Now, in the measure that this image of market power conveyed a new sense of vulnerability to the fluctuations of commodity exchange, it was not entirely misplaced. As Bernard
Supple has shown, the exceptionally high liquidity of commercial
capital, coupled with the equally high mobility of entrepreneurial
talent and (to a lesser degree) of skilled labor, left early-seventeenth-century England far more responsive to commercial dis-
turbances than it had been a century before or than it would be
a century later.[123] In many respects, the detached assets of England's mercantile estate bore a closer resemblance to the mobile
resources of twentieth-century finance capital than to the relatively fixed investments of nineteenth-century industrial capital.
Indeed, it could be said that the same money market experience

that had moved merchant-bankers closer to a modern concept of capital had also kept that concept just beyond their grasp. To most seventeenth- and eighteenth-century merchants and tradesmen, capital remained theoretically inseparable from the short-term credit and transfer instruments that had nurtured their first expectation of constant returns. "Capital" continued to be defined, as late as Smith's *Wealth of Nations,* as the money invested in an enterprise, not as the machinery and materials in which the money was invested. Money, not capital, was the "visible God."[124]

Consequently, when commercial crisis struck, as it did in the 1620s, Britons were offered a choice of two providential explanations: one visible and secular; the other, invisible and divine. Both the mercantilist and the Puritan versions of events rooted the catastrophe in a theory of debasement and corruption, and both accordingly sought to purify, clarify, and rectify what each regarded as the critical conditions of belief: commercial and religious. Mercantilism and Puritanism embraced representational strategies aimed at righting a world that money (among other things) appeared to have upended, a world that threatened to become, in effect, a permanent carnival. For this very reason, perhaps, the theater quickly became the terrain on which this struggle to redefine the grounds of exchange relations was most vividly and vigorously joined. Separated, like the market, from its original ritual and hierarchical aegis, the Elizabethan and Jacobean theater furnished a laboratory of representational possibilities for a society perplexed by the cultural consequences of its own liquidity. The theater, too, promised the "fraternization of impossibilities." For this alone, it would have invited the hostility of those who sought to cleanse their world of all symbolic promiscuity.

Still, these elective affinities between market and theater might never have become effective affinities had the new geography of exchange not placed the antagonists in such explosive proximity. It was no accident that the common players of the English Renaissance sought the same immunities of London's liberties as the alien craftsmen who constructed their playhouses and fashioned their costumes; nor was it wholly fortuitous that a significant number of these craftsmen should have been drawn from the growing ranks of radical religious separatists. Liberty and license lay at London's threshold. Masterless artificers, petty chapmen, vagabonds, sailors, criminals, players, and Puritans – all of them marginal figures in the Tudor–Stuart landscape – found themselves crowded together in the strange, extraterritorial zone outside the walls but inside the "bars" of the City.

It had been to London's suburban liberty of Southwark, for example, that Wat Tyler had brought his rebels in 1381, Geoffrey Chaucer his pilgrims in 1387, Jack Cade his insurgents in 1450, Edward Alleyn his players in 1588, and Cuthbert Burbage the timbers for his Globe Theatre in 1599. And it was to Southwark that wayfaring preachers came to lecture the thousands of Protestant refugees who eked out a living (and an occasional prison sentence) cheek by jowl with Bankside prostitutes and cutpurses from the Clink. *"London,"* Nashe lamented, "what are thy Suburbes but licensed Stewes?"[125] Yet it was just this hothouse atmosphere of art, piety, criminality, and entrepreneurialism that moved some of England's most articulate, imaginative, and inspired citizens to find forms and figures adequate to the new and vexing "economy" that had brought them so indiscriminately together.

More than two millennia had passed, meanwhile, since Aristotle had first broached his initial and altogether modest definition of "economy" as the rules regarding proper household management. In that time, neither the practices of merchants nor the exegeses of scholastics had done much to alter that classical understanding. Only under the pressures of Europe's seventeenth-century crisis did the constituents of a new definition of economy – as an autonomous and self-regulating process of resource allocation – begin to coalesce in the minds of commercial and courtly policy makers.[126] By this time, however, the relation between the marketplace and the society in which it had been for so long materially and metaphorically lodged had so drastically changed as to require not just a recalculation but a refiguration of all exchange. Small wonder, then, that those confused by the vicissitudes of exchange value in their own lives should have invoked the "second nature" of the stage-world to express their sense of inverted causality, of a world turned upside down.

The curious intellectual career of the *theatrum mundi* emblem is, in this respect, but one of many evidentiary sources in which we can still make out the lingering imprint of a culture's efforts to grasp this nearly Copernican redefinition of economy. The cosmological metaphor of the "theater of the world" captured the scale if not the detail of England's new map of commodity circulation, one where markets were no longer seen to revolve around the periodic and cyclical needs of the commonwealth but were rather understood to generate permanent pressures and attractions of their own, around which the commonwealth now gravitated.

This historical shift in the market's meaning – from a place to a process to a principle to a power – suggests a gradual displacement of concreteness in the governing concept of commodity exchange. The attributes of materiality, reality, and agency ordinarily assigned to the sphere of social relations (or to God) were implicitly reassigned to the sphere of commodity relations, as supply and demand took on a putative life of their own. It remains a matter of some debate, of course, whether the market's concreteness was displaced by events or misplaced by theory, but it is nonetheless useful to bear this shift in mind when traversing the seemingly unbridgeable divide between the colorful mythologies of antiquity and the relatively pallid folklore of capitalism.

2. Another nature

That, for which many their Religion,
Most men their Faith, all change their honesty,
Profit, (that gilded god) Commodity,
He that would grow damn'd rich, yet live secure,
Must keep a case of faces...

> Thomas Dekker and John
> Webster, *If It be not Good, the
> Devil is in It* (1610–12)

ENGLAND'S LITERATE CITIZENS steeped their response to the placeless market in mythological and magical allusions. But it is difficult to know what to make of these references when scholars themselves are at odds over the meaning and functions of mythical and magical thinking, even within the relatively stable confines of "primitive" societies. We are told by some anthropologists, for example, that myths are best understood as legitimating "charters" for the social institutions and practices of a particular culture and that magic serves as a propitiatory technology used by believers, albeit misguidedly, to control a world defined by myth.[1] Now we have already seen that such definitions can shed light on the meanings with which various societies have, in effect, annotated the record of their exchange relations. Hermes was, after all, a divinity who embodied the equivocal character of the trade he was charged with protecting. Still, the illumination that these definitions offer is at best partial for early modern England, because the character and conditions of belief were themselves in flux. In the same measure that the English fell back on their mythical and magical resources to explain and order the social consequences of a burgeoning agricultural and commercial capitalism, those same resources were falling away before them. What is more, the very sense of a charter, mythical or otherwise, acquired a new ambiguity during the sixteenth and seventeenth centuries as the fundamental terms of authority and authenticity were challenged and subverted from within. Structures of meaning and feeling that had long anchored themselves in a distinctively landed set of social relationships began to lose their moorings as those relations shifted toward new forms of tenantry. To many eyes, these new and often elusive forms of exchange were gradually emptying ancient warrants of their legal substance, leaving behind only the hollow mask or shell of entitlement. "Here lay / a mannor bound fast in a skin of parchment," the villain of Philip Massinger's *The City Madam* (1632) exclaims. "The wax continuing hard, the acres melting."[2] Behind the outward authority of ancient writ and conveyance now lurked the specter of sudden alienation and forfeiture.

Perhaps the commonest form of land tenure in early modern England was the copyhold, a title that drew its name from the copies of the manorial court roll entries given to tenants as a record of their rights and obligations. Because the adjudication of these rights and obligations depended to so great an extent on the particular "custom of the manor," however, copyholds were among the most manipulated and disputed forms of title. Not surprisingly, the word and its cognates began to display the darker and more ironic colorations of this protracted and litigious contest over custom, memory, and authority. To "change one's copy," for instance, became a common sixteenth-century expression for any alteration of "style, tone, behavior, or course of action" so abrupt and startling as to suggest that a person had assumed an entirely new character. To attempt a pretense or imposture, according to standard usage, was to make "a copy of one's countenance."[3] In this fashion, language metaphorically translated a narrow, technical conflict over legal forms into a more figurative and therefore encompassing sphere of self-representation. Embedded within the idiomatic analogy between legal and social forms of identity was a new and somewhat sinister implication that the human face, like the "skin of parchment," was an autonomous, even alien, instrument of misrepresentation. For those disposed to put such thoughts in writing, it seemed as if the personal properties of the self were becoming as ambiguous as the "real" properties to which that self, as a "freeborn Englishman," might lay claim.

Ancient myth and magic were slim resources indeed to cope with the mysterious powers of a price system that appeared to have set an entire countryside – its inhabitants and its estates – into motion, and yet popular writers resorted to both in their determination to give order and meaning to the unsettled and unsettling character of their social relations. At the same time, they drew on the more topical, moralizing tradition of satire and complaint inherited from the fiery sermons of itinerant preachers during the Middle Ages.[4] Older archetypes thereby mingled with newer conceits to form a distinctively Elizabethan and Jacobean repertoire of imagery about social exchange. Not surprisingly, one of the most popular images in that repertoire was the figure of the theater, albeit a detached and deritualized theater. Such a theater offered a more or less precise idiom with which to describe the transfigured countenance – the "altered copy" – of social relations as well as to anatomize the process of their transfiguration: its strategies and mechanics. Even in those social commentaries that did not directly allude to the theater, the figures of speech deployed to capture the seemingly wayward impulses of market exchange amounted to an inventory of misrepresentations that audiences were increasingly prepared to identify with the stage. As both world and stage changed during these years, the metaphor of the *theatrum mundi* was resurrected and, in its own quite literal sense, transfigured so as to accommodate more fully the crisis of representation that a volatile and placeless market had occasioned.

The new liquidity of mercantile relations, like the growing fluidity of social relations in general, made itself most vividly felt in those literary genres devoted to social description and moral instruction. Most conspicuous among these popular literary forms were the literature of estates, the literature of rogues and vagabonds, the literature of characters, the literature of conduct and courtesy, and the "philosophical" anatomies of passions and physiognomies. Whatever the differences among these genres – and there were many – each one underwent a formal shift during the sixteenth and seventeenth centuries, jettisoning the stock character types of ritual and festive allegory for what Bakhtin has called the "petty," "voyeuristic," or "alcove realism" of carefully observed social types. By these epithets Bakhtin meant to dismiss the numerous Renaissance catalogues of social types as derivative, indeed "degenerate," versions of the surrealist and grotesque personae of the medieval carnival.[5] Yet the figures to be found in Elizabethan jest books, character collections, and courtesy manuals were scarcely less theatrical than the classic archetypes of vice and virtue present in lay sermons and mystery cycles. What had changed was the perceived character of the theatrical itself.

No longer was the sense of theatricality confined exclusively to the deliberate representation of common ideals in the negotiated relations between the individual and God; more and more, it suggested the calculated *mis*representation of private meanings in the negotiated relations among men and women. Where publicity had distinguished the theatricality of the medieval marketplace, privacy became its animating principle in the marketplace of the Renaissance. The festive mask was "stripped of its original richness," according to Bakhtin, "and acquire[d] other meanings alien to its primitive nature"; now the mask hid something, kept a secret, deceived.[6] As a result, the *theatrum mundi* became a peculiarly contradictory and unstable term of placement during the English Renaissance, signifying, as it did, a world at once empty and saturated with meanings. Within the traditional emblem, an older reference to man's vanity and futility vied with a newer reference to man's multiple and all too effective purposes – purposes that invited the penetrating, "voyeuristic" scrutiny of an absorbed yet critically distanced spectator. The changing conventions of sixteenth- and seventeenth-century literature, like those of popular drama, revealed a movement toward a realism (and eventually a romanticism) that was at its heart theatrical – theatrical in the sense that such realism took the social world to be so thoroughly "staged" as to make its truths accessible not so much by what those performances claimed to display as by what they unwittingly betrayed.

The social and political crisis of representation that agricultural and commercial capitalism introduced into England's semifeudal society raised the issue of personal intentions in new and disturbing ways. What a person could be said to "have in mind" grew in importance as the signs of his or her social identity grew in obscurity. Hence, religion broke with ritual and embraced the

direct scrutiny of conscience; hence, law abandoned its preoccupations with the acts of oath, conveyance, and delivery so as
to focus on those fleeting promissory moments when minds were
understood to meet in contract.[7] The new conventions of the
Renaissance marketplace, like those of the Renaissance theater,
encouraged participants to see their profit and pleasure as requiring the willing suspension of their disbelief. Yet, few were
prepared to credit the evidence of their eyes in this way without
first arming their vision. To meet this need, a series of guides
began to appear in the hands of English booksellers in the waning
years of the sixteenth century, each of which attempted to brief
its audience on the mechanics of representation and misrepresentation in society. From these primers, readers were expected
to con the rudiments of a histrionic calculus. Whether or not
they did, they undoubtedly confirmed their impressions of the
shape-shifting nature of social exchange in the new world of
commodities.

I

Among the earliest literary forms to take note of the fluidity of
England's social world were those fourteenth- and fifteenth-century versified laments that systematically catalogued the character
and defects of each social class. The literature of estates, as it was
called, owed much to the satirical tradition of sermon and jest
book. The genre's antipathy toward those who would rise above
their estate, for example, was of a piece with the medieval jer-
emiad, so that it is difficult to know when the truculence of estates
literature betokened a genuine change in social structure as opposed to a mere rising of the bile. Still, it is clear from the work
of Ruth Mohl that the genre's sensitivity to estatelessness was
far keener in England than on the Continent and that it was in
the widening maelstrom of England's social mobility that the
genre ultimately foundered during the sixteenth century.[8]
   The metaphor of the ship is used advisedly here, for it was
one of the favorite tropes of and for medieval society.[9] It appeared
in countless sermons and jest books, and it was no doubt out of
the latter that the German satirist Sebastian Brandt drew the
materials for his *Narrenschiff* (1494) and Hieronymous Bosch the

inspiration for his painting, *Ship of Fools* (ca. 1500). In 1509, Alexander Barclay, an English friar, published his free translation of Brandt's soberly written but vividly illustrated narrative. Barclay's points of departure from the original were revealing, for what distinguished his *Shyp of Folys* from the German, Latin, and French versions was its weightier emphasis on the faults of each estate and its almost obsessive attack on the sins of those with social ambitions above their rank.[10] Barclay imagined that Democritus – often considered (with Pythagoras and Epictetus) to have been the creator of the theatrical analogy – would have laughed at

> The wayes of men in this our tyme lyuynge
> Howe they with vysers dayle disgysed be
> Them selfe difformynge almost in euery thynge
> When they are disgysed to them it is semynge
> That no syn is gret; nor soundynge to theyr shame
> Syns theyr foule vysers thereof can cloke the fame[11]

The structure of society was intimately bound up in Barclay's mind with the structure of his feelings, his certainty. For him estatelessness undermined the very foundations of judgment about the self and its world. A man could so wear "vyle counterfayte vesture / Or payntyth his vysage with fume in suche case / That what he is hym selfe is skantly sure."[12] Social mobility implied social disfigurement, a donning of masks and a sloughing off of the feudal framework of accountability as "eche seruant fayne wolde a mayster be."[13] Mobility suggested a corruption of "utterance" in its sixteenth-century meaning as the issuance of both wares and words:

> All suche as ceueyt the buyers to begyle
> With flaterynge wordes fals and dysceyuable
> Disceyuynge other, disceyue them selfe the whyle
> And all other are greatly reprouable
> Whiche make theyr warke not true and profitable
> But counterfayte and pleasaunt to the iye.[14]

Barclay's preoccupation with the themes of mobility and deceit, his pattern of rhetorical excess, his methodical inventory of occupational abuses (the sheer variety of which foreshadowed the end of estates literature), all seemed to point toward an inward disequilibrium that was, in a way, the expression of the friar's sense of lost proportion in society.[15] By its very overreaching, Barclay's *Shyp of Folys* marked off a place for itself between the formulaic medieval lament and the improvisational Renaissance conceit. Small wonder, then, that Barclay should have found in the Ship of Fools, with all of its associations with fantasy and madness, the aptest metaphor for the social consequences of England's feudal decline.

Indeed, Barclay's work, published in the same year as Erasmus's *Praise of Folly,* conformed to the general tendency in late-fifteenth-century European literature and painting to substitute the theme of madness for the theme of death. As Michel Foucault has observed, this substitution did "not mark a break, but rather a torsion within the same anxiety."[16] That is to say, it removed the burden of worldly futility and meaninglessness from the revelatory moment of death and judgment and transported it into the continuity and flux of everyday life. In this way, the sense of death as a final threshold or ultimate boundary was made to yield to a more overarching sense of life as a permanent threshold experience, a fool's journey to Narragonia, the Land of Fools. Ironically, Barclay's sharpened focus on the details, if not the mechanics, of man's petty deceits threatened to dissolve the very asceticism in whose service the literature of estates had been enlisted. In a society where poverty, blindness, disfigurement, and even madness itself could be feigned for profit, the conventional tokens of *contemptus mundi* were themselves open to doubt.[17] Barclay's "petty realism" anticipated a long and lively tradition of reportorial exposés, revelations whose motives would always remain ambiguously divided among the punitive, the prudential, and the prurient.

As it was, the descriptive, almost sociological side of the *Shyp of Folys* made it one of the earliest models for the fashion of rogue literature that flourished in late-sixteenth- and early-seventeenth-century England.[18] And like Barclay's book, the cony-catching (or trickster) pamphlets owed much to German forerunners.[19] The most celebrated of these was the *Liber Vagatorum: Der Betler Orden,* published in the same year as Barclay's translation of Brandt's *Narrenschiff.* A stinging indictment of Europe's mendicant orders and their fraudulent imitators, the "Book of Vagabonds" went through eighteen editions in Germany alone before Luther wrote his famous preface to it in 1528 and several more before an English variation appeared under the hand of John Awdeley. Tricks and sleights were legion, but theft remained the principal crime in all rogue literature. The rogue's "main business," according to Frank Chandler, was "to obliterate distinctions of *meum* and *tuum*."[20] Yet for all the vituperation the genre hurled at thieves and confidence men, rogue books transgressed the very same boundaries of property they earnestly claimed to uphold. Awdeley's *Fraternity of Vagabonds* (1561) was plagiarized by Thomas Harmon in his *Caveat for Common Cursitors* (1566), and Harmon was in turn plagiarized by Thomas Dekker, the dramatist. As another playwright, Thomas Tomkis, put it in 1615:

> This Poet is that Poets plagiary,
> And he a third's, till they end all in *Homer*.
> And *Homer* filtch't all from an Ægyptian Preestesse.
> The world's a Theater of theft.[21]

Copyholds did not as yet have their counterpart in copyrights; so that narratives that had once belonged to the commonwealth of oral culture now, as printed texts, opened themselves to the possibility of theft.

The boundaries whose transgression the rogue books described and enacted were more than imaginative constructions; they framed real relations of power and authority, and their violation was taken seriously. Here, literature and life rivaled one another, for the proliferation of rogue pamphlets toward the end of the sixteenth century accompanied one of the sharpest rises in vagabondage in England's history. Indeed, the period between the parliamentary act to brand vagabonds (1547) and the act to put them to work (1576) has been called by one historian the "palmiest days of vagabond life in England." Few literate contemporaries, however, were so benign toward the swelling numbers of masterless men and women in the streets and countryside. If anything, urban merchants and rural yeomen were more likely to adopt the accusatory tones of the medieval lay preacher. But categories originally framed with an eye to the tricksterism of the mendicant monk creaked audibly under the weight of the multiple offenses against property and authority that sixteenth-

and early seventeenth-century itineracy produced. "England had never so much work for a chronicle," one observer wrote after the murder of a chancery worker in 1616, "never such turnings, tossings and mutabilities in the lives of men and women and the streams of their fortunes."[22] In the face of the accumulating pressures of enclosure, disestablishment, and demobilization, new forms of social, political, and imaginative order were improvised to keep people and things in their place. Like the estates literature that preceded it, rogue literature served as a figurative act of settlement: exposing, dissecting, and classifying all that threatened to confuse the social relations of Elizabethan England, tying the loose ends of commerce and crime back to the frayed fabric of society.

The cony-catching pamphlets, as they were called, enumerated some twenty-four orders of rogues. The list, partially anticipated in Barclay's earlier inventory of fools, included fraters (proxy beggars), counterfeit cranks (sham victims of falling sickness), dommerers (sham deaf-mutes), whipjacks (sham shipwrecked sailors), and Abraham Men, the counterfeit madmen later memorialized in Shakespeare's tragedies. Though demographic evidence indicates that most sixteenth- and seventeenth-century wayfarers were solitary, subsistence migrants, the literature of roguery projected an image of organized regiments of confidence men methodically infiltrating the city and countryside from their favorite staging areas in culvert, hayrick, and tippling house.[23] The effect of these fictions was to assimilate an otherwise erratic pattern of itineracy and trespass into a more familiar notion of deliberate, if dubious, guild activity: a freemasonry of crime whose arts and mysteries the pamphlets purported to lay bare.

Deception emerged as the common feature of the rogue portraits of the 1590s and early 1600s. The literary rogue's greatest resource was his capacity for "deep dissimulation." So it was, for example, with the legendary counterfeit crank who went by the names of Nicholas Jennings and Nicholas Blunt and who was pictured in two of his roles in *The Groundwork of cony-catching* (1592). The caption warned:

> These two pictures lively set out
> One body and soul. God send him more grace!

This monstrous dissembler, a crank all about,
Uncomely coveting, of each to embrace
   Money or wares, as he made his race;
And sometimes a mariner, and a serving-man,
   Or else an artificer, as he would feign then.
Such shifts, he used, being well tried,
   Abandoning labour, till he was espied.
Condign punishment for his dissimulation
   He surely received, with much exclamation.[24]

As the verse makes clear, only the faintest of lines separated the multiple by-employments of the rural outworker from the multiple impostures of the professional rogue. To the jaundiced Elizabethan eye, the casual laborer and the wandering rogue were virtually indistinguishable from the itinerant actor, so that few could have been entirely surprised when, in 1572, players themselves were placed under the force of the Vagabond Act.[25]

The sheer number and variety of social deceits practiced by England's vagrant bands tended to abstract the notion of deception from its context and, on occasion, to encourage its romanticization as a form of clever "cozening" of "gull" by "gallant." In Thomas Dekker's *Gulls Horn-Book* (1609) as in other cony-catching texts, roguery and theatricality were intertwined, the breath of criminality was passed over the illusions of art, and a seventeenth-century prototype of Bohemianism was born.[26] To be sure, the numerous hints of mock-heroic rascality thrown out by the rogue pamphlets indicate the genre's ties to the outlaw legends and trickster parables of popular tradition. Nevertheless, these chapbooks and broadsides expressed a new sense of psychic and social distance from that tradition, one that encouraged readers to reconceive plebeian culture as a strange and sinister underworld. Taken as a whole, rogue literature projected the impression of a mobile and predatory subculture the occupational mysteries and arcane idiom of which required careful and methodical translation before a literate audience could be expected to understand them.

This pattern was as true of the Continent as of England. Seventeenth-century France, for instance, produced its *genre poissard,* booklets that claimed to reproduce and translate the actual dialect of French peasants and fishwives, while across the Channel, Elizabethan writers compiled so-called canting dictionaries. These were crudely illustrated and occasionally versified lexicons of the jargon purportedly used by rogues and petty chapmen when talking among themselves.[27] Such glossaries marked, among other things, a widening breach between the "great" and "little" traditions in England across which the ornate euphemisms of aristocratic poesy now countered the equally elaborate argot of the streets. The marketplace no longer mocked and overturned social differences but rather affirmed a new kind of difference that required "Englishing" to be understood. By the end of the seventeenth century, for example, "billingsgate" became a general term to describe foul and abusive language, thus eclipsing its original reference to the London fishmarket where such language continued to be heard.[28]

Indeed, if for a moment we consider the various rogues' dictionaries within the characteristically private context of the act of reading, we can see how such works could have reinforced the common impression of England's migratory subculture as an exclusive and esoteric one: a set of expressive codes more likely to be overheard than to be shared by the glossaries' readers. For this reason, perhaps, Bakhtin has treated the printed lexicons as auguring a new " 'alcove realism' of private life, a realism of eavesdropping and peeping" that would not be fully realized, in European art or literature, until the nineteenth century.[29] As early as the seventeenth century, however, one can see the formative conventions of literary realism already presuming a social world (or a portion of that world) from which the reader was made to feel at once excluded and privy. For rogue literature as for other popular genres, the consequence of these literary conventions was to establish the author as a proxy for the reader in what was an avowedly and, at times, provocatively vicarious experience.

The simultaneous impression of presence and exclusion that rogue literature conveyed was something more, however, than a mere acknowledgment of the sharpening division between plebeian and patrician cultures in Elizabethan England. It was also a feature of new material relationships among individuals, specifically those in which buyers and sellers transacted their business along principles and with instruments that rendered the participants conveniently yet distressingly opaque to one another. Whether consolidated in a bourse or exchange or dispersed throughout a network of petty traders, commodity exchange was gravitating during the sixteenth and seventeenth centuries toward a set of operative rules that fostered a formal and instrumental indifference among buyers and sellers. To be indifferent in this respect was not, of course, to be wholly disinterested nor, for that matter, wholly self-interested. All sorts of interests beyond the self might be thrown into a bargain. Stripped of its ritual, communal, and personal integument, market exchange did not become a simple egoistic exercise, a case of autonomous, rapacious selves unleashed from all social restraints. A "pure" market or "economic" relation, in Philip Wicksteed's words, "does not exclude from my mind every one but me"; rather, "it potentially includes every one but you."

> You it does indeed exclude, and therefore it emphasises, though it does not narrow or tighten, the limitations of the altruism of the man who enters into it; for it calls attention to the fact that, however wide his sympathies may be, they do not urge him to any particular effort or sacrifice for the sake of the person with whom he is dealing at the moment.[30]

Words like "altruism" and "egoism" are nineteenth-century inventions, but the bipolar typology of motives that both terms imply reaches back to the first efforts of Elizabethans to impute intentions to a form of exchange that yoked partners together in a rhetoric of reciprocity while dividing them by means of a logic of mutual indifference. Brotherhood and otherhood, to use Benjamin Nelson's dichotomy, were thus coupled in this new and impersonal form of exchange, yet coupled in such a way as to resurrect the very question of motives that impersonality had presumably removed.[31]

From this perspective, we can see rogue literature as one of several forms of imaginative writing that sought to penetrate the new and exclusionary conventions developing within the class and market structures of English capitalism. Yet the pamphlets' promise of special access was at the same time a reminder of the social and psychic distance to be traveled within the interior of England's new exchange relations; their very effort to transport the reader behind the rogue's rhetoric of mutuality and through his or her logic of instrumentalism merely reenacted, where they did not in fact deepen, the reader's sense of estrangement – of distance from the multiple and shifting intentionalities concealed behind the outward face of all exchange.

It was just such suspicion that led Martin Luther, a writer familiar with rogue literature, to attack all monastic charity as a ruse to purchase salvation. That such a purchase should have been considered a sin was itself a novelty, however, for in the two centuries before Luther's *Long Sermon on Usury* (1520), the church had metaphorically promoted itself as a treasury of grace: a repository of merit into which the faithful paid their taxes and from which they withdrew their salvation. Exchange itself had to alter its form before such a figurative vindication of faith could become, in a twinkling of a sermon, a symbol of faith's violation.[32] Before the Reformation, churchmen had regarded charity as a form of self-sacrifice for God rather than humankind, and they could do so because relief for the poor and disabled was administered, however inefficiently and exiguously, through the monastic foundations. And though it is true that donations had already begun to dwindle before the dissolution of the monasteries in the early sixteenth century, the process of disendowment, disafforestation, and enclosure, coupled with dramatic increases in population, accelerated the formation of a class of masterless and migratory wage laborers who confronted not only each other but a ruling principle of charity wholly inappropriate to their circumstances[33] – hence the steady growth of secular philanthropy and the ragged experimentation in Tudor poor laws, on the one hand, and the equally steady, if ragged, attempts at roguery and deceit, on the other.[34]

The utilitarian solutions to the problem of poor relief toward which the Elizabethan and, in particular, the Puritans eventually inclined were designed to circumvent just those deceits that rogue literature faithfully reproduced. As the sixteenth century advanced, English policy makers adopted an ideology of philanthropy that used the same method of ledger-book accounting by which the pious kept their conscience. William Perkins was but one of many reformers to use the merchant's idiom to prod the reluctant philanthropist toward direct, rationalized charity. Perkins claimed he could not understand the individual who "upon good securitie lends to another an 100. pounds, hoping for the principall with the increase at the yeares end," yet who would "skarse deliver an 100. pence to the poore members of Christ vppon the promise and bonde of God himselfe."[35] In a sense the numerous charitable trusts that sprang up during these years posed as the institutional analogues of the private trading syndicate, an entrepreneurial alternative to the corrupt and over-ritualized monopoly of the monastic foundation. The rhetorical effect of this analogy, however, was less to spiritualize the marketplace than to monetize the spirit. Each benefaction was a "loan to God," as another Puritan divine put it. "Charity to the poor," Thomas Jacomb declared, "'tis your bill of exchange; pay down your money here, and you shall receive it again in glory."[36]

Drawing their funds from the more or less constant returns to land and capital, the charitable trusts that sprang into being during the early seventeenth century amounted to a rudimentary form of social engineering. "Reason" (which Hobbes derived from the Latin word for accounts) was to be elevated over "imagination" (which Hobbes called the "decaying sense") in the administration of relief. Imagination surely did enter into the Tudor–Stuart response to dislocation and immiseration, but it was largely in the sense of the mind's capacity to conceive, scheme, or formulate "projects" for the poor rather than in its inclination to fantasize, sympathize, or identify with them. Across the shifting social boundaries of commodity and labor exchange, England's "projectors" and their aristocratic sponsors strove to impose a new pattern of accountability on the masterless men and women who roamed the English countryside; they were to be subjected to a workhouse calculus of labor exchange drawn from the model of a merchant's daybook. Against the colorful tricksterism of the begging orders, the new men of Tudor–Stuart England pitted their own bland brand of ledger-demain. As the tissue of traditional obligation dissolved, the Elizabethan workhouse became, to borrow Philip Massinger's phrase, "a new way to pay old debts."

Ironically, the very promise of certainty that the mercantile model of philanthropic policy brought to the problem of England's disabled and dispossessed reminded Elizabethans of the same magical and occult powers already associated with roguery.

Even the word "policy" had become freighted with sinister meanings by the fifteenth and sixteenth centuries, for as one Elizabethan merchant put it, the term suggested one's "seeking a certaintie even in uncertainties." And nowhere was such policy better (or worse) exemplified than in the cunning expedience of rogues and usurers.[37] Because usury was considered a riskless profit, it was therefore regarded as unnatural or at best supernatural. Thomas Wilson's famous *Discourse Upon Usury* (1572), for example, singled out usury's claims to certainty. The assurance of constant and extortionate returns, he warned, would eventually induce all Englishmen to abandon their vocations and, as a consequence, their manliness.[38] Claiming to look on the knight as the ordained protector of widows and orphans, Wilson recoiled from those "projectors" who sought to secure the welfare of the helpless and the hapless through the aggregate interest on loans that the charitable trusts were mobilizing.[39]

Writing at the time of the statutory decriminalization of interest, Wilson expressed the misgivings of an age bemused by what Huizinga once called the "spectral impalpability" of money capital in a moral economy.[40] The perplexing absence of solidity in the transactions of the money market – transactions that Wilson and others referred to as "dry exchange" – merely accentuated the growing obscurity of new commercial relationships. Wilson, for his own part, was unable to fathom how a standard of value could become a thing of value, for "moneye was not first devised for thys ende, to bee merchaundize, but to bee a measure and a beame betwixte man and man, for the buyinge and sellinge of weares."[41] Money seemed increasingly disembodied, a means abstracted from its original intent, a sorcerer's apprentice. "Ha!" cries the villain of John Webster's *A Cure for a Cuckold* (ca. 1625),

> ... ready money is the prize I look for,
> It walks without suspition any where,
> When Chains and Jewels may be stayed and call'd
> Before the Constable.[42]

Notwithstanding the denials of scholastic theologians, money did appear to reproduce itself in the new Elizabethan markets; indeed, it never ceased to reproduce itself. Its plough, as Francis Bacon put it, worked Sundays.[43] But if money licensed a new boundlessness in exchange, it also offered itself as the most potent resource available with which to cross or close that psychic space, a resource no doubt enhanced by gold's traditional alchemical associations.

Money was alchemy and roguery conflated and abstracted; it was a "visible God / that solder'st close impossibilities, / and makest them kiss!" And like the rogue Nick Jennings, money spoke "with every tongue, / To every purpose."[44] When the playwright Ben Jonson borrowed the deity Pecunia from Lucian and Aristophanes in order to satirize the contemporary conversion of news to a commodity, he added to her character an alchemical dimension she had never possessed in classical drama. Similarly, when Giambattista Della Porta's play *Astrologo* (1606) was turned by Thomas Tomkis into *Albumazar* (1614), Tomkis added the figure of a "would-be gentleman" who saw himself magically elevated to the gentry.[45] Money thus gave upward mobility the character of a spurious miracle. Its liquidity seemed metaphorically and materially indistinguishable from the disturbingly deliquescent features of Tudor–Stuart society.

But just as magic provided a convenient metaphor for the abstract powers of a nascent commercial capitalism, so it promised a method for the demystification of commerce. In the same fashion that mercantilists attempted to divine the hidden sources of prosperity and depression, so popular writers sought to penetrate the social face of the new marketplace, where clothes and coats of arms no longer operated as the unequivocal insignia of rank. The changing English social structure, with its new patterns of distance and proximity in exchange and deference, invited decipherment, and magic (according to Mary Douglas) has always offered a means to define external boundaries.[46] So when English readers began to cast about for some sociological Rosetta Stone, they understandably looked beyond the rogue pamphlets to several other kinds of magical and semimagical texts, some of which put into print and thus into the form of private experience the collected wisdom (and ignorance) of generations of wandering palmists, physiognomists, players, and preachers. In this respect, cony-catching books were but one of several genres of literature that managed to extract out of the communal complaint of estates writing an inventory of social strategems and social types from which yet others would create the specialized manual of self-help.

Yet what sort of self was it, we may well ask, that these guidebooks sought to help? If the rogue pamphlets are any indication, it was a private self, a self already constituted *behind* the many public masks it delighted to wear. To the readers of these pamphlets, the self existed not just in the measure that it *had* something to hide but in the measure that it *was* something to hide. This was an answer of sorts, although one that, adequately scrutinized, raised almost as many questions as it seemed to resolve. If, for example, the human self could be said to exist only as the imagined vessel or vehicle of the interests its many masks implied, then that existence was likewise as conjectural as the motives to which those masks obliquely pointed. Such questions were moot, of course, for the conventions of rogue literature were never intended to be interrogated in this way. That readers' doubts remained only strengthened the hold of a genre that thrived on the promise of their imminent resolution. Rogue literature was thus part of the problem (and the problematic) it purported to resolve.

Still, the genre would not have succeeded at all had it not provided a new, more intelligible, and ultimately more satisfying form for its readers' diffuse and inarticulate anxieties. The model of selfhood that the pamphleteers offered up did in fact give a shape, however fluid, to interests and intentions that would otherwise have remained frustratingly indeterminate and unattached, given the indifferent and impersonal logic of the placeless market. In this, we can see rogue literature as forming part of a general effort by popular writers and dramatists to contrive new definitions of self, new forms of dialogue, indeed a whole new array of literary and dramatic conventions with which to body forth their solutions to Britain's growing crisis of representation. Together, these solutions amounted to a new vision of the *theatrum mundi*. A worldly theater, these writers seem to say, was best able to represent a theatrical world.

II

During the late sixteenth century, England's literature of estates underwent a quick if not altogether painless death. Philip Stubbes's

Anatomie of Abuses (1583), a work best known for its brief but influential attack on the stage, figures as one of the genre's last authentic examples. There Stubbes complained of how difficult it had become "to knowe who is noble, who is worshipfull, who is a gentleman, who is not: for you shall have those which are neither of the nobilitie, gentilitie, nor yeomanry; no, nor yet anie Magistrat, or Officer in the common welth, go daylie in silkes, velvets, satens, damasks, taffeties, and such like, notwithstanding that they be both base by byrthe, mean by estate, & servyle by calling."[47] The lament was none the less poignant for its being old, for it now signaled the end of a genre truly confused by the changing configuration of classes and occupations, by their seemingly arbitrary arrangement and their alien social countenance. As a distinct genre, estates literature eventually gave way to new undertakings in political theory, drama, courtesy manuals, and, most important, character sketches.[48]

The tradition of character sketches extended back to Theophrastus, a Greek *metic* and pupil of Aristotle who had once published a set of thirty "ethical" characters, each of which portrayed a particular departure from the governing norms of social behavior. The first English translation of the Theophrastan characters is believed to have appeared under Isaac Casaubon's hand in 1592, followed by Joseph Hall's *Characters of Vertues and Vices* in 1608. But by far the most influential work of this revival was Sir Thomas Overbury's character sketches of 1614. Character, he wrote, has to be "taken for an Egiptian Hierogliphicke, for an impresse, or shorte Embleme."[49] There was a striking difference, however, between the "impresse" of the Theophrastan characters and their Overburian counterparts. The former were preeminently depictions of moral types; the latter were visibly social types.[50] The characters of Theophrastus and Hall were, at bottom, personifications of moral vices and virtues. Overburian characters were epitomes of recognizably social traits. The remarkable growth in the catalogue of Overburian portraits – from twenty-two to eighty-two over the six editions that spanned the first year of publication – attests to the appeal of their topicality. And though the cony-catching pamphlets captured just those social types that eluded the grasp of the Overburian collection (the thief, swindler, cutpurse, and bawd), only the drama cast its net sufficiently widely to draw into its folds the whole motley assortment of Elizabethan and Jacobean society.[51]

Character books offered their audiences a witty, sociobotanical excursion (Theophrastus had been a botanist) around contemporary English society. If they forebore from outright moral instruction, perhaps it was because there already existed manuals of appropriate conduct for every order and degree of that society, from Baldesar Castiglione's *Il libro del Cortegiano* (1529) to Thomas Dekker's *Gulls Horn-Book* (1609). Dekker's satirical guide to the conceits and deceits of the Elizabethan underworld parodied the whole courtesy genre, at the apex of which stood *The Book of the Courtyer* (1561), Sir Thomas Hoby's translation of Castiglione's great work. Yet both the translation and the reception of *Il Cortegiano* in England revealed the extent to which the English reading public, high and low, had departed from older notions of theatricality and ritual in the conduct of social relations. Castiglione's work, as Wayne Rebhorn has shown, attempted to sketch out an aesthetics of society. Written in the form of an extended and lighthearted conversation among members of the court of Urbino, *Il Cortegiano* aspired to represent society as a symposium, a deliberate and decorous version of the carnivalesque in which, according to Rebhorn, the skill and delight with which the participants played their allotted parts indicated the seriousness they attached to the obligations of social courtship in a stratified society.[52] The masks courtiers wore were to be taken as texts, not pretexts; they were figurative expressions of communal ideals, not mere dissimulations of private motives.[53]

Much of this Neoplatonic aspect of Castiglione's work was sacrificed in Hoby's translation; still more was lost to the English reader's determination to extract out of the Italian author's artful dialogues a set of practical political rules and guidelines.[54] Elizabethan dramatists thus struck a familiar chord when they used "Castiglione's vision to create a superficially brilliant, but essentially hollow, image of civilization and refinement."[55] Here, they had but to select the occasional passage on courtly expedience to make their case. Hadn't Castiglione advised his readers, after all, to follow "the example of the good marchaunt men, that to gaine much, adventure a little, and not much, to gain a little"?[56] The effect of this selective reception of Castiglione's ideals was to convert his masterpiece from a model of collaborative meditation to a model of individual premeditation. Like so many things Italian, *The Courtyer* became for English audiences a symbol of grace *and* guile, propriety *and* policy.

These felt contradictions had sprung from within English society and culture, but they were accompanied by an equally pressing compulsion to project the source of such unacceptable conflicts on figures already identified as foreign. For the English as for the French before them, Italian writers became convenient symbols of shrewd, almost magical, manipulation. Thus one anonymous pamphlet of 1591 advertised itself as "a Discovery of the great subtiltie and wonderful wisedome of the Italians, whereby they beare away over the most part of Christendome, and cunninglie behave themselves to fetch the Quintescence out of the peoples purses."[57] Words like "cunning," "art," and "craft" no longer evoked the unequivocal meanings of ingenuity, skill, and workmanship. Instead, they implied a capacity for misrepresentation and treachery that, by the late sixteenth century at least, was popularly identified with Machiavellism.[58]

As with Castiglione's courtier and Della Porta's astrologist, English dramatists forced on Machiavelli's principles an association with commercial trickery that would have horrified the Florentine.[59] Thomas Heywood's portrait of the "modern projector," for example, appeared under the title *Machiavel* (1641). It featured a sharp-edged character sketch of the Elizabethan entrepreneur as a latter-day Proteus, but a figure far more sly and sinister than the Protean ideal of Castiglione's courtier. The projector, Heywood declared, "is made all of Cringes and Complements, as if he dropt out of the Docke of a Courtier, and can change himselfe into as many shapes as Painters can doe colours, either a decayed Merchant, a broken Citizen, a silent Minister, an old maym'd Captaine, a forejudged Atturney, a busie Soliciter, a crop-ear'd Informer, a pick-thanke Pettyfogger, or a nimble pac'd Northern Tike, that hath more wit than honestie."[60] Under Heywood's pen, the chapbook portrait of the sixteenth-century whipjack dissolved into the seventeenth-century image of the "old maym'd Captaine," but there the playwright's invention stopped. The projector seemed to invite and thereby defy all labels. Words were inadequate. Language had yet to identify

honesty with policy, much less the best policy. If anything, the
two terms would have struck most Elizabethans as antithetical.
Machiavellism, as one pamphleteer saw it, turned "the Art of
Government, into the Art of Jugling and dissembling."[61] Political realism had yet to attain the status of a theory in England or
to emancipate itself from the thrall of medieval homiletics. Popular audiences were less likely to identify the "Machiavellian
moment" with the precarious destinies of republics than with the
predatory ambitions of rogues and usurers. Indeeed, most Elizabethans preferred to grasp the obscure and distant strategies of
the Tudor state in the equally obscure but more readily available
terms of their market experience.[62] Vivid analogies and elaborate
conceits had to bear the strain that new social relations imposed
on traditional conceptual categories.

It was not long before Hoby's *Courtyer* inspired the translation
of other manuals of even greater appeal to England's growing
middle class. Prominent among these handbooks were Robert
Peterson's translation in 1576 of Giovanni della Casa's *Il Galateo*
(1554) and George Pettie's translation in 1581 of Stefano Guazzo's
La Civile Conversatione (1574).[63] Conversation was for Guazzo
the representative social relation, but where Castiglione situated
his symposium in the palace chamber, Guazzo chose the marketplace as the ideal locale. There he found "a numberlesse mul-
titude walking upp and downe in euery place, keeping a continuall
mercate, where there is bargayning for all things."[64] Words, not
money, were the relevant currency, and selves the objects of
exchange. Dialogue forced people to "put of[f] as it were our
own fashions and manners, and cloath our selues with the conditions of others, and imitate them so farre as reason will permit."
These last words, with their tantalizing intimations of unreason,
suggested the risks Guazzo associated with civil conversation.
Still, the possibility of madness lay at either extreme of the con-
versational spectrum: "We *must* alter our selues into an other,"
Guazzo insisted. "And he, which shall not frame him selfe to
doe this, shall bee driven to curse Conuersation, and to pray unto
God with the snayle . . . that to auoyde all neighbours and naugh-
tie companie, hee will giue him the grace to bee able to carrie
his house about with him."[65] Sociability was for Guazzo a civil
religion, with its own moments of transport and its own threats

of excommunication. Stripped of its hierarchical frame, the deritualized marketplace of discourse offered the choice of sympathy or solitude.

To be sure, neither Guazzo nor Pettie ever used the word "sympathy," but the older, occult connotations of the word were clearly present. Altering oneself into another presumed a knowledge of the other that went beyond the ordinary, if not beyond the claims of the self-help manual. Without entirely dispelling the aura of magic that clung to such wisdom, English handbooks plucked physiognomy, metoposcopy, and kindred popular arts out of the jealous hands of itinerant astrologers and "cunning men" and transformed them into commodities available to all "pragmatical men" who "wished to raise and make their fortune."[66] Nestled snugly in the same pockets with the dog-eared character catalogues, these manuals offered their owners a mode of divination for a new and perplexing secular realm – the realm of commodity relations where man, not God, lay concealed.

For the late-sixteenth-century reader, the word "commodity" still signified, above all, a profit or advantage, and it was just such an advantage that the Renaissance handbooks held out to their prospective purchasers. In *The Contemplation of Mankinde* (1571), for example, Thomas Hill stressed the utility of physiognomical skills in business, calling them a "necessarie and lawdable science, seeing by the same a man may so readily pronounce and foretell the natural aptness unto the affections, and conditions in men, by the outwarde notes of the body."[67] Similar claims were to be found in Thomas Wright's *The Passions of the Minde in Generall* (1601), a work at once more philosophical and influential than Hill's. In it Wright sought to bring together the Renaissance anatomy of the emotions, the tradition of classical rhetoric, and the pseudoscience of physiognomy. And though Wright, as a former Jesuit, must have drawn on the dramatistic spiritual exercises of Ignatius Loyola, he did not hesitate to address his work to philosopher, physician, orator, ambassador, lawyer, and magistrate, for whom he hoped the book would bring "a goodly and faire glosse of profit and commodity."[68] Wright's guide appeared to serve the very same ambitions that Elizabethans could gleefully malign as Machiavellian upon the stage.

Wright devoted the third and fourth books of his treatise on the passions to the method of their discovery in the changing configuration of man's countenance and gestures. This "extraordinary apparell of the bodie," as he called it, "declareth well the apparell of the Mind."[69] In a similar vein, Francis Bacon accounted "the discovery of a man's self by the tracts [traits] of his countenance" to be "a great weakness and betraying, [as shown] by how much it is many times more marked and believed than a man's words."[70] Neither author left any doubt that the truth of social relations was a matter more likely to be disclosed than displayed. As a consequence, their readers were expected to take the conventional signs of social identity in a stratified society less as cues to action than as clues to motive. The curiosity that had arisen to meet the impersonal conventions and instruments of the new marketplace had inevitably magnified the suspicion of multiple and hidden interests at work behind the deliberately blank face of mercantile relations. The rub, if any, came from the reader's sense of inadequacy and lack of preparation in such matters. Social relations, particularly those touched by the market, had themselves become a "mystery" toward which the reader was made to feel at best a callow and untried apprentice.[71]

Books on characters and passions may have ministered to a conservative or nostalgic impulse among their readers, as some scholars have suggested, but they also fed the hunger for what Bacon called "the knowledge of present actions" in a world where "more trust be given to countenance than to words."[72] An instance of this double vision, at once retrospective and prospective, can be found in William Scott's *An Essay of Drapery* (1635), the first English work to extoll the business life. Subtitled *The Complete Citizen,* Scott's essay took its inspiration from the vogue of gentlemanly courtesy literature, though it contained none of the disdain for mercantile matters found in Henry Peacham's *The Complete Gentleman* (1622) or Richard Brathwaite's *The English Gentleman* (1630). Where Bacon had taken pains to distinguish between the honest gains of "ordinary trades and vocations" and the "doubtful" gains of bargains "when men shall wait upon others' necessity," Scott – a merchant and "cautious puritan" – asked "what man almost profiteth, but by the loss of others?" Did not "Traders thrive by the licentiousness of youth? the Husband man by the dearth of Corne: the Architect by the ruin of houses, the Lawyer by contentions betweene men, the Physitians by other sicknesses?"[73] The world was for Scott a zero-sum game, one that drew effective and affective boundaries between and within its participants. Dissimulation, which Bacon had called "a faint kind of policy or wisdom," was for Scott "a thing more tollerable with a Citizen."[74] The Citizen could "mingle profit with honesty," and though he could "never turne his back to honesty," he could "yet sometimes goe about and coast it, using an extraordinary skill, which may be better practis'd than exprest."[75] The popularity of such guides doubtlessly drew on their repeated hints of a mercantile craft so deft as to resist the most earnest and deliberate efforts to set it down.

For the aspiring draper of Scott's essay, dissimulation was merely the face assumed by distrust in a world "wholly composed of lyes, fraud, and counterfet dealings." An open and avowed distrust was ineffectual in the marketplace, Scott reasoned, because it merely strengthened the determination of others to find more devious and undetectable forms of fraud. Instead, Scott recommended that his readers combine "a professed trust" with "a concealed diffidence" so as to deprive another's intent to defraud of its inner rationale by a public and preemptive expectation of the other's fidelity. Out of this intricate pattern of strategem and deceit, in which older notions of honor mixed with more recent concepts of credit, Scott managed to extract for himself and his readers a vocation whose practice rested on an "ordered distrust." What honesty there was to be found in the draper's trade grew largely out of the publicity of the tradesman's life, "living as if he were alwaies in publique, rather fearing himselfe than others."[76] Here, *The Essay of Drapery* seemed to suggest that the emotional boundary or threshold between individuals had its counterpart within the individual. The merchant was to fear himself as much as, if not more than, his competitors. Indeed, he might do well to number among his rivals the selves or characters he was prepared to present within his shop, for each self was, in a manner of speaking, a capital risk and thereby subject to the same calculus of opportunity costs that applied to any other venturable resource. Estranged from himself and from others, Scott's draper was, in a new and entirely secular sense, weaned from the world.

Nowhere was this threshold experience more sharply evoked

than in the recurring image of the tradesman poised between the possibilities of silence and speech. In one of the earliest English mercantile manuals, *The Marchants Avizo,* John Browne had recommended that his readers "deale closely & secretly in all your affaires and busynes" and that they "be earnest in noting & marking euery thing" they uttered. But, he added, "be yourselfe as secret and silent as is possible."[77] Scott's *Essay* similarly observed that the taciturn man had an advantage over the voluble one "in having all he knowes without paying of him any thing for it." Speech, like Bacon's celebrated example of the family, was an impediment to the ambitious man, for if children were the hostages such a man offered to fortune, his words also "let loose many prisoners, which betray him to disadvantage."[78] One talked for a price, but one talked at a price as well. Yet whatever risks speech might run, silence brought with it the unwanted reputation or "character" of being a "too idly reserv'd Man." As the character writer John Earle put it, such a type was "a foole with discretion: or a strange piece of Politician, that manages the state of himselfe."

> His Actions are his Priuie Consell, wherein no man must partake beside. He speakes vnder rule and prescription and dare not shew his teeth without *Machiavell.* He converses with his neighbours as he would in Spaine, and feares an inquisitiue man as much as the inquisition. . . . Hee ha's beene long a riddle himselfe, but at least finds Oedipusses; for his ouer-acted dissimulation discouers him, and men doe with him as they would with Hebrew letters, spell him backwards, and read him.[79]

In the end, the *Essay of Drapery* opted for speech. Indeed, Scott concluded that a merchant's words should flow like honey, especially when the seller's conversation was "tyed to his Commerce, for therein his Customer will commonly take more delight to heare, than hee to speake." To this eloquence, the reader was expected to add "a grave naturall action" of the hands and face, since to persuade "his Customer to the liking of his commodity, hee must put on the same liking himselfe." The speaker had not merely to alter himself into another, as Guazzo had suggested; he had also to produce in himself the same state of mind toward which he wished to bring his customer, "for putting on the same passion hee would stir up in others, he is most like to prevaile."[80] If this was sympathy, it was a fellow-feeling trained in the rhetorical traditions of Cicero and Quintilian – an eloquence without portfolio that, years later, Daniel Defoe would christen "shop-rhetoric."[81] The rhetorical analogy was hardly lost on Scott's seventeenth-century contemporaries, however. Thomas Wright, for example, compared the lyrical salesmanship wherein "all Tradesmen excell" to the verse of "fantasticall and lascivious Poets," and Scott himself warned the ambitious tradesman that "in as much as hee is to deale with men of divers conditions, let him know that to speake according to the nature of him with whom he commerceth, is the best Rhetorick."[82] To deal in goods, it seemed, was to dabble in psychology.

Once again language registered changes in consciousness. The word "deal," for instance, now began to carry hints of subtle negotiation that substantially altered its older and more commonplace definition as a public, physical distribution of goods.[83] It was as if the new rules of indifference governing the placeless market had inspired a compensatory impulse to personalize the popular understanding of the commodity transaction. Advice manuals of the English Renaissance consistently infused the act of exchange with multiple and often hidden intentions. At the same time, the juridical test of a contract (like the literary sense of a "deal") increasingly focused on evidence of a "meeting of minds," to the neglect of earlier preoccupations with the physical delivery or transfer of goods or property.[84] Contracts, like the commercial and conduct manuals that dissected the process of their negotiation, were becoming more fully promissory instruments. They now looked to a future unsecured by the repetitive operations of ritual or the recognizable imprimaturs of kin and clan.

To prepare their readers for the uncertainties of such a future, the popular writers of Tudor–Stuart England drew up a new inventory of human motives that far outstripped the modest scholastic catalogue of the passions. Topical, accessible, and teeming with detail, the popular chapbooks of sixteenth- and seventeenth-century Britain supplied a conspicuously secular psychology that quickly displaced the musty axioms of medieval clerics. Character books, together with the novels they eventually helped to spawn, introduced a model of the autonomous self as the most expedient and plausible repository of the motives they enumerated.[85] Still, the self they improvised to contain these accumulating interests was in no wise a firm and settled entity; it was, if anything, a serial self, not a cumulative self – that is to say, a self composed in, of, and for successive performances. As if to accommodate this novel definition of subjectivity, the word "performance" itself acquired new connotations of illusion and imposture, connotations that complemented and, at the same time, subverted the word's earlier meaning as the ceremonial execution or discharge of a command or obligation. As time passed, the "self" that popular writers imagined became increasingly mercurial. Behind the countenance of the projector, as behind Massinger's "skin of parchment," much more than acres were melting.

For these and other reasons, advice manuals urged on their readers a skepticism and empiricism that refused to take the world at face value. "Be not carefull to please thine eye," the reader was warned, "for it is the deceiptfullest enemie thou hast."[86] The ruses of others were of little consequence to the tradesman if his own vision were playing tricks on his mind. How futile it would be to alter oneself if, while doing so, one failed to observe the shifts of others. Close observation was therefore the condition of success in the marketplace. "A superficiall knowledge of it" was not enough, as Scott insisted;

> a man must penetrate into the inside, and see things in themselves, with the accidents and consequents that belong thereunto; joyning both these together, it will be easy for him to profit, if according to the divers natures of the persons and afaires, he change his stile, and manner of preceeding; as a wise Sea-man, who according to the divers state of the Sea, and change of winds, doth diversely turne his sayles and rudder; knowing every mans nature and fashions, hee may lead him; knowing his ends, he may perswade him; knowing his weaknesse or disadvantage, he may awe him.[87]

Time has scarcely blunted the edge of this passage; it is as pointed now as it was when William Scott first plagiarized it from Francis Bacon's celebrated essay, "Of Negociating." In the seventeenth-century "theater of theft," Scott showed himself to be a shrewd judge of quality, for in choosing Bacon, he was selecting not only a superior wit and stylist, but a writer who was prepared to speculate on the practical uses of misrepresentation. Like other popular writers, Bacon was quick to remark that a knowledge of physiognomy could be "a great discovery of dissimulations, and a great direction in business."[88] But even more important was his conviction that facial and bodily movements were reducible to habit, both in the word's contemporary meaning as a characteristic inward disposition and in its original meaning as a characteristic outward dress or demeanor. In an epoch when clothes themselves were becoming an increasingly manipulable and therefore equivocal sign of rank, Bacon openly treated the mind's own inclinations as subject to the manipulation of their customary outward expression. The same overweening social ambitions that had successfully challenged the traditional statutory connection between class and costume could, in Bacon's view, be turned upon the body and, by extension, the mind that inhabited it. Writing in the same year that Parliament repealed the last remaining sumptuary laws on clothing, Bacon was optimistic. If custom could indeed be conceived as a kind of costume – something to be put on and off at will – then man could literally make himself.[89]

True, Bacon conceded, Greek philosophy had recognized that vices and virtues were but habits long before the publication of his *Advancement of Learning*. But having done so, he added, Aristotle "ought so much the more to have taught the manner of superinducing that habit: for there be many precepts of the wise ordering the exercises of the mind, as there is of ordering the exercises of the body."[90] Accordingly, Bacon offered a few techniques of his own by which the mind could be slipped into a harness of its own making. One of these "precepts" held that "the mind is brought to anything better, and with more sweetness and happiness, if that whereunto you pretend be not first in the intention, but *tamquam aliud agendo* [as if doing something else], because of the natural hatred of the mind against necessity and constraint."[91] In the theater of the mind, the will was to set about its task in disguise; in effect, the mind was to misrepresent itself to itself in order to bring forth "another nature" – a new and improved nature.[92]

That the provenance of human action lay less in nature than in "another nature," that such action could indeed be shaped to a second nature, that virtuosity could, in short, beget virtue – this was the cutting edge of Bacon's argument. Expressive behavior appeared to him "as a garment of the mind, and to have the conditions of a garment." For that reason, he went on, such behavior "ought to be made in fashion; it ought not to be too curious; it ought to be shaped so as to set forth any good making of the mind, and hide any deformity; and above all, it ought not to be too strait, or restrained for exercise or motion."[93] It was as if Bacon had appropriated Thomas Wright's "extraordinary apparell of the bodie" as the aptest metaphor for the plasticity of behavior his pragmatic cast of mind demanded. "Small profit the knowledge of our Passions would afford vs," Wright himself had declared, "if we could not attaine vnto some good means to direct them."[94]

Given these practical interests, it was not to Aristotle but to Machiavelli that Bacon ultimately looked for guidance, for, as he saw it, the Florentine had written about "what men do, and not what they ought to do."[95] Far from regarding the various anatomies of affections and inventories of characters as statements about the moral inadequacies of men and their estates, Bacon insisted on treating them as formulas or "receipts" (recipes) for social transactions. Thus, to set down the "sound and true distributions and descriptions of the several characters and tempers of men's natures and dispositions" was the first object of his scheme of learning, because, as he put it, "we cannot fit a garment, except we take measure of the body."[96] "Characters and tempers," then, were to be regarded as *investments,* both in the sixteenth-century sense of a garment, insignia, or office into which one was installed by ritual or communal fiat and in the seventeenth-century sense of a commercial asset that, properly deployed, might yield more than a "small profit." Bacon's "precepts" treated the expressive surface of the human body as a sphere of risk, but of a kind that went beyond the "thousand natural shocks" that flesh was heir to. As a locus of representation and misrepresentation, the body had become, in effect, a commodity – a double-stitched garment the social value of which fluctuated according to the mysterious movements of a placeless market. In its own, albeit figurative way, the human body had become the newest of England's new draperies.

III

Beneath the complacency of the popular handbooks there lurked a skepticism that could occasionally break out into bitter expressions of irony and melancholia. How often, one wonders, did the singular hopes that such sociological detection nourished in the short run dissolve, over time, into a more general despair and paranoia? Elizabethans were undoubtedly aware of the contradiction embedded at the heart of the characterological and physiognomical manuals, for how could any reader remain assured that what misrepresentations the handbooks discovered and deciphered would not, once learned, merely deepen the dissimulations and impostures they purported to unmask? If every literate Briton could acquire the knowledge contained within the handbooks' pages for the paltry price of purchase, each reader would then have to seek his or her advantage on a different, more inaccessible plane. The promise of disarmament thus brought with it the prospect of immediate rearmament; reciprocal detection raised, in its turn, the specter of mutual, assured deception. The reader's feeling of distance and estrangement could only have sharpened as the handbooks' promise of a transparent social world gave way, once again, to the familiar image of cross-purposes: the Tower of Babel.

The tower was, of course, an ancient emblem; yet seventeenth-century popular writers used it almost exclusively to describe the contemporary marketplace. Thomas Dekker's pamphlet *The Dead Tearme* (1608) conjured up an image of St. Paul's church – where merchants struck deals and masters hired servants – complaining to Westminster about the surge of fraud and deception within its bounds during the regular terms of court.

> What damnable bargaines of vnmercifull Brokery, and of vnmeasureable Vsury are there clapt up?... and such humming (every mans lippes making a noise, yet not a word to be vnderstoode,) I verily beleeue that I am the Tower of *Babell* newly to be builded up, but presentlie despaire of euer beeing finished because there is in me such a confusion of languages. Thus am I

like a common Mart where all Commodities (both the good and the bad) are to be bought and solde.[97]

A year later, in *The Gulls Horn-Book*, Dekker advised the gallants on Paul's Walk to "observe your doors of entrance and your exit not much unlike the players at the theatres, keeping your decorums even in fantasticality."[98] The image was an arresting one, yet altogether commonplace. Two decades later, John Earle could still call Paul's Walk a microcosm of England, the "Lands Epitome."

> It is a heape of stones and men, with a vast confusion of Languages, and were the Steeple not sanctifyed nothing liker Babel .... It is the great Exchange of all discourse, & no business whatsoeuer but is here Stirring and a foot. It is the general Mint of all famous lies, which are here like the legends of Popery, first coyn'd and stampt in the Church.... [Men] all turne Merchants here, and trafficke for Newes.[99]

Yet for all the irony of these descriptions, their general effect was to naturalize the relations of the marketplace. Despite the confusion of tongues and the conflict of purposes, a natural and universal language was understood to bind buyers and sellers together. Indeed, according to the English physician and pro-topsychologist John Bulwer, it was precisely in the Babel of the marketplace, he insisted, that the best evidence was to be found for his theory of gesture as the universal communicative medium. In his *Chirologia: or the Naturall Language of the Hand* (1644), Bulwer declared that the "whole trade of the universe" was "driven by this driving stroke of the Hand":

> [He] that shall (as I have sometimes done) walke upon the Royall Exchange among merchants, meerly to observe their intercourses of buying and selling, shall soon be sa[t]isfied in the naturall force of this expression. But he that would see the vigour of this gesture in *puris naturalibus*, must repaire to the Horse cirque, or Sheep-Pens in Smith-field, where those crafty Olympique merchants who need the *Hand* of no Broker to speed the course of their affaires, will take you for no chapman, unlesse you strike them for good lucke, and smite them in earnest in the palme. And I have sometimes in consort with my friend had good sport to set him to observe the pure and naturall efforts of these men in the heat of their dealings, and have suffered my selfe to bee a little smitten

with the *Hand* of deceit, to gaine the curiosity of an experiment, a kinde of solace, pleasing to Philosophicall complexions, and such who hunt after the subtleties of Nature: wherein though I cannot brag of my bargain, yet I can afford my Reason a good penniworth. Their cunning managing of the *Hand* in time and tone, I have sometimes call'd the Horse-Rhetorique of Smithfield.[100]

At Bartholomew Fair, men struck their hands in surety and deceit, a transaction Bulwer referred to as a "nexus" long before Carlyle made the word a term of opprobrium.[101] In the knot of exchange, the natural language of the heart and the artificial language of commodities were interwoven. The hand, acting in natural sympathy with the mind and "willing to goe out and set a glosse upon the inward motion, casts itselfe into a forme extending to a semblance of the inward appetite." Accordingly, the hand would then receive its favor and good will back again "by a naturall bill of exchange in the *Hand* of another, which verily is a signe of mutuall agreement, and of a perfect conjunction."[102] The handshake was, for Bulwer, the natural representation of a contract, a gestural meeting of the minds.

This figurative assimilation of market exchange into nature was not uncommon in the seventeenth century. It was present, for example, in Shakespeare's Sonnet 87 and in John Hall's *Pastoral Hymn* ("Great Lord, from whom each Tree receaves / Then pays againe as rent, his leaves").[103] And more than a century and a half before Adam Smith wrote of the natural human propensity to "truck, barter, and exchange one thing for another," a former secretary of England's Merchant Adventurers, John Wheeler, declared:

> ... for there is nothing in the worlde so ordinarie, and naturall vnto men, as to contract, truck, merchandise, and trafficque, one with an other, so that it is almost vnpossible for three persons to conuerse together two houres, but they will fall into talke of one bargaine or another, chopping, changing, or some other kinde of contract. Children, as soon as euer their tongues are at libertie, doe season their sportes with some merchandise, or other: and when they goe to schoole, nothing is so common among them as to chaunge, and rechaunge, buye and sell of that, which they bring from home with them: the Prince and his subiects, the Maister and

his seruants, one freend and acquaintaunce with another, the
Captaine with his souldiers, the Husband with his wife, Woman
with, and among themselues, and in a woord, all the world
choppeth and chaungeth, runneth and raueth after Martes,
Marketes and Merchandising, so that all things come into
Commerce, and passe into trafficque (in a manner) in all times,
and in all places: not onely that, which Nature bringeth foorth, as
the fruits of the earth, the beastes, and liuing creatures, with their
spoiles, but skinnes and cases, the metalles, mineralles, & such like
things, but further also, this man make the merchandise of the
workes of his own handes, this man of another mans labour, one
selleth woords, another maketh trafficque of the skins and blood
of other men, yea there are some found so subtill and cunning
merchantes, that they perswade and induce men to suffer
themselues to bee bought and sold, and we have seen in our times
enowe, and too many which haue made merchandise of men's
soules.[104]

Bulwer's work never struck such a resounding or celebratory
note as that of Wheeler's in this encomium to trade, but his
Chirologia found many of the same harmonies. For one thing,
his observations on gesture were situated squarely within the
pattern set by Bacon's sanguine prospectus for learning. The
book's dedicatory poems boasted that Bacon's soul could now
"sleepe sweet; the time is come / That *Gesture* shall no longer
now be dumbe."[105] Moreover, Bulwer's introduction, like that
of William Scott, borrowed freely from Bacon's text.[106] But where
Bacon had pointed to the sign language of "barbarous peoples"
as proof of its universality, Bulwer brought the example even
closer to home. Evidence of the natural language of gesture lay
in "that trade and commerce with those salvage Nations who
have long injoy'd the late discovered principalities of the West,
with whom (although their Language be strange and unknowne)
our Merchants barter and exchange their wares, driving a rich
and silent Trade, by signes, whereby many a dumb bargaine
without the Crafty Brocage of the Tongue, is advantageously
made."[107] Natural language, it seemed, promised to unlock much
more than lips, and Bulwer's friends and patrons were careful to
preserve this bright commercial prospect in the poetic afterwords
they contributed to his *Pathomyotomia* (1649), a detailed treatise

on the muscular bases of emotional expression. There, Bulwer was addressed as

> Thou Grand Adventurer, wits *Magellan,*
> To whom our Microcosme or Isle of man
> By thy all searching Pen's so thoroughly scand
> There's now no part in us an unknown land;
> How thriving is thy Fleet in new Designes,
> To bring home not the Minerall but the Mines?[108]

"Here the Affections keep an open Marte," the poem concluded, the "Patent seal'd by thy Cephalick Art." The poem's imagery ideally suited the task Bulwer had set himself, for his book proposed nothing less than a systematic strip mining of the emotions. *Chirologia,* together with its companion volume, *Chironomia: Or, the Art of Manuall Rhetorique* (1644), pared the language of feeling down to the revelatory movements of the hand, which Bulwer called the "vicegerent of the Tongue" and "Vicar of the Heart."[109] *Pathomyotomia,* written five years later, went even farther. It removed the flesh, as it were, in order to reveal the "Moral Anatomy of the Body" – the motion behind the emotions. Bulwer's "Corporeall phylosophy" claimed to examine "the Clock-work of the Head, or the Springs and inward Contrivance of Instruments of all our outward motions, which give motion and regulate the Dyall of Affections, which Nature hath placed in the Face of Man."[110] Motion was the governing idea in Bulwer's work. Perfection was attainable only through motion, the soul was known only in motion, passions were nothing but motions. Indeed, without the "moving virtue" of the muscles, "the countenance" would lie inert, "like a watch, whose spring or Principle, and the wheeles that served for motion, were taken out."[111] Bulwer had truly attempted "to penetrate into the inside" of the self and to "see things in themselves." He had stripped away the "garment of the mind" so as to expose the true physiognomy beneath, the muscular infrastructure of all expression.

What is especially noteworthy here is how closely Bulwer's own imagery – his metaphors of mechanics and motion – prefigured Hobbes's famous Galilean (or Telesian) opening to the *Leviathan* two years later. There Hobbes used the same "corporeall" analogies to give a rhetorical life to man's social and technical creations, from his watch to his night watchman's state:

> For seeing life is but a motion of limbs [Hobbes wrote], the beginning whereof is in some principal part within; why may we not say, that all *automata* (engines that move themselves by springs and wheels as doth a watch) have an artificial life? For what is the *heart*, but a *spring*; and the *nerves*, but so many *strings*; and the *joints*, but so many *wheels*, giving motion to the whole body, such as was intended by the artificer?[112]

Hobbes's imagery still affects us today; his models or representations of human activity actually seem to detach themselves and take on a life of their own, a second nature so to speak. Bulwer's work displayed the same tendency. In the *Chirologia* he had written of the human hand as setting "a glosse upon the inward motion, cast[ing] itselfe into a forme extending to a semblance of the inward appetite." But in the *Pathomyotomia* he reversed himself, turning the causal order on its head. There he portrayed the "inward motions of the mind" as setting "a representative shape and glosse upon the outward motions of those parts which are moved by the Muscles."[113] The same behavior Bulwer had once taken as the sign, symptom, or expression of various humors and passions he now recast in the form of their effective cause. Despite Bulwer's insistence that all man's gestures were initiated by the will and that habit was not a cause but a quality of motion, he had nonetheless advanced a theory in which the mind was compelled to wait on the habitual movements of the body in order to discover its own "intentions." Man, it seemed, was so constructed by nature as to pursue his projects in accordance with Bacon's precept, which is to say *tamquam aliud agendo*. Behaviorists would embrace just such a formulation some three centuries later, but in the mid–seventeenth century Bulwer could at best but wrestle with its unwanted and unexpected implications. It was, he conceded, "a thing hard enough to believe, that any one should command and not know that he doth command."[114] The quest for motives, like the search for a Northwest Passage (both of which owed much to the pressures of a placeless market), had yielded only further questions. All that could be said on behalf of the "Grand Adventurer" and "wits Magellan" was that the answers, whatever they might be, still resided "in some principal part within" that mysterious continent of the body. Having come this far, however, Bulwer eventually drew back from the behaviorist conclusions toward which his research and his argument were leading him, perhaps because his metaphorical naturalization of commerce had served only to reintroduce the very artifice and duplicity his search for a universal gestural language had sought to remove.

In any event, whether it was a courtier giving his "countenance" to an industrial project or a merchant lending his "hand" to a commercial venture, it was now a face and hand that many seventeenth-century writers suspected of being significantly *denatured*. And nowhere were these suspicions and misgivings more sharply expressed than in Bulwer's last published work, *Anthropometamorphosis* (1653). Profusely illustrated and polemically written, *Anthropometamorphosis* amounted to a vigorous anthropological arraignment of all nations before the "Tribunall of Nature." Their crime? "High-treason, in Abasing, Counterfeiting, Defacing, and Clipping her Coine, instampt with her Image and Superscription on the Body of Man."[115] To meet the false and blasphemous standards of ceremony and fashion, Bulwer argued, men and women the world over had deformed their bodies and thus debased themselves. In the "open Marte" of the affections, mankind had made itself an unacceptable coin.

Published in the first year of Oliver Cromwell's Protectorate, *Anthropometamorphosis* betrayed an anxiety over man's "pragmaticall invention" absent from his earlier work. Bulwer lingered, for example, over the hypothesis of a "too scepticall" philosopher that "man was a meer Artificiall creature, and was at first but a kind of Ape or Baboon, who through his industry (by degrees) in time had improved his Figure & his Reason up to the perfection of man."[116] So far as is known, this passage stirred up nothing remotely resembling the kind of reaction that met Darwin's (faintly) kindred proposals some two hundred years later, which leads one to wonder, conversely, whether it was not Bulwer's already vivid sense of the upheaval in England's social order that impelled him to venture his "too scepticall" theory in the first place. One wonders, in other words, whether his hypothetical "descent of man" was not meant as much to figure as to figure out the crisis of representation that had turned the Tudor–Stuart world upside down. *Anthropometamorphosis* indicted the self-made man in a way that pointed to the man-made state. Subtitled the "Artificiall Changeling," the work stood in some measure as an implicit critique of Hobbes's proud endorsement of his Commonwealth as an "artificial man."

In another sense, *Anthropometamorphosis* was little more than a long rumination on the theme of decorum, for it was this principle more than any other that restrained writers like Bulwer and Bacon from embracing the ideal of an autonomous performing self.[117] Educated in the classical rhetorical tradition, Renaissance writers naturally assumed that each emotion had its appropriate expression, an expression that was at once a compromise between the inward, "subjective" intensity of the feeling and the outward, "objective" pressures of status and situation. Moreover, to stir others to a particular emotion, one had to be aroused oneself.[118] The hand might seem to have conceived the thought, it might even by its movement strengthen the sentiment within, but it was ultimately dependent on a socially given character or temperament. Decorum could assert the identification of life with art – the garment of behavior with the garment of style – but it balked at artifice. "That which one does without Art," Bulwer announced, "cannot wholly be delivered by Art."[119] Decorum aestheticized the distance between the estates of English society. It prescribed the rules by which that distance could be given form, shape, and detail and thereby endowed it with a tangible and, more important, a legitimate presence, an authority made all the more palpable on those dangerous occasions of the carnivalesque when propriety was deliberately and systematically overthrown.

Whether the principles of decorum are best understood as a residue of ritual or oral culture, they may nonetheless be seen to have checked the tendency of the Renaissance advice manual to draw out of the pseudosciences of physiognomy, metoposcopy, and chirologia the constituents of an autonomous, performing self – a polymorphous second nature.[120] The self that propriety imagined remained fixed within the gilt frame of rank and status. Across the social distance that status presupposed, decorum permitted only certain emotional liberties: One could feel the "vertical" sentiments such as admiration, envy, and pity but not the "lateral" sentiments of sympathy or curiosity. Thus, although decorum furnished boundaries for the action of man's second nature, it also policed the impulse to decipher that action, especially as that impulse threatened to intrude on the protocols of class and gender. In Thomas Wright's discussion of the "silent speech" of the countenance, for example, he held it wrong for women, children, and servants to look into their betters' eyes "because it were presumption for [them] to attempt the entrance or priuie passage into [their] superiors minde, as contrariwise it is lawfull for the superior to attempt the knowledge of his inferior."[121] Bacon was similarly disposed toward the "custom of the Levant," which forbade subjects from fixing their eyes on their masters, particularly from trying "to pierce and penetrate into the hearts of kings which the scripture hath declared to be inscrutable." Decorum declared such scrutiny out of bounds.

Some Italian writers, emboldened perhaps by more deeply rooted Platonic and Hermetic traditions, moved more comfortably, if unobtrusively, in this ambiguous terrain. In conversation and negotiation, they recommended the mobilizing of whatever resources were at hand to take (and evade) the soundings of another. The playwright Della Porta, for instance, wrote works on the arts of cryptography, memory, physiognomy, and chiromancy: *De Furtivis literarum notis vulgo* (1563), a manual of codes and ciphers; *Arte del ricordare* (1566), a memory book for actors; *De humana physiognomonia* (1586), a treatise applying the "doctrine of signatures," or plant physiognomy, to animals and humans; and *Chrifisonomia* (1581), a work on palm reading not published until 1643. John Bulwer was especially impressed with Della Porta's gestural cipher system, which he thought promised uses for diplomacy and foreign trade. Bacon, too, had been deeply influenced by Della Porta's *Magia naturalis* (1548), as had Della Porta's fellow magus, Tomasso Campanella, whom the former met in 1589.[122]

Of all the instructional writers of the Renaissance, it was Campanella, a Dominican scholar, reformer, and magician, who took the possibilities of man's second nature to their farthest reaches. In his writing, the imperatives of virtue and virtuosity, simulation and dissimulation, sympathy and scrutiny converged to form a model of the self as a placeless and Protean entity – a liminal being always on the verge of becoming something or someone else. The first English account of Campanella's discoveries appeared in 1650 under the title *Unheard-of Curiosities,* a translation of a French work, *Curiosités inouyes* (1629), by Jacques Gaffarel, librarian to Cardinal Richelieu. A priest deeply immersed in cabalist and orientalist studies, Gaffarel, like Bacon, had read Campanella's *De sensu rerum et magia* (1620) with great interest and in 1626 had visited the author in Rome, where Campanella had been imprisoned on charges of heresy and conspiracy.

Campanella, who still bore the visible marks of torture by his inquisitors, was found in his cell making "certain wry faces" over a letter of supplication he was composing to one of his superiors, a Cardinal Magaloti. These facial expressions, as Campanella explained them, allowed him to enter into the cardinal's mind by exactly reproducing the cleric's physiognomy. In other words, by observing his own feelings at the same time that he assumed the outward appearance and bearing of another, Campanella claimed direct access to the other's state of mind and thus a privileged insight into the ways in which he might be moved.[123] By "altering his copy" – to recur to the seventeenth-century idiom – Campanella hoped to alter his fate. By escaping the prison of his body, he sought to escape the prison in which his body had been lodged.

A logic of this order resembles nothing so much as the homeopathic or sympathetic principle in magic: the conviction that one can produce any effect one wants simply by "imitating it in advance."[124] But Campanella's reasoning was equally indebted to an epistemological position first marked out by the anti-Aristotelian philosopher Bernardino Telesio, a sixteenth-century precursor of Bacon and Hobbes. That position, summed up in Telesio's dictum *cognoscere est esse,* assimilated the knower into the object known.[125] "We do not perceive anything by which we are not affected and by which we are not changed," Campanella declared in his Ninth Doubt. "When we perceive something, we are in some way alienated and changed into something else, so that we know when we become something else." "But," he added, "this is insanity, for when man is changed into something else he is said to be insane."[126] Bulwer, the protopsychologist, agreed. No one, he insisted, could "put off his own, and put on another's nature."[127] And what was madness for the individual to contemplate was, by extension, apocalyptic for a society. Looking about the strife-torn England of the mid–seventeenth century, Bulwer concluded that man's presumptuous self-fashioning had already left him "shoared upon the Continent of Change and confusion, where the inconstancy of his actions, and the various shapes he entertained, by the new modelling of his person, justly brought upon him the judgment of dereliction."[128] Whatever place *Anthropometamorphosis* can be said to occupy in the early history of anthropology, it still belongs to an even older tradition of lament that had taken root in the literature of estates. "All other creatures keep their ranks, their places and natures in the world," Bulwer observed; "only man himselfe disorders all, and that by displacing himselfe, by losing his place."[129] Campanella's method for *self*-displacement could make but little headway against an opposition, Puritan or patrician, that continued to cling to the pristine social signs and symbols by which classes were supposed to represent themselves to one another.

As it was, Campanella came to be regarded by his English critics as an eccentric philosopher and magician whose extraordinary self-control had inured him to the pain of torture and had enabled him to escape the death sentence of the Inquisition by feigning insanity. For English skeptics, there was as much method to Campanella's madness as madness to his method. Little wonder, then, that they should have preferred to think of the beleaguered Dominican philosopher as a Machiavellian or that the label should have been first applied to him by the arch-enemy of the English stage, William Prynne.[130] Campanella had taken the physiognomical skills of the Renaissance handbook and made them the characteristic possessions of a Protean and essentially homeless self. Only the most obtuse of readers could fail to see in that portrait the mobile features of the stage player.

IV

To survey the sixteenth- and seventeenth-century literature of moral and social instruction, as we have just done, is to see at once how consistently it subverted its deepest conservative in-

stincts. The various forms of sociological and psychological realism that it urged on its readers merely heightened the suspicions
of fraud and factitiousness it was intended to protect against.
Beneath all the pseudoscientific anatomies and inventories of the
self, the popular handbooks acknowledged the onset of a national,
if not global, crisis of representation, one wherein traditional
social signs and symbols had metamorphosed into detached and
manipulable commodities. Copyholds could be tested in the
courts, but where was the tribunal that could try the "copies"
men and women made of their countenances? The playwrights'
answer was, of course, the stage, and in a sense their contemporaries agreed, for not only did the former seize upon the problem of social representation and misrepresentation as the theme
and touchstone of their drama, but their audiences, equally perplexed by the fluidity of social relations, used the idiom of the
theater to frame the problem for themselves. "Man in business
is but a Theatricall person, and in a manner but personates himselfe," the poet John Hall wrote, adding that "in his retired and
hid actions, he pulls off his disguise, and acts openly."[131]
Hall's observation suggests a number of things, not least of
which is a new concept of privacy, one centered within the self
rather than within the household, as had earlier been the convention. No longer was the household seen to mark the formal
boundary of kin and kindness. So far, in fact, had the traditional
threshold convenant decayed in sixteenth-century England that
the ritual obligations of hospitality and protection long connected
with it were gradually removed from the near-bankrupt guilds
and offered as commodities by the new professional theaters and
suburban inns – sometimes the two together.[132] As for the threshold *experience,* its specific associations with the standard boundaries and break points of the life cycle were gradually falling
away, leaving the sense of transition a permanent feature of personal life. It is therefore not altogether surprising that the secrecy
and withdrawal long identified with moments of ritual passage
should have survived in the new image of the private Protean
man that the handbooks (and the theater) set forth. With the
emergence of a placeless market, the threshold experience threatened to become coextensive with all that a deritualized commodity exchange touched. Life now resembled an infinite series

of thresholds, a profusion of potential passages or opportunity costs running alongside experience as a constant reminder of the selves not taken. And just as London's Exchange enforced an ideal of financial liquidity, so London's theaters enacted a vision of this new sociological and psychological fluidity. And why not, since the world was at once a market and a stage?

John Hall's portrait of the "man in business" collapsed these two worlds into one another and, in doing so, acknowledged the problem of accountability in the placeless market. With decisions over purchase and sale increasingly removed from the immediacy of the traditional marketplace, commercial transactions had already begun to take on the perceived character of a script drafted elsewhere and enacted by proxy. The professional theater offered itself, ironically, as the most credible instrument with which to visualize, so to speak, the lost transparency of these ordinary acts. Indeed, it was Shakespeare who first gave to the word "act" the peculiarly "theatrical coloring" it has ever since retained.[133] And it was during Shakespeare's life that the original sense of the word "actor" as a general agent or representative – a steward, attorney, or factor – began to give way to its modern definition as a player or performer.[134] This complex play of meanings betokened not just a change of definition but a certain loss of definition, a new bewilderment about the boundaries and conditions of representation in a society where impersonality and impersonation were suddenly thrusting themselves forward as vexing issues. To understand the sources of this confusion is to appreciate why the efforts to express and resolve it were so frequently couched in the language of the stage.

When Thomas Hobbes undertook to assure his readers in 1649 that neither political authority nor commercial accountability need be lost if England embraced a new and thoroughgoing contractualism, it is noteworthy that he first looked to the contemporary theater for an appropriate analogy. There he found a model of social relations he was anxious to legitimate, one in which the ownership and responsibility for specific acts could be contractually transferred. Like John Hall, who was himself a Hobbesian, Hobbes identified the person in business with the actor. But unlike Hall, Hobbes was prepared to develop the analogy at some length. The word "person," he observed, was derived from the word *persona,* which had originally referred to the outward appearance or mask of a player. "So that a *person,* is the same that an *actor* is, both on the stage and in common conversation; and to personate, is to act, or *represent* himself, or another." There was, however, a further distinction to be made. "Natural persons," Hobbes declared, were those individuals who could be said to represent themselves; "artificial persons," on the other hand, were those whose words and deeds were "owned" by those whom they represented. The former were authors; the latter were actors, but actors in the sense of mere hirelings.[135] Human commodities that they were, Hobbesian individuals lived a twofold existence – a first and second nature – in the new marketplace. It was a duality for which Hobbes could find no more appropriate representative than the figure of the player.

Had it not been for the gradual secularization of the theatrical metaphor in the years before the publication of *Leviathan,* Hobbes's use of the *theatrum mundi* might have drawn him perilously close to a blasphemous analogy between human and divine authorship. As it was, however, the vocabulary of the stage perfectly suited his aim of identifying contractual ownership with contractual authority in the social relations of civil and political society. His reference to the actor intended least of all to point up the meaninglessness of secular society. Rather it implied the presence of a society surcharged with meanings and intentions, meanings and intentions that only contract could render tangible, realizable. In such transactions, actors and factors were interchangeable.

This connection was as critical for the opponents of secular contractualism as for its champions. Because of this, it is difficult to see the seventeenth-century attack on the English stage – an attack that eventually succeeded in suppressing it – as having been somehow divorced from the more general crisis of representation within English society as a whole. Critics of the theater looked upon the frequent swearing of oaths on the stage as a covert preparation for the equally casual forswearing of oaths within society[136] – all the more so since such oaths were uttered, as in the placeless market, "by way of Proxie, or Representation onely, not as the Words, the Oathes and Imprecations of the Poets, or Actors, but of those parts they represent."[137] The contractual grant of immunity that Hobbes was prepared to assign, within stipulated conditions, to the commercial or political "actor" was an outrage in the eyes of men like William Prynne, an authorization without foundation in scripture. Prynne's actors were, like Hobbes's actors, "artificial persons," but they were so precisely because they could claim *no* author, contractualism being an insufficient ground of authority. Like John Bulwer, Prynne saw actors as apostates from themselves and from God, "artificiall changelings" who obscured and escaped the imputation of sin itself.

William Prynne's massive antitheatrical polemic, *Histrio-Mastix* (1633), then, was something more than an envious and literal-minded reaction to the recreational pastimes of others. It was the response of a man, histrionic in his own right, to the problem of theatricality reconceived as a dimension of secular life; it was, in other words, an effort to solve the crisis of representation by purging *its* most vivid representation: the theater.[138] By 1642, if not 1633, the *theatrum mundi* was no longer the simple, sacred emblem of the divine cosmos. Society had changed sufficiently since the *Shyp of Folys* to appropriate the image entirely to itself. The theater had changed as well.

3. Artificial persons

A Player is a representatif by his calling, a person of all qualities;
and though his profession be to counterfeit, and he never means
what he says, yet he endeavours to make his words and actions
always agree. His labour is to play, and his bus'nes to turn
passion into action – The more he dissembles, the more he is in
earnest, and the less he appears himself, the truer he is to his
professions. . . . He assumes a body like an apparition, and he can
turn himself into as many shapes as a witch. . . . When he is off
the stage he acts a gentleman, and in that only makes his own
part himself. . . . He is like a Motion made by clockwork, the
Poet winds him up, and he walks and moves till his part run
down, and then he is quiet. . . . His profession is a kind of
metamorphosis, to transform himself out of one shape into
another, like a taylors sheet of paper, which he folds into
figures.

Samuel Butler, *Characters* (ca.
1667-9)

I am not that I play.

Twelfth Night, I, v, 184

THOMAS HOBBES'S INTEREST in the theater as a model
of authority had little or nothing to do with the stage's
ancient emblematic status as a microcosm of the divine
or natural order of things. The polity that he envisaged in *Leviathan* was a creature not of nature but of second nature, an
"artificial man" whose aura of authority was no more (and no
less) than an "artificial soul." Skeptical as he was of all analogical
explanations, Hobbes sought, if anything, to relieve the *theatrum
mundi* of its cosmic associations in order to see more clearly the
ordinary performative acts and agreements by which men – as
artificers – fashioned their own social and political worlds. Hobbes
regarded every human act as an act of representation, either of
oneself or another. And because men "personated" themselves
in this way, the one momentous transaction whereby they con-
tracted among themselves to authorize a sovereign to represent

and thereby to rule them was entirely consistent with their nature as men: their fears, their desires, and their performative capacities.

From its pit to its heavenly canopy, the design of the London playhouse reproduced the *structure* of rank to which men, in Hobbes's view, had freely submitted themselves. But, more important, the impersonations of its players reproduced the *process* by which these same men had transferred their authority to one "actor." With every performance, the player enacted in miniature the genesis and transmission of authority in civil society; his freedoms and immunities were therefore a perfect representation of those that had accrued to Hobbes's sovereign. His was indeed a "player-king" but one relatively untroubled by the misgivings and miscastings that plagued Shakespeare's anguished monarchs.[1] Thus, the same "personations" that Puritans (and playwrights) stigmatized as the source of England's disorder, Hobbes defended as the condition of its future security. What William Prynne anathematized as a problem, Thomas Hobbes thematized as a solution.

To achieve this solution, however, Hobbes attempted to graft a particularly narrow concept of absolute authority on an increasingly elastic understanding of representation. Indeed, by the time of *Leviathan*'s first publication, the word "representation" had already drifted out of the figurative idiom of ritual, art, and religion and into the legal lexicon of politics and commerce, although this shift appears to have occurred much later in English than in Latin and French. English texts, for their part, indicate that between 1580 and 1650, the term "representative" (or "representatif") came to encompass both the traditional, static definition of a person or token chosen to *stand for* another and a more recent and dynamic definition of a person chosen to *act for* another. It was just this new, albeit equivocal, sense of surrogate agency that led Hobbes to select the theater out of all the mimetic arts and rituals to serve as his master trope of representation. The state had its vicegerents, the church had its vicars, but only the theater projected a whole world of vicarious relations. What more appropriate metaphor could one find to epitomize and resolve the problem of representation in the placeless market than the vivid, engaging example of the theater, where "artificial persons"

ranged widely, freely, and with the delighted assent of the assembled multitudes? There, if anywhere, was the true habitat of
man's second nature, his Protean capacity not only to personate
others but, in Hobbes's terms, to represent (and misrepresent)
himself.

Here, unfortunately, Hobbes's metaphorical strategy served
him less well than he imagined, for it was never entirely clear
whom the seventeenth-century player could be said to represent.
He certainly never claimed to represent himself on the stage, nor
did he purport to represent the playwright. Nor, finally, did he
represent his "character." He *was* the character as long as the
action of the play went forward, and he could expect to be taken
as such by his audience.[2] Notwithstanding the many ceremonial
and cosmological residues to be found in Renaissance drama,
people streamed to the London theaters in order to watch the
professional presentation of an entertainment, not to participate
in the amateur representation of a communal ritual.[3] The rudimentary conventions of seventeenth-century dramatic realism
(which is to say the conventions of a mutually acknowledged
fiction) confuted Hobbes's figurative theory of authorization as
thoroughly as the conventions of an earlier, ceremonial drama
had appeared to confirm it. Performers could now enact authority
in their dramas without ratifying it. With the single, though
important, exception of the court masque, theater had relinquished its claims of ritual efficacy.

As a masterless man consigned to the limbo of London's liberties, the common player occupied a margin or threshold in
English society and culture from which most ritual and ceremonial protections had been systematically stripped. His warrant
to act was at best dubious, hanging as it did on the whims of
courtly patrons, the sufferance of municipal officials, and the
ambiguities of civic jurisdiction. With every outbreak of plague
or disorder, his social contract with society had, in effect, to be
renegotiated so that his thought, like that of William Scott's
draper, returned again and again to the practical and imaginative
conditions of his credibility in society. These ruminations yielded,
in turn, new dramatic conventions by which the player sought
to establish his stage persona in the absence of a ritual rationale.

Predictably, these devices reproduced the same confusions over identity that the actor was himself encountering within the recreational marketplace of early modern England.

The social confusions that playwrights sought to satirize and that instructional writers strove to anatomize, others preferred to sanitize. In this, the theater provided a convenient, if not exactly obliging, target. Of course the desire to purify, clarify, and restore lost boundaries has always inhabited the "antitheatrical prejudice," at least since Plato, but never did it seem more compelling than during the controversy that erupted over the English stage in the 1570s and that, some seventy years later, culminated in its complete suppression. In this struggle, Puritans and their allies sought to reorder English society by purging its culture of its most visibly Protean tendencies; in other words, they attempted to resolve the complex problematic of market exchange by repressing its most vivid figurative expression: the stage.

In the pages that follow, I shall explore the changes that placed the theater in such a congenial relation to the new market and, at the same time, in such a volatile relation to the new religionists. Viewed against the background of these changes, the suppression of the English stage in 1642 appears to have been one of the most striking acts of symbolic displacement in the history of market societies.

I

Of the many pressures propelling the English drama out of the church and streets and into the protective confines of the playhouse, none was more insistent or effective than that brought to bear on the drama by the players themselves. As the ritual and ceremonial ground of drama dissolved beneath their feet, actors stretched a safety net of story and spectacle across the widening chasm of disbelief. Innovations in character and plotting, novel arrangements of theatrical space, and new rhetorical and authenticating devices – these were the players' answer to the material problems growing out of a declining civic patronage, to the political tensions produced by a deepening religious conflict, and, not least of all, to the performative exigencies imposed by the changing expectations and responses of occasional audiences.[4] Few improvisations were ever more successful than the ones players made in their own behalf in the face of religious reformation and economic dislocation. And though that success may have seemed frail indeed to the silenced performers of the mid–seventeenth century, it remains instructive, for it alerts us to the link between the rise (and fall) of Renaissance drama on the one hand and the career of the common player on the other.

Medieval actors, for example, had identified with their parts in an emblematic rather than an existential sense. Theirs was not a theater of illusion, as V. A. Kolve has reminded us, but instead a ritual or quasi-ritual enactment in which no clear line divided performers from spectators.[5] The former did not seek to present a story and its characters to the latter; rather, they sought to represent a foreshortened and symbolic narrative keyed to the governing typology of biblical time and to the surrounding structure of social rank. The guilds regarded dramatic roles as ceremonial offices and hence chose their incumbents according to their extratheatrical occupations. Bakers would perform the Last Supper, shipwrights the story of Noah, and cooks the Harrowing of Hell. Doubling in parts was uncommon, though "not unknown."[6] The aim in every instance was to heighten the reality, as opposed to the realism, of the play. "Medieval drama," as Anne Righter notes, "drew its boundaries between a fragmentary secular environment and the cosmos of the play. While the performance lasted, audience and actors shared the same ritual world, a world more real than the one which existed outside the frame."[7] Though the vernacular drama of the Middle Ages did not itself employ the *theatrum mundi* as an emblem, it nonetheless embodied, as a matter of its formal properties, the emblem's principle of otherworldliness. It has long been argued that the theater is the cultural form best equipped to bring into presence that which is absent. If so, its powers were never more effectively exercised than in the mystery cycles, where the numinous reality of God's invisible cosmos was triumphantly posed against the hollow pretensions of man's visible existence.[8]

It was to this common and profane existence that the fifteenth-century morality plays turned, but, in so doing, they reversed the relation of reality to illusion that the mysteries had earlier assumed. Now the stage became the locus of a fabricated and essentially didactic illusion aimed at an identifiable "audience." "A barrier that had been non-existent in the mystery cycles now divided the play world from the place where the audience stood."[9] Within the moral interlude, new forms of extradramatic address emerged to pierce this barrier and to allow the spectators a privileged moment of communion with the popular character of "Mankind." But such gestures were, by their very nature, tacit acknowledgments of a new theatrical relation whose growing palpability would eventually earn it the title of the "fourth wall." In this respect, the morality initiated the long journey of the English theater toward the perfected physical and psychological enclosure – a journey not completed until the invention of the footlit box setting of the nineteenth century.[10] Still, when the players brought the moral interludes into the banquet hall and guild hall at the beginning of the sixteenth century, they could do so with some confidence that a space had already been prepared for them in the minds of their expectant audience.

Scholars have generally taken the passage of vernacular drama into the Tudor hall as marking the emergence of a class of professional players in England.[11] With this entrance into the theater of the hall, the players began to cast off the increasingly cumbersome legacy of abstract representation for the freedom to present recognizably social and moral characters. The effect of this emancipation was to leave the players free to appeal to the social idiosyncrasies of their audience, indeed to create and manipulate their audience through the power of illusion.[12] In Henry Medwall's *Fulgens and Lucrece* (1497), the earliest secular comic interlude to be preserved, characters misrecognize one another, act as spectators to one another, and eventually invite the audience to amend the play.[13] As a dramatic form, the interlude "was constantly pretending to burst its artistic limits, skillfully affecting to be on the verge of extemporization."[14] In the context of the banquet hall, this theatricality could be most palatable, suggesting as it did a bittersweet delight in the arbitrary and complicitous character of social ritual and convention. Its aftertaste can still be savored in the early writings of Thomas More, whose whole career, according to Stephen Greenblatt, was haunted "not only [by] the shadow of the designing consciousness manipulating the mask but [by] the shadow of other selves crouched in the darkness." Like More, the professional player was beginning to entertain the thought of a self contrived against the imagination of its own opportunity costs – a consciousness of "the possibility of other identities unfulfilled by the particular role" that one was "in the act of projecting."[15] In dramatic as in nondramatic literature, the rudiments of a histrionic calculus were falling into place.

Had he wished, the player might well have used such a calculus to assess the personal cost of the freedom and power he had purchased through the popularity of the secular interlude, for by its performance, he had effectively made himself over into a servant of the hall, a property like any other stage machinery appropriated on behalf of an aristocratic spectacle of power.[16] Nevertheless, the protection afforded by livery was one that actors continued to seek, if only fitfully, throughout the sixteenth century. As a consequence, their fate, like that of any retainer, became increasingly identified with that of their lordly patrons, even as the substance of that patronage steadily diminished with the proliferation of public theaters in London after 1576.[17] Aristocratic values undoubtedly percolated downward in the process of this exchange between players and patrons. For example, the traditional stage image of the usurer as battening upon the generous impulses of a rural aristocracy owed much to the players' vested interest in the hospitality of their lord.[18] Still, the attachment was not entirely one-sided. By the early seventeenth century, both common player and lordly aristocrat could find in each other and in their masque a figurative expression of their own sense of power.

Moreover, the cord of retainership was often an exceedingly light one for the player, a matter of safety in times of controversy and of provision in times of dearth. "Under the protective shield of their lord's badge, invoking a declining, obsolescent form of service, which was in their case sometimes little better than a legal fiction, the players established themselves as purveyors of a commodity for which the general public was prepared regularly to put down its cash." Ancient badges of seigneurial obligation ornamented a relation that was often no more than an affair of mutual convenience, just as they cloaked the players' more prosaic aspirations "to the condition of merchants and citizens."[19] The same empty ceremonies of patriarchy that formed the thematic center of so many of Shakespeare's plays furnished the screen behind which the common players strove to break the pattern of their own dependence. Livery sealed off a social space within which the player could fashion for himself a professional identity, with enormous consequences for the theater itself. The impulse to enclosure in the theater thus came as much from the performers within as from the reformers without.[20]

Inside the banquet hall and guild hall of the sixteenth century, the players experimented sporadically with dramatic forms, developing new conventions that would enable them to communicate with an audience at once physically present and psychologically distant.[21] Detached as they now were from the seasonal rhythms of the festive calendar, the liturgical requirements of ritual enactment, and the status expectations of local guilds, the small touring companies that performed the moral interludes found themselves in a position to refashion the drama to fit the image and needs of their own mobile existence. Because the companies were small, they turned to doubling and disguising to fill out their ranks, especially after the midcentury suppression of the remaining mystery cycles. The social morality *All for Money* (1559–77) allotted five parts to every actor, for example. Players increasingly doubled as their characters' alter egos, and different human attributes came to be compressed into one character. A change of costume no longer served as an unequivocal indication of a change of heart or part but could just as easily signal a character's intention to deceive. "An assumed dress, like an assumed name," became, according to T. W. Craik, "a means whereby evil characters [could] purchase credit." The change applied to virtuous characters as well, for as the eschatological vision of the early moralities yielded to the ethical perspective of the later plays, "virtue's credit with heaven for heavenly redemption" no longer satisfied an audience increasingly attuned to the here and now. In the moralities written after 1500, Bernard Spivack notes, virtue became "a negotiable instrument of currency" in the secular world, a commodity to be negotiated for fame and honor in the present. In this way, the figures of the morality (like those of the character books) changed from simple personified abstractions of vice and virtue into more complex and composite social types.[22]

The small size of the companies likewise necessitated multiple entrances and exits from the stage as actors scurried to change their costumes behind a curtain that now concealed a portion of the play's contrivance from the eyes of the spectators. These appearances and disappearances implanted a sense of intrigue within the form of the play itself, as David Bevington points out, and thus edged drama away from its traditional panoramic displays and toward a more episodic unfolding of plot. Relationships among the characters, long assumed to be static properties of the characters themselves, were now allowed to develop in a more or less linear sequence of scenes.[23] Gradually, the synoptic and timeless viewpoint of the religious mystery gave way to the fragmentary and historical viewpoint of the secular chronicle.

These changes, in turn, prompted the introduction of dramatic conventions that could keep the audience abreast of the play's action and attuned to the motives that the new plot devices were signaling. Long soliloquies enabled the players to use the rich rhetorical traditions of the drama to convey some of this information in what was, increasingly, an extradramatic form of address. As the boundaries of the play world grew more distinct during the late sixteenth century, moments of direct address tended to become grouped around the periphery of the play, in prologues, inductions, and epilogues. Though soliloquy preserved many of its extradramatic properties well into the Jacobean period, it also began to project the impression of a solitary rumination set well within the frame of the play's pretense. In effect, the audience was being invited to eavesdrop on the characters in much the same way that the characters eavesdropped among themselves. Faithful to the new social relations it was attempting to enact on the stage, Elizabethan drama presented a world that was less likely to be heard than overheard.[24] Once again, familiarity and distance were joined in a way that reproduced the new sensibility of commodity exchange.

This was not the only resemblance. The same suspicion of multiple and concealed intentions that haunted the new marketplace found an even stronger evocation in the drama of late-sixteenth-century England, where players used verbal asides to reveal the motives that their disguises merely insinuated. What had been an occasional device of Greek and Roman drama (largely comedy) quickly became a standard convention of English drama, as playwrights interpolated asides into comedies and tragedies alike.[25] The immediate effect of the disguise, the soliloquy, and the aside, however, was to allow the truths of a play to emerge as imminent rather than immanent revelations, as impending disclosures of fact rather than as indwelling figurations of meaning. In the best of plays, of course, these two forms of discovery can scarcely be distinguished, but when viewed across the whole corpus of sixteenth- and seventeenth-century plays, these conventions and devices seem only to rehearse the warning that popular instructional literature never tired of issuing: that Elizabethan society operated in a state of diminished and diminishing transparency.

The mystery cycles had functioned, above all, as ceremonial enactments of religious and mythic charters, carefully designed to replicate governing patterns of social authority within the city and the larger society. Theirs was a relatively static tableau drama performed to propitiate a divine and unseen audience through the ritualized representation of widely held principles of ecclesiastical and social order. Renaissance plays, on the other hand, offered an elaborately plotted, polymorphous drama performed to amuse, enthrall, and edify a secular and all too visible audience.[26] Conservative lessons abounded in Renaissance drama, to be sure, and the defenders of the stage never hesitated to point out these homilies. But, as their opponents were equally quick to note, these were messages that the medium itself resisted, subverted, and at times openly contradicted. Despite its many ties to the court, the seventeenth-century stage was in some measure constitutionally disposed to enact the representational crisis of authority occasioned by England's increasingly boundless market; it was by that same measure constitutionally incapable of providing all but the most ambiguous answers to the problematic of exchange that the market had brought with it. The Renaissance stage was an experimental, not a propitiatory, institution.

Whereas the theater of the Middle Ages had formed part of an ongoing communal ritual, the theater of the Renaissance more closely resembled an occasional discretionary compact struck between performers and audience. The transaction consisted of two "partners" who agreed, in effect, to authorize one another for the determinate duration of the play and, at the same time, to immunize one another from any extratheatrical consequences that would follow from a literal or, for that matter, a ritualist reading of their collaborative fiction. The spectacular proportions of carnival that a redemptive and retributive tradition of travesty had once marked out for itself were trimmed down to fit "the two hours' traffic" of the stage, for which the audience was of course expected to pay. Thus, to use Victor Turner's formula for the evolution of "leisure goods," a liminal ritual was converted over time to a liminoid commodity. The new theater effectively offered itself as a joint venture of limited liability. Small wonder, then, that so many more Londoners assisted at *The Tempest* (1611) than at the expedition of the Virginia Company (1609) that had inspired its opening scene.[27]

Renaissance dramatic form thus figured, when it did not actually prefigure, the emerging relations of a market society. The introduction of a device like the soliloquy or the aside signaled, in Raymond Williams's view, "new conceptions of the autonomous or relatively autonomous individual, new senses of the tensions between such an individual and an assigned or expected social role." A "formal innovation" of this kind, Williams warns, should not be treated as a mere reproduction or derivation of social changes occurring elsewhere but rather as a "true and integral element of the changes themselves: an articulation, by technical discovery, of changes in consciousness which are themselves forms of consciousness of change."[28] Flanked on one side by Southwark's notorious brothels (the "licensed Stewes") and on the other by the equally notorious shops of "interloping" artificers, the Bankside theaters were in a perfect position to incubate the embryonic *mentalité* of an increasingly commercial society.

As we shall see, Renaissance dramatists did not shrink from comparing their own conventions of performance to the new contractual relationships arising outside the theater. A conditional credibility, not faith, was the playwright's aim, much as it was for his fellow artisans (most men of the theater were drawn from the ranks of artisans and tradesmen) who sought credit in the marketplace.[29] The worst of dramatists nonetheless distinguished himself from the best of tradesmen by his willingness to make credibility not just the dream but the theme of his art, a theme explored in countless episodes of mistaken identity, misplaced trust, and misdirected suspicion. Together, players and playwrights improvised conventions of performance that deliberately acknowledged the fabricated character of the play world and that, in doing so, mooted the authority of all appearances. *Hamlet,* for example, required the performer to divulge the very process of his own enactment and to do so in a setting, real and fictive, where ritual itself had been explicitly desacralized.[30] The effect, however fleeting, of this pointedly deconstructive exercise was to subject all claims to authority to a deeper and in many ways unattainable standard of authenticity. The new drama showed, as no other genre could, how precarious social identity was, how vulnerable to unexpected disruptions and disclosure it was, and therefore how deeply theatrical it was. Everyone, dramatists seemed to say, was a player-king embroiled in a ceaseless struggle to preserve his legitimacy. In this fashion the player-playwright managed to return, with equal measures of malice and geniality, the challenges hurled at *his* illusion by gallants and groundlings alike.

By thus disclosing the peculiarly roguish construction of his stage persona, the player arrived at a theater of unprecedented realism and, pari passu, a realism of unprecedented theatricality. Such a theater was, in Jonas Barish's apt phrase, "ontologically subversive," for it resurrected all the existential doubts that earlier generations had lodged in the theatrical metaphor without at the same time restoring the ancient assurances of a final cause or indeed a final curtain.[31] The emblem of the *theatrum mundi* entered English drama for the first time, in fact, during the sixteenth century, where it served playwrights as an ideal vehicle with which to convey the changing character of stage and society: preserving the older, stoic melancholy of a Jaques on the one hand while introducing the newer worldly aestheticism of a Richard II on the other. "Thus play I in one person many people," Richard muses, "And none contented."[32]

Did such deep brooding about the theater's own theatricality indicate a deliberate withdrawal from the hurly-burly of life into some solipsistic, Neoplatonic void? Yes, at least to the degree that the drama had managed to extricate itself from the ritual and ceremonial imperatives of medieval town life in favor of the "liberties" and the protective confines of the "wooden O." But it was just this physical and imaginative segregation, in a sense, that made the theater's realism a feasible ideal, for no theater can claim to hold the mirror up to a society from which it is still widely regarded as inseparable. At the same time, the mirror that Renaissance dramatists held up to their society served less to reflect the "real" than to expose the posturings its own reflective surface invited. True, audiences did expect to see their social and temperamental quirks as credibly typified on the stage as they were in the character books, but to watch such types enacted within the context of a plot, with all that word's connotations of intrigue and scheming, was to confront the possibility that the self was a contingent, arbitrary, and instrumental affair, not a natural or supernatural calling. By deliberately effacing the line between the self's iconic representation in art and ritual and its instrumental presentation in ordinary life, Renaissance theater formally reproduced the same symbolic confusion that a boundless market had already introduced into the visual codes and exchange relations of a waning feudal order. The theater's most iconoclastic reflection, then, was the one it made on itself.

Not that audiences were prepared, on that account, to renounce the theater's vicarious pleasures of misrepresentation. Even at the point of a dramatist's darkest epistemological speculations, he could still count on the lingering attractions of tricksterism to deflect the most sobering implications of his defamiliarized play world. Spectators could applaud the ingenuity of the protagonist in the anonymous university interlude *Jack Juggler* (1553–8), who manages, at the risk of his own name, to assume the identity of a fellow servingman in so convincing a manner as to make the servant doubt himself.[33] And they could marvel at Anthony Munday's *John a Kent and John a Cumber* (1594), which featured two wizards who assume each other's countenance in order to further their schemes.[34] Without entirely sacrificing its older, folk legacies, the drama began to build on its own theatricality, on an ideal of "pure acting" expressed in the confrontation of "Self with Rival Self."[35]

Despite its continuities with the medieval folk play, the new drama projected a certain unfamiliar and disquieting aspect. The same dramatic devices and conventions that had partitioned the performers from their audience began to divide the characters as well. Since soliloquies and asides were perfectly suited to signal various forms of duplicity, playwrights placed them chiefly in the mouths of their villains.[36] Verbal asides, grimaces, and other facial expressions became ways in which characters could represent their "role distance," that is, their detachment from a self or situation to which other characters (and the audience) might presume them to be committed. But from an acknowledgment of a character's detachment, only a short distance remained to arrive at a recognition of the actor's detachment, especially when audiences alternately challenged the player to step in and out of his role.[37] Soon the very idea of playing a part "acquired a new and sinister quality," and Vice – the "first Protean figure of the stage" – became more and more identifiable as an actor: a deceiver and master of disguise.[38] For that reason, one cannot retrace the career of the Vice figure in English drama without at the same time recapitulating the rise of the common player in the sixteenth century.

II

Appropriately, the origins of the Vice figure remain as shrouded in the mysteries as those of the professional actor. Lucifer stands among the Vice's possible ancestors, as does the consummately evil Pilate of the Towneley Cycle. There are also distinct affinities with the fool of medieval folk plays and with the Lord of Misrule. Yet neither Pilate nor the Devil nor the fool compares with the character that came to dominate virtually all the later English moralities apart from those dealing with the themes of death and judgment.[39] The Vice was unique. It had no counterparts in French or German moralities, and in the hybrid English moralities it played a singular role. It was, for example, the only character permitted to bridge the play's two distinct worlds of allegory and historical chronicle, and it alone continued to address the audience across the slowly rising scaffolding of the theater's fourth wall. As the sixteenth century advanced, the various personae of the Vice began to crowd the figure of Good out of the morality play, leaving the stage free for the exercise of the character's dazzling versatility.[40] Understandably, leading players continued to seek out the role, even when, toward the end of the century, the Vice lapsed into extradramatic silence. Confined to the illusionary bounds of the play world, the Vice still remained a chameleon, a tempter, a schemer, a rogue, and a "manipulator of plot," in short, an actor who constantly sought to extend and complicate the action of *his* play.[41] To the aspiring player, the challenge of the role may have seemed irresistible: To become a luminary, he had first to become, in anthropological terms, a *liminary* – a transitional self permanently stationed at the threshold of otherhood. But since events had already conspired to render the actor a peculiarly estateless and masterless man, the role of Vice lay well within the ambit of the player's experience.

Short of an edict requiring the outright suppression of the stage, no measures of state seemed capable of modifying the course that the player had charted toward the ideal of pure acting. Statutes and ordinances there were aplenty, and many of these did indeed place impediments in the way of England's common players, especially the unlicensed ones.[42] Yet the very measures that a watchful Parliament designed to fit the Protean actor to the mold of the Elizabethan settlement served largely to detach him further from the ancient ritual and ceremonial frameworks of dramatic performance. If M. C. Bradbrook is correct in arguing that the whole problem of the common players during this period "turned on the question of who should control them, and in what respects," then the Elizabethan solutions (the Vagabond Act of 1572, the Leicester Patent of 1574, the Burbage Theater of 1576, and the new office of Master of Revels of 1581) succeeded only in enlarging their franchise. Taken together, these measures helped to concentrate the diffuse powers of a provincial drama within that dangerous marginal zone between town and country: the London suburbs or liberties.[43] Sporadic efforts at social control merely accentuated the singularity of England's new dramatic forms, isolating and framing them in a way that focused rather than deflected the public's attention. In this, the theater was indebted as much to the symbolic efficacy of royal and municipal regulation as to its practical laxness.

Given the rather capricious record of Tudor regulation, however, critics of the stage had little patience with proposals (such as that put forward by dramatist Thomas Heywood) for a well-ordered theater. It was futile to think of ridding the drama of its abuses, Puritans insisted, when corruption belonged to the very form of a theater that could, without blinking, identify the Vice with the player and the player with the Vice. "Vice hath the whole, at least the greatest share in all our stageplaies," William Prynne complained in 1633. "Vice oft times acts it part alone upon the Stage with great applause, whereas Virtue seldome comes upon it but accompanied with a cloud of sundry spredding vices."[44] In Hobbesian terms, Vice inhabited the play world as the only character who could claim to be both author and actor of its own designs, the only "natural person," ironically, among the "artificial persons" of the play. "The personifications of evil," one critic has noted, "were the most 'human' personifications in the moralities." And when even the Vice grew too abstract and fleshless for an audience hungering after more recognizably social types, characters, and humors, dramatists did not hesitate to slip the character into the costume of a "Machiavel" and thence into the garments of a Volpone or an Iago.[45] "Thus, like the formal Vice, Iniquity," Richard III confesses, "I moralize two meanings in one word."[46] Even as playwrights looked abroad to name the targets of their art, they were drawing closer to home.

Strictly speaking, Elizabethan drama shared in the movement from moral abstraction to social type that had marked the late medieval sermon and that was beginning to influence the literature of characters.[47] Critics, however, were troubled less by the realistic pretensions of theater than by the theatrical qualities of its realism. Mostly they were nettled by the player's capacity to enact stereotypical social traits as "roles," his ability to treat expressive behavior as an "investment" to be worn and discarded at will. One observer actually compared the common player to a "garment which the Tailor maketh at the direction of the owner; so they frame their action, at the disposing of the Poet." "They are reciprocal helpes to one another," he added, "for the one writes for money, and the other plaies for money, & the spectator payes his money."[48]

Controversy had made the actor worthy of inclusion in the

character books, but what hieroglyphic could capture his contradictions? "All men have beene of his occupation," the playwright John Webster wrote in a gesture toward the tradition of
the *theatrum mundi,* but, more important, the actor had been of
all occupations.[49] By the mastery of his trade, the actor encom-
passed the whole dynamic of social and economic mobility in
Tudor–Stuart England. His was not a vocation but an equivocation, a point not lost on the Puritans.[50] The time had long
passed when a writer like John Chrysostom could use the paradoxes of the player's life as an unambiguous lesson on the futility of profane ambition. There were some dramatists, to be
sure, who preserved this older sense of the theatrical *topos.*
Shakespeare was one. George Chapman, a deeply classical
playwright, was another. In his *Revenge of Bussy D'Ambois* (ca.
1626), Chapman wrote:

... if but for this, then,
To make the proudest outside, that most swells
With things without him and above his worth,
See how small cause he has to be so blown up,
And the most poor men to be griev'd with poorness,
Both being so easily born by expert actors.
The stage and actors are not so contemptful
As every innovating Puritan
And every ignorant sweater-out of zealous envy,
Would have the world imagine.[51]

The sticking point, however, was that such things *were* "so
easily born by expert actors," that the hieroglyphics of character
could be recreated with such freedom, facility, and finesse. The
theater seemed suddenly to promise a *recreation* that not only
restored and refreshed its spectators but refashioned them in the
bargain – or at least offered them the means and models by which
they might refashion themselves. The ancient trope of the *theatrum mundi* was thus stood on its head. What had once served the
church fathers as a homily on human vanity now threatened to
become a model of manipulative opportunism. Men became actors, after all, by mastering just those skills of simulation and
dissimulation, detection and imposture, skepticism and sympathy that preoccupied the handbook writers of the English Renaissance; they performed the very sleights that writers, at once

more guarded in their aims and limited in their means, claimed only to reform; they presented what others purported only to represent.[52]

Shades of the Christian commonplace lingered in both dramatic and nondramatic literature, of course. They darkened the ruminations of a Jaques, a Prospero, or a Hamlet and colored England's rich literature of melancholy. Yet this Stoicism no longer signaled a clear and unequivocal recognition of man's microscopic place in the divine order; instead, it bespoke a sensibility that could as well embrace an ethos of self-fashioning as of self-effacement. Indeed, so deftly does *Hamlet* combine its ancient allusions to a divine script with its contemporary imagery of men's deliberate impostures that Shakespeare's *theatrum mundi* has been likened to Calvin's own contradictory vision of willful individuals in a predestined world.[53] That players should then escape the burden of moral, if not divine, censure for their "acts" was all the more distressing to those Puritans whom Calvin's paradoxical freedom condemned to perpetual anxiety.

For the seventeenth-century enemies of the stage, then, the actor seemed more a threat than a lesson, and a threat as much for his action as for his inaction. The distinction, as it turned out, was not at all clear to contemporary observers. The player's life "is not idle," John Earle wrote, "for it is all action."[54] Like the usurer, whom Earle satirized unmercifully, the player and his business fell outside the conventional categories of his time: He reproduced himself (or his selves), labored on the Sabbath, and engineered "close impossibilities." If stage plays were the "common shops of all wickedness" and "very markets of bawdry," they yet cheated "mens money out of their purses by dishonest means, not giving *quid pro quo.*" They engaged, figuratively speaking, in a form of "dry exchange," offering "shadowes instead of substance."[55] Where dishonest tradesmen adulterated their goods, actors sophisticated and perverted the works of God, "putting a false glosse upon his creatures."[56] If the market was a theater of exchange, a "Iugling in Trades," then the theater was itself a market.[57]

Dramatists, once again, freely acknowledged the analogy. "Were but the vaine names of commedies changed for the title of commodities, or of playes for pleas," one anonymous author wrote, "you should see all those grand censors, that now stile them such vanities, flock to them for the maine grace of their gravities."[58] Not one to leave a commonplace unused, Thomas Dekker extended the comparison:

> The theater is your poets' Royal Exchange upon which their Muses — that are now turned to merchants — meeting, barter away that light commodity of words for a lighter ware than words — plaudits and the breath of the great beast which, like the threatenings of two cowards, vanish all into air. Players are their factors who put away the stuff and make the best of it they possibly can, as indeed 'tis their parts to do so. Your gallant, your courtier and your captain had wont to be the soundest paymasters and I think are still the surest chapmen.[59]

But it was Dekker's rival and enemy, Ben Jonson, who drew the closest parallels between the new theater and the new market of the English Renaissance. In his induction to *Bartholomew Fair* (1614), Jonson constructed an elaborate conceit — one unthinkable in medieval drama — analogizing dramatic convention to commercial contract, the willing suspension of disbelief to the "natural bill of exchange" wherein partners consent to suspend their skepticism for the sake of profit.

"Articles of Agreement, indented between the *Spectators* or *Hearers* at the *Hope* on the *Bankside,* in the county of *Surrey,* on the one party, and the *Author of Barthol'mew Fayre,* in the said place and county, on the other party," the induction begins. Having disposed of the formalities of time and place, Jonson's "Scrivener" then spells out the main features of the agreement. Among other things, it entitles spectators to criticize the play only in an amount commensurate with the price of their tickets, while at the same time committing them to remain "fixed and settled" in their initial judgment — all this with the stipulation that "how great soever the expectation be, no person here is to expect more than he knows, or better ware than a *Fayre* will afford, neither to look back to the sword-and-buckler age of *Smithfield,* but content himself with the present." Neither custom nor politics are to govern the expectations brought to the comedy. In keeping with the spirit of contract, every man is instructed to "exercise his own judgment" within the broad limits set by the agreement, as opposed to the predictably narrower limits set by those not party to the compact: the state, for example, or the equally meddlesome Puritans. In other words, the induction seeks to negotiate its own good-humored rules of valuation, to substitute its own histrionic economy for the prescriptive moral economy that official and self-appointed censors had for so long applied to the stage.[60]

Here, the issue of the theater's warrant or license passes beyond the status of mere conceit, however, for authority is, as Ian Donaldson argues, the central theme of *Bartholomew Fair*. The plays' comic effects and satirical powers all spring from the characters' determination to counterfeit, conceal, or caricature their social credentials.[61] The zealous Puritan who spouts casuistry to disguise his own greed and ambition is but one example. There is likewise a pie-powders justice who dresses as a fool to trap malefactors at the fair, as well as a genuine lunatic who wanders about the grounds dressed as a market searcher and who demands of the characters a written warrant for everything they wish to do. All is confusion. There are plenty of plots in the play but no plot to it; no one, villainous or virtuous, appears to be in charge. *Bartholomew Fair* lacks anything remotely resembling a Vice figure to move the action along, for the fair itself is the engine that precipitates the action of the play. The characters merely find their private desires turned to other purposes, as one scheme cancels another.[62] Jonson's market operates, in effect, as an "invisible hand," diverting private vices to the public benefit.

Clearly, Jonson never intended to use *Bartholomew Fair,* in 1614, as an illustration of the aggregate utility of a competitive market. Nothing in his plays or his past suggests any but the deepest revulsion toward the acquisitive urge.[63] Nevertheless, the forms and conventions that Jonson introduced to achieve his dramatic purposes in the play do adumbrate the solutions that Adam Smith would later propose to those who feared the divisive social consequences of unrestricted competition. Like *The Wealth of Nations, Bartholomew Fair* imagined the market as a power capable of generating its own legitimacy through a negotiated process of mutual authorization. By making the fair itself the occasion of countless private calculations and, at the same time, the vehicle of their ultimate public reconciliation, Jonson was taking a step, however tentative, toward a functionalist legitimation of a free and placeless market, a step that the new economic publicists were only beginning to contemplate.[64] In a sense, the formal, narrative, and thematic experiments of England's professional theater were moving authors and audiences alike toward an imagination of social exchange that neither party would have been prepared to articulate, much less justify, on their own.

For all of its formal innovations, however, *Bartholomew Fair* reveals a strong residual attachment to earlier notions of usury and of the corrective powers of carnival – to "Lucke and Saint *Bartholomew*."[65] To Jonson as to most Jacobeans, in fact, usury still wore a countenance imprinted with the features of Avarice, Envy, and Pride. Overuse had blurred this impress, usury having become at times a catchword for any inequitable bargain. And those who used the epithet frequently revealed their common bewilderment before the new forms of "semi-capitalism," as R. H. Tawney called it, namely, the operations of the international money and credit markets.[66] To them usury appeared to produce no tangible commodity, yet it was labor that never rested. It was "dry exchange," yet it begot itself. It was ascetic (Shylock reviled masques as "shallow foppery"), yet it thrived on the expenditures of others.[67] Usury was hypocritical, then; it was theatrical in the way that all roguery was seen to be theatrical: making its profits by making itself over in the image of its victims' deepest desires. To Thomas Lodge, the usurer was not a large-scale creditor but rather a "subtill underminer" who penetrated every "secret corner" of a gull's heart, "framing his behaviour to the nature of the youth."[68] Usury had grown so strong, according to the Puritan zealot William Burton, that it had "sinews and bones like a man and walked up and down the streets like a serving man, like a gentleman, like a merchantman," perhaps even "like an alderman."[69]

Burton's image of the usurer was more than mere animism, however. It compressed into one "character" the same forebodings about the market that writers like Alexander Barclay and Thomas Wilson had already voiced. Here, the figure of the usurer was as much a rhetorical touchstone for the debate over a secular economy as the figure of Machiavelli had been in the debate over a secular polity.[70] Burton's metaphor localized and personalized a set of social relations – commodity exchange – that were everywhere growing more diffuse, abstract, and impersonal; it conveyed a recognition of moneylending not only as a widespread by-employment but as a vehicle of upward mobility assimilable neither into the tradition of estates nor into the doctrine of vocations. The figure of the usurer incarnated the characterlessness and "infinite purposiveness" of the money he lent out at interest.[71] A placeless market thus found its most appropriate avatar in an avowedly disembodied social type, an "artificial person" without feudal or scriptural authority, a puppet "with sinews and bone like a man." "If you prick us," Shylock feels obliged to ask, "do we not bleed?"[72]

This curiously bloodless yet living abstraction of the usurer summed up in one image the felt correspondence between the new stage and the new market. On the one hand, the chameleonlike usurer was a perfect expression of the performance principle of capital: It bodied forth the ideal of full liquidity as a standard by which the inescapable costs and rewards of life could be measured. On the other hand, the usurer was also the figurative counterpart of the Vice and, as such, a perfect expression of the performance principle of the secular stage. He was, in this respect, a fungible man, a "universal equivalent" whose self was effectively interchangeable with any or all of the selves to be found in the seventeenth-century repertoire of "characters." The usurer was, like the actor, a liminary: a marginal man perennially poised in midpassage, a figure situated "betwixt and between" the conventional boundaries of social identity in early modern England.

To an audience already familiar with the instructional literature of the Renaissance – from the courtesy book to the cony-catching pamphlet – the player was a little shop of characters. His extraordinary plasticity offered a living lesson in the mechanics of social mobility and assimilation.[73] And whereas the social pretensions of an aspiring stage character usually went unrewarded in the drama, the social talents of the player earned him a living, if not, as in Shakespeare's case, the insignia of a gentleman. The skills of the player were, in fact, identical to those touted in the self-help manuals. The new theater was built on such paradoxes

– reproaching its audience for talents it delighted in displaying – and it required a certain complacency and assurance (which many did not possess) to abide them.

Seventeenth-century playwrights, it should be said, did impart to their work a conservative and cautionary perspective they had inherited from a long tradition of homiletic writing and teaching in England. Like their literary forebears, the lay preachers and estates writers, dramatists looked to an imagined past for models against which to judge the shortcomings of their own epoch. This nostalgia may have run more deeply in some than in others, but on stage it ran afoul of conventions (spatial, rhetorical, narrative) that complicated, when they did not actually subvert, its meaning and force. What kind of dramatist was it, critics wondered, who could affirm the importance of decorum by making its loss the form and content of his play? And what kind of play was it that could counsel the virtues of remaining in one's vocation by means of the equivocations of the estateless actor – the image of the Vice itself? These were questions for which there were no easy answers, and few dramatists (Heywood excepted) were disposed to pretend that there were.

A century earlier, writers of the moralities had used the rhetorical resources of extradramatic address "to prod the audience into dissociating itself from the Vice." Having more or less relinquished the practice of direct address, however, Renaissance dramatists were left to achieve their "alienation effects" through more oblique and ironic measures. As the transparent and didactic meanings of the old drama yielded to the dense verbal and visual puns of the new, the play became an entirely different kind of "mystery," one that quietly brought the spectators to *discover* a relation to the play world that an earlier drama had merely directed them to recall. The gain to art was of course immeasurable, but the perceived risk to the spectator of his "sustained imaginative collusion" in the theater's pretense was correspondingly increased. All other evils "pollute the doers onlie, not the beholders, or the hearers," Anthony Munday observed in his *Second and Third Blast of Retrait from Plaies and Theaters* (1580). "Onlie the filthines of plaies, and spectacles is such, as maketh both the actors & beholders giltie alike."[74]

It was not just the suspicion that spectators unwittingly became what they beheld that irked the foes of the stage. It was that audiences freely assented to a spectacle whose conventions of performance declared the spectator's complicity in the stage illusion as of a piece with the collusive arrangements that formed the interior action of the play. Here, in the intricate relation between players and spectators, the repercussions of the actor's own struggles for survival found their most sensitive sounding board. Consciously or unconsciously, the player-playwright had refashioned the play in the shape of the compact he had struck with his paying audience: allowing his plot to develop both with and against the formulaic stipulations of his "indenture" with the audience, using the disruptions and discrepancies of his characters' performance to convey the precarious state of his own promissory understanding with the spectators – and of their understandings with each other.

Taken together, these understandings or conventions tended, if anything, to extract and isolate the actor's persona from its ritual and representational origins, transforming it from a prescribed identity to a demonstrably fabricated one. By these measures, the actor managed to endow his stage characters with the same liminal and mercurial properties he had acquired in the course of his own professionalization. Thus, the social and economic circumstances that had driven the common player to the margins of the old order thrust him at the same time to the forefront of the new theater. It is scarcely surprising, then, that the drama should have appropriated as one of its principal themes the experience of the player's new and precarious exchange value, his ceaseless effort to win, in Jonson's terms, the two parts of the audience's "suffrage": their money and their applause.[75]

It is even less surprising that those most disturbed by the prospect of a fabricated and boundaryless society should have found in the theater's play of mirrors a source of dismay. The motives behind the Puritans' hostility toward the stage were of course many and complex, but they found a common target in the actor. Because the fortunes of the Renaissance theater had been so inextricably tied to the rise of the common player, there was a logic to the Puritan determination to evict the theater's most visible agent. The irony was that, in so doing, Puritan polemicists were only completing a process of enclosure that the players themselves had initiated when they first sought the protection of the suburban playhouses. Now, the liberties too would be purged, for in the regenerate society there could be no margin for error. Indeed, there could be no margins at all.

III

Throughout the long and bitter debate over the English stage, it was the player, not the play, who aroused the Puritans' greatest hostility.[76] Sixteenth-century Protestant reformers, Calvin included, had rarely sought to attack the drama as a genre or the theater as an institution; many, in fact, had taken a special delight in the polemical interludes that flourished at midcentury. John Bale, a Protestant bishop, was but one example. He was known to have performed at least one violently anti-Catholic play at a market cross, composed several other such dramas, and protested the suppression of stage polemics in his *Act for the Advancement of true Religion* (1543).[77] Even the prohibitions on polemical plays by Elizabeth in 1559 aimed more at soothing the feelings of indignant Catholic diplomats than at placating dissenting Protestants. In fact, the Protestant Inns of Court continued to produce dramas during this time, and as late as 1581 moderate Puritans such as Philip Stubbes had little difficulty in clearing a space for such productions within the narrowing confines of their religious conscience. Even at that, the security of class could still assuage the anxieties of a proscribed faith. Two of the greatest patrons of the English stage, the Earls of Leicester and Essex, were sympathetic to the Puritan cause.[78]

The frontal assault on the common player did not get fully underway (nor was it deemed worthy of response) before Stephen Gosson's *The School of Abuse* (1579), a work quite probably commissioned by London authorities.[79] But even in the dust and confusion raised by this opening salvo, one can make out the pattern of the contest that was to follow. Above all, it is possible to see how the parties to the conflict were themselves deeply implicated in the accusations they hurled at one another. In the years between 1570 and 1640, players and Puritans locked themselves in a battle to determine, among other things, the depth of each other's inauthenticity. Had each side to this conflict not harbored its own profound self-doubts on this issue, and had the surrounding society not deepened these misgivings by voicing suspicions of its own, it is unlikely that the controversy would have been taken up with such vehemence and tenacity. To the extent that both Puritans and players sought to put the vast question of political, social, religious, and economic representation in an accessible, compelling, and original cultural form, they were yoked together in the public mind as examples of the very ambiguities and contradictions they wished to resolve. But to the degree that each side wished to dispel, if not displace, this stigma, they became indispensable enemies.

There was a deep, albeit brittle intimacy to this dispute, then, a subtle collusiveness that belied the bombast of the public debate. Each side indicted the other for that of which it stood publicly accused; in a similar fashion, each party appropriated to its own purposes the devices and arguments of its opponents. Puritan pamphleteers, for example, managed to use satirical dialogue so shrewdly in the Martin Marprelate controversy of 1588–9 that the church felt compelled to hire dramatists to respond in its defense, causing Bacon himself to wonder how it was that matters of religion had come to be handled "in the style of the Stage."[80] While Puritan polemicists drafted their attacks on the theater in the form of plays and scenes, playwrights used the figure of Machiavelli to unmask the suspected impostures of their religious and political enemies. In fact, the earliest recorded instance of the use of Machiavelli's name as a general term of abuse appeared in Thomas Lodge's reply to Gosson's School of Abuse. There Lodge tweaked Gosson for his hypocrisy; alluding to "Machiavel" as an "advocate of dissembling," he reminded his readers that Gosson himself was a former player and playwright and that his attack on the stage was not all that it seemed.[81]

For his part, Gosson accused the stage of being a canker of privatism on the body of the commonwealth. It was an institution that, like usury, tempted men to abandon their callings for the vain dreams of instant wealth and rank.[82] Curiously, the same message appeared twenty years later in John Marston's moral play Histrio-Mastix, Or the Player Whipt (ca. 1599). Its plot revolved around a group of feckless artisans who decide to desert their trades, only to find themselves banished from their community in the end. It is an intriguing play, to say the least, for it pronounces a judgment on itself by criticizing the "offensiveness of men taking it upon themselves to image on stage essential social activities which for the life of them they could not perform in reality."[83] This ambivalence about the theater's own theatricality was even more pronounced, as we shall see, in Jonson and Shakespeare.

To be fair, however, this suspicion of the theater ran throughout the theater itself. At bottom, players shared with their Puritan foes an abiding distrust of all surfaces and a corresponding impulse to probe and penetrate the outward cast of things.[84] They sought to expose the theatricality of ordinary life, from the deceits of cony catchers to the artificial tears of monarchs who framed their faces "to all occasions" and who, like actors, sought power as "steward, substitute, / Or lowly factor for another's gain."[85] What distinguished and presumably redeemed the actor's pretense from the performances to be seen in daily life, however, was the former's frank and open acknowledgment of his theatricality. As Christopher Marlowe put it in *The Jew of Malta* (1589):

As good dissemble that thou never mean'st
As first mean truth and then dissemble it:
A counterfeit profession is better
Than unseen hypocrisy.[86]

Here was the nub of a controversy in which both sides affirmed the virtues of constancy, decorum, loyalty, and social stability, while at the same time enacting new theatrical and religious conventions that challenged the givenness of these ideals as they had theretofore been understood. Although the Shakespearean hero was disinclined to "flatter and look fair," to "Smile in men's faces, smooth, deceive, and cog," Puritans nonetheless saw in him a master teacher of vice. No other school was necessary, Philip Stubbes insisted, "if you will learn cosenage; if you will learne to deceiue; if you will learn to play the Hipocrit, to cogge, lye and falsifie."[87] Theaters were indistinguishable from their neighbors, the brothels, according to Gosson, because they enacted the prostitution of the self and occasioned the prostitution of others; they were "the very markets of bawdry, where choise without shame hath bene as free, as it is for your money in the royall exchaung, to take a short stocke, or a longe, a falling band, or a french ruffe."[88] Even moderate Puritans found the homiletic cures of the theater worse than the disease.

Puritans were truly affronted by the kind of moral and sociological homeopathy that the public theaters purported to practice; hence, they remained unmoved by the actors' claim that they inoculated their audience against the entrapments of a disordered social world. What was the theater, as even Thomas Dekker admitted, but a place where the "stinkard" enjoyed the "selfsame liberty to be there in his tobacco fumes" as the "sweet courtier?" If the playhouse was indeed a microcosm, as its design, its inscription, and its sliding scale of prices implied, then it was one in which the Great Chain of Being had been snapped, link by link, and heaped together in an unrecognizable jumble. What, then, could the theater's motley audience hope to learn there but "trickes, deuises, and mad Herogliphickes?"[89] What could it find in a play like Henry Chettle's 'Tis No Deceit to Deceive the Deceiver (1598) but a primer on falsehood?

"Let us therefore consider what a lye is," Stephen Gosson wrote in a passage that was to resound though all subsequent attacks on the stage.

> ... a lye is, *Actus cadens super indebitam materiam,* an acte executed where it ought not. This acte is discerned by outward signes, every man must show him selfe outwardly to be such as in deed he is. Outward signes consist either in wordes or gestures, to declare our selves by wordes or by gestures to be otherwise than we are, is [an] act executed where it should not, therefore a lye.
>
> The profe is evident, the consequent is necessarie, that in Stage Playes for a boy to put on the attyre, the gesture, the passions of a woman; for a meane person to take upon him the title of a Prince with counterfeit porte and traine, is by outwarde signes to shewe themselves other wise then they are, and so within the compasse of a lye, which by *Aristotles* judgement is naught of it selfe and to be fledde.[90]

Despite its stolid phrasing and laborious rhythms, the passage betrays a deep-seated anxiety about the social implications of the actor's mutability. We have already traced part of this anxiety to the cumulative impact of a placeless market on the perceived boundaries of self and society in England. Other factors, such as the outcome of specific class and religious struggles, also figured in England's crisis of representation. Yet, for all that, it is difficult to disentangle these upheavals — at the plane of culture — from the formless and polyvalent properties of a deritualized pattern of commodity exchange. Mobility begot confusion over the structure of rank and occupation; confusion over the division of labor, in its turn, bred perplexity over the place of gender in the assignment of tasks, and that, in turn, raised questions (of which *King Lear* is the most eloquent example) concerning the conditions and future of patriarchal authority.

It was not just that the market was seen to draw women out of the household and into the public sphere of petty commodity exchange. Women had for centuries engaged in household marketing.[91] It was rather that this traffic *of* women now seemed to intersect with the traffic *in* women. With the simultaneous growth in prostitution and in the marriage markets of the seventeenth century, Elizabethans began to look to the theater to represent a society thus opened to considerations of price. Concern for the welfare of lower-class women was scarcely the issue, for the sexual and marriage markets had almost always operated as cross-class enterprises. As such, they had reproduced and, in effect, underwritten the less explicit but no less febrile forms of social courtship then prevailing among men of power and authority.[92] For such men to be themselves visibly implicated in a form of social exchange hitherto confined to women would have been for them to risk the very authority that the trade in land and titles was intended to secure. Yet this trade and the "courtship" accompanying it were never so extravagant as during this epoch. Of Elizabeth's fifteen hundred courtiers, no more than thirty were women, and the scramble for preferment only intensified under the Stuart kings. "Gentlemen be made good cheape in England," Sir Thomas Smith declared in 1565, but the price of titles and offices soon rose as the numbers of England's gentry and peers underwent a threefold increase in the century before 1640. Few chroniclers failed to remark on the theatricality of the Stuart court, whose offices, relative to those of its predecessors, were freely bought and sold.[93] England's indignant Country party regarded court masques and other flamboyant displays as signs

of the court's effeminacy, but the suspicion of sexual ambiguity
– at least insofar as it appears in the literature – may have had as
much to do with a rural gentry's distaste for warrantless social
mobility as for its envy of courtly prerogatives.[94]

Gosson's effort to convict the player for his sexual fictions can
be seen, therefore, as part of a broader campaign to restore social
boundaries that circumstances seemed to have erased.[95] Though
Puritan casuists (like the Schoolmen) consistently hedged the
biblical injunction against usury (Deuteronomy 23:19), they were
determined to revive the Mosaic rule (Deuteronomy 12:5) against
cross-dressing and to bring the injunction to bear on the player.
Actors were accused of willfully fostering sexual confusion in an
age already sensitive on the point. "To weare the Apparel of
another sex," Stubbes raged, was "to participate with the same,
and to adulterate the verite of his owne kinde." Therefore, he
added, "these Women may not improperly be called *Herma-
phrodita,* that is, Monsters of bothe kinds, half women, half men."[96]
Fears of sexual transmutation nourished a distinct subgenre of
popular literature, encompassing not only the various pamphlets
against the stage but also such works as *Hic Mulier: Or, the Man-
Woman* (ca. 1620) and *Haec-Vir, or the Womanish-Man* (ca. 1620).[97]
It was into this tradition, for instance, that John Bulwer's *Anthropometamorphosis* (1653) fell.

Together these books help to situate the Puritans' simultaneous
fascination and revulsion toward the boys who played women's
roles on stage. Because these youths were in a literal sense "hirelings" and in a figurative sense "changelings," they failed to
display the traditional signs of social identity. Mindful of this,
perhaps, Ben Jonson had his stage Puritan, Zeal-of-the-Land-
Busy, inveigh against the puppets of *Bartholomew Fair;* Busy
accuses them of having no calling and of wearing women's clothes,
only to have one of the puppets reply that they have "neither
male nor female amongst us." So saying, the puppets lift their
garments to reveal their sexlessness, a gesture scarcely designed
to comfort the true Puritan, though Jonson has it persuade Busy.[98]

What precisely is to be made of the Puritans' obsessive attacks
on the androgyny of the professional actor?[99] David Leverenz
suggests, for example, that *Histrio-Mastix's* long and rambling
attack on the sins of effeminacy reflected an "unconscious am-

bivalence about the father's authority" in an age marked by the "weakening of traditional male norms of identity." Puritans, Leverenz argues, were projecting the source of their own inner conflicts on an external object: the actor.[100] This is an important insight and one consistent with the general approach ventured here; yet it must be both amplified and qualified in the light of the difficulties the evidence does present. We need to recall, for instance, that it was the Puritans who, by their deliberate austerity of dress and demeanor, elected to forego the traditional signs and expressions of male and female eroticism. Relative to the governing standards of masculine and feminine display in Elizabethan and Jacobean society, theirs was an androgynous, almost asexual style, and as such it resembled, for all its asceticism, the ambiguous sexual identity of the common player.[101] In pitting his stage Puritan against the sexless puppets, Jonson may have been striving for the humor of an unexpected likeness as much as for the burlesque of cherished incongruities.

Of course we can never be certain that the "Puritans saw themselves in what they hated."[102] The classic defensive responses of projection and displacement seldom acknowledge themselves as such in the documents; nor can the historian readily specify the grounds on which such motives might be disproved. What is clear from the protracted debate over stage transvestitism, however, is the Puritans' utter disbelief in the traditional corrective virtues of travesty. How could they countenance a remedy that was so difficult to distinguish from the disease? Festive misrule no longer served as a periodic ritual designed to throw the commonly accepted boundaries of honor and authority into greater relief. Removed to the theaters of the liberties, carnival had become a permanent institution that – for Puritans at any rate – threw such boundaries into greater confusion. "Wanton and excessive apparell" was sinful, William Perkins declared, because "it maketh a confusion of degrees and callings as God hath ordained, when as men of inferiour degree and calling, cannot be by their attire discerned from men of higher estate."[103] To the Puritans, all changes and extravagances of dress were a species of transvestitism. Where travesty once punctuated the life of society, now it seemed to permeate it.

To the beleaguered dramatist, Puritan hostility to stage costume was at best misguided, at worst hypocritical. Thomas Randolph's *The Muses' Looking-Glasse*, published in 1638, was but one of several plays to mock the Puritan feathermakers of Blackfriars for furnishing the theater with the very vanities they allegedly abhorred.[104] In much the same spirit, Henry Chettle's *Kind-Harte's Dream* (1592) used the beloved figure of the clown Richard Tarleton to snipe at the double standards of the stage's enemies, to expose those who would mingle profit with honesty by a skill "better practis'd then exprest." Chettle's Tarleton imagined his enemies complaining:

> Out vpon them [the players], they spoile our trade . . . they open our crosse-biting, our conny-catching, our traines, our traps, our gins, our snares, our subtilities: for no sooner haue we a tricke of deceipt, but they make it common, singing Iigs, and making iests of vs, that euerie boy can point out our houses as they passe by.[105]

Since players and Puritans lived side by side in the liberties that lay within and without the "bars" of London, such mockery undoubtedly came close to home.

The ridicule of the stage Puritan struck home on more than one account, moreover, for hypocrisy remained "one of the most persistent and damaging of the Anglican's indictments of the Puritan."[106] "Puritan" became a cant word for hypocrite and, in some instances, whore. To act puritanically was, in the slang of the streets, to act secretly or deceitfully, a usage the stage did much to popularize. Ananias, Goggle, Zeal-of-the-Land-Busy, Languebeau Snuffle, and Tribulation Wholesome were only a few of the stage caricatures that pilloried the Puritans on the scaffold of the public playhouse.[107] The Puritans, for their part, accused the player of being "like a Marchants finger, that stands sometime for a thousande, sometime for a cypher."[108] Each side seemed anxious to isolate and identify the other with the sharp practices and impostures of unlicensed artificers and tradesmen.

William Prynne's immense volume, *Histrio-Mastix, the Players Scourge, or Actors Tragedie* (1633) was, among other things, a painstaking effort to rebuff this accusation. Taking his title from John Marston's hybrid morality play, Prynne sought to refute the view that antitheatrical sentiment was a Puritanical and thus hypocritical idiosyncrasy. If the devil could quote scripture to his own purposes, Prynne, whose footnotes won him the so-briquet Marginal Prynne, was determined to quote pagan writers to God's purposes[109] – or more accurately, to Prynne's purposes, for his attack on the hypocrisy of the stage was at bottom a defense of the sincerity and authenticity of religious dissenters. Was it any wonder, Prynne complained, "for Puritans to be reputed hypocrites and imposters now," when "even our Saviour Christ himselfe was not only counted, but *called a Deceiver, and one who did but cheate the people.*"[110]

It is surely in this light that the length and bitterness of Prynne's harangue against the player must be scrutinized. Actors were the "blemish of our English Nation," he charged, ". . . crafty shifting companions, who purchase money, not by their generositie, but by their tongues and impudency; they being wise to dissemble, apt to counterfeit."[111] Simulation and dissimulation were ingrained in the actor's nature, or rather in his second nature. "For what else is *hypocrisie* in the proper signification of the word, but the acting of anothers part or person on the Stage; or what else is an hypocrite, in his true etimologie, but a Stage player, or one who acts anothers part?*" The problem lay not in the play but in "the very forme of acting Playes," which was "noght else but grosse hypocrisie," since players were "alwayes *acting others*, not themselves."[112] More than any other passage in *Histrio-Mastix*, Prynne's etymology (like Hobbes's) pointed up the new dimensions of theatricality – of the *theatrum mundi* – in the new forms, the new representations of society and stage in Tudor–Stuart England.

Hypocrisy, ambition, conceit – these were the epithets that players and Puritans traded back and forth among themselves during their seventy-year-long war. The social aspirations of the Puritan were a commonplace of dramatic satire, but then so were the pretensions of the common player. Critics – Shakespeare not least among them – suspected that stage actors had woven for themselves an illusion of power out of their own powers of illusion, a suspicion not entirely without foundation. "Prestige" – a new word – signified, in English as in French, a conjurer's trick or illusion, and as such it captured in one simple image the precarious influence of the common player.[113]

To the degree that the seventeenth-century actor did in fact enjoy a moderate if fragile authority in his society, it no doubt sprang from the still deeply rhetorical culture in which he practiced his art. In the emphasis that Renaissance education placed on the "social function of a proper training in the art of expression," A. G. H. Bachrach has written, "so much importance came to be attached to delivery that one could almost put it that a nation was being pre-conditioned for the stage."[114] Thomas Heywood neatly reversed the terms of this argument in his *Apology for Actors* (1612), where he supported the stage as a preparation for life. University dramas, he wrote, emboldened the scholar, instructing him "to fit his phrases to his action, and his action to his phrase, and his pronunciation to them both."[115]

Heywood did not stop there. A playwright himself, he went on to compare actors to the "cunning folk" of the sixteenth century: itinerant men and women who used mirrors and conjuring glasses to discover criminals and other malefactors by crystallizing, in effect, the suspicions of their victims. "A play's a true transparant christall mirror," John Taylor's dedicatory poem read; thus actors, Heywood continued, were able to provoke spontaneous confessions from criminals concealed in the audience through the reenactment of their crimes on the stage[116] – hence, Hamlet's "Murder of Gonzago." Still, the drama was not all that transparent; its claim to unlock the hearts of the guilty presupposed an audience prepared to unlock the heart of the play. Dramas *à clef* were common. Despite his protests against the canny *"State-decipherer"* and "politique *Picklocke of the Scene,"* Ben Jonson populated his plays with thinly disguised contemporary figures, whether rival playwrights like Anthony Munday or rival stage designers like Inigo Jones.[117] Justice Overdo, whom Jonson has investigate Bartholomew Fair incognito, might easily have been modeled after Sir Thomas Middleton, lord mayor of London, who as part of his reforms visited "lewd houses" in disguise the year before Jonson's play opened.[118] The prospect of censorship deepened the allusions of the playwright, just as it thickened the casuistry of the dissenter.

London's municipal authorities repeatedly complained of those citizens who ran "streight from prayer to playes," but those who did were as well prepared to search out concealed meanings there as in the sermons of separatist lecturers.[119] In company with the drama and the literature of characters, Puritan sermons had shifted from a preoccupation with abstract moral categories to an emphasis on social types, their purpose being "to mirror the individual consciousness of spiritual grace, to make him feel worse in order to purge him of those passions." In this moment of catharsis, reflection, and *recreation*, as William Haller has observed, the Puritan and the player found yet another point of rivalry.[120]

IV

Not even "the most accurate Chymist," Prynne insisted, could purify the stage, nor for that matter was the stage about to seek the "blessed Alcumist" of God's grace.[121] Instead, the purification of the stage was to be accomplished through the suppression of the player; it was to be undertaken, according to Prynne, as an exercise in mortification. Faith and labor, the twin foundations of William Perkins's doctrine of vocations, were to purge and restore a deformed and diseased social organism. Faith would protect the individual from the malign influences of the stage by breaking his or her personal relation to it.[122] Labor would protect society from the actor who had forsaken his occupation "to lyve by playing." Stephen Gosson's imagery was identical to Perkins's in this respect:

> A common weale is likened to the body, whose heade is the prince, in the bodie: if any part be idle, by participation the damage redoundeth to the whole, if any refuse to doe theire duetie, though they be base, as the guttes, the gall, the bladder, howe daungerous it is both to the bodie, and to the heade, euerie man is able to coniecture. . . . So in a commonweale, if priuat men be suffered to forsake theire calling because they desire to walke gentlemanlike in sattine & velvet, with a buckler at theire heeles, proportion is broken, unitie dissolued, harmony confounded, & the whole body must be dismembered and the prince or the heade can not chuse but sicken.[123]

Should players refuse to return to their occupations, Gosson recommended that they be "cut off from the body as putrified members for infecting the rest."[124] Perkins argued in a similar vein on behalf of the Elizabethan Poor Laws. Men who were "of no civil society or corporation, nor of any particular church," he wrote, were "as rotten legs and arms that drop from the body."[125] As a symbol of deceit and disproportion in society, the player was to be severed from the social organism. The problem of theatricality, in all its forms, was to be recast and resolved as a problem of the appetites. One's life was not Christ's, Gosson declared, "excepte we crucifie the flesh, with the affections and concupiscences of the same."[126] The histrionic calculus was to give way, therefore, to a hedonistic calculus, but one that reduced, rather than maximized, the claims of the pleasure principle. England's crisis of representation would be ended, then, by a collective resolution to pare away, as if they were flesh, the specious and shameful surfaces of things.

An individual's sense of shame, psychologists suggest, is intimately bound up with experiences of personal incongruity and disharmony; it is especially responsive, they say, to a perceived loss or confusion of personal boundaries. Shame appears to involve a "stagelike" act of self-attention in which the surface of the body is felt to shrink in an involuntary protective reflex. Shame, Dostoyevsky wrote, safeguards the self against the indifferent gaze of the marketplace.[127] If these observations are true, they may help to explain why medieval festivals of misrule were set within the tumult of the public market. Carnival, as we have already seen, served as a symbolic resource whereby a society's perceived disjunctures and disorders could be countered by their periodic and deliberate caricature. It was a remissive festival that appropriated the structure of a rite of passage to correct and regenerate a social order beset by its own incongruities and injustices.

Situated as they were within an increasingly boundless market, those who became Puritans were even more deeply distressed by the same sense of social disproportion and promiscuity that had once preoccupied the authors of estates literature. Yet, when the new religionists looked about them for some sign of outrage against this state of affairs, they found only complacency, a response they saw incarnated in the apparent shamelessness of the Renaissance stage. Another, less carnivalesque form of purification was called for. If the sense of shame could not revive the individual's sensitivity to sham in social and religious life, then the oblique and homeopathic remedies of burlesque would have to give way to the more direct and heroic measures of social purgation, amputation, and mortification. Boundaries would be clarified so that their transgression could be recognized by all. Individuals would be made answerable or, in the late-sixteenth-century coinage, accountable to each other and to God by the dichotomous logic of the ledger book. A fair and conscientious spirit of bookkeeping would differentiate that which the market had indiscriminately mixed together. In this way the symbolic incongruities endemic to the placeless market would be resolved, or so it seemed, by the very principle of commensurability that lay at their root.

A methodical and ascetic faith did not, of course, ensure a unity of self or society, nor did it dispose of the lingering doubts about sincerity and authenticity, either in the eyes of the religious dissidents or in the eyes of their foes. If anything, asceticism deepened the Puritans' anxiety on this point, driving them, as one historian has noted, "into a concern with outward appearances, into hypocrisy."[128] "The final paradox of the search for purity," Mary Douglas writes, "is that it is an attempt to force experience into logical categories of non-contradiction." Because experience is not ordinarily amenable to these efforts, she adds, "those who make the attempt find themselves led into contradiction." Hypocrisy, she concludes, "is the new contradiction that arises out of the "act of purification itself."[129]

The predicament was spelled out in William Perkins's view of the individual as a "double Person" serving under "two regiments." In the first regiment, the person was a self-abnegating private being related only to Christ; in the second regiment, the person was a temporal being living "in respect of another."[130] If temptation drew one to the second regiment, suspicion might as easily thrust one back into the first. "We may not trust men upon fair pretences that they make to us without further trial," Perkins warned.[131] Men's wickedness and "the depth of hypocrisy" were such "that a man may and can easily transform himself into the counterfeit and resemblance of any grace of God."[132] God's first regiment thus welcomed to its ranks those whose experience of man's mutability had already weaned them from a social world conceived as a stage. Caught between the omnipotent stagecraft of God and the ubiquitous puppetry of man, however, Puritans could never be fully confident of the regiment in which they had enlisted; its colors were too easily reproducible by that chameleonlike being, man.

Man's mimetic talents made all ritual suspect in the eyes of Puritans, who derided the repetitive "patter" of paternosters for much the same reason that they condemned the lines an actor committed to memory. Both kinds of performance required the mechanical recitation of formulaic phrases rather than the direct and spontaneous expression of feeling and intention; both, therefore, smacked of "insincerity," a term that was itself first introduced in the sixteenth century.[133] All liturgies were inherently theatrical or "scenical" since they reduced the individuality of personal piety to a collective and reiterative type; they were not hallowed rites but hollowed rites, ceremonies emptied of any meanings that might be deemed sincere. Yet to antinomians and Anglicans alike, the weight that Puritans placed on a *professed* faith, a *visible* sainthood, and a *covenant* theology (modeled after contracts "among men of business") threatened to reintroduce the very hypocrisy that had provoked the first cries for reformation.[134]

Regardless of the passive character of grace (as Calvinists interpreted it), a concept of belief so inextricably tied to its own deliberate and distinctive expression implied, as one of its own conditions, "the possibility of deliberate reticence . . . and of insincerity."[135] Understandably, skeptics seized on this possibility, insisting that Puritans had merely exchanged the burden of going through the motions for the onus of inventing them. This explained why, according to one character writer, the Puritan was "so cautious to have all his *Exercises* seem to be done Extempore, that his spiritual Talent may not be thought to receive any Assistance from natural or artificial Means, but to move freely of it self, without any Care or Consideration of his; as if Premeditation and Study would but render him, like the false Witnesses, the more apt to contrive and imagine, how to betray and abuse the Truth."[136] To the Puritans' foes, improvised prayers were no less deliberate and calculating than the litanies they supplanted; they too bore the marks of a histrionic calculus.

Yet of all those who commented on the problem, Puritans were clearly the most disturbed by the paradox of their own theatricality. Preachers warned incessantly against the spurious facsimiles of grace and insisted that the authenticity of religious experience be subjected to a grueling process of self-scrutiny and public witness. For most Puritans, the "conception of private experience was real, but not of private expression."[137] Only in the most ecstatic effusions of the radical sectaries do we find even the remotest hint of the private languages of meaning and feeling that romantic poets and novelists would later celebrate. English culture was still in many respects an oral or rhetorical culture, so it was assumed that religious belief needed to be stirred by wide and repeated public expression as well as by private readings of the Word. Even in the writings of one of the most rigorous Puritan theologians, William Perkins, the attractions of the plain style had yet to overwhelm the appeal of venerable principles – hence, the odd echo of Ciceronian rhetoric (as opposed to Ramist logic) in Perkins's advice to the preacher to "stir up privately in his own mind, that he may kindle the same in his hearers."[138]

Perkins advised the preacher that "the lifting up of the eye and the hand signifieth confidence," but critics like Thomas Nashe warned that no "heaving uppe of the eyes to heaven . . . shall keepe these men, from having their portion in hell."[139] Puritans could rail against the "scenic apparatus" of eucharistic vestments, but Catholics like Jonson could point with equal contempt to the handiwork of the Blackfriars feathermakers.[140] The irreligious crowds that flocked to Bartholomew Fair were the same throngs that filled the market-day lectures of the Puritans; if their number concealed the misdemeanors of bawd and cutpurse, it also concealed the secret gatherings of Presbyterians. And just as the puppets sold at the fair were known as Bartholomew Babies, so the Puritan pamphlets distributed there were called Bartholomew Fairings.[141] Puritan lecturers, as Haller has put it, "were mendicants and had like the wits and playwrights to coin their gifts and learning in order to live."[142] Accordingly, they described themselves as free traders in spiritual goods hitherto engrossed by the established church.[143] This, at least, was how Perkins sought to portray himself in a sermon delivered at Sturbridge Fair in 1593:

> Everybody brings hither something to be sold. This is the merchandise that I bring and set to sale unto you. Whatever

commodity any of you bring it is from some quarter of this land, but all is from the earth. But this that I bring it is from heaven and all the earth cannot yield it: and as it is from heaven, so it is of a heavenly virtue and will work that which all the wealth in this fair is not able to do.[144]

The passage of nearly four centuries may have muted the ironic inflections of Perkins's declamation, but its themes are by now familiar. The Puritan lecturer was, in effect, a spiritual "factor," paid out of the endowments of a merchant aristocracy. If he was not the usurer that popular literature imagined, he was still an alien artificer who sold the fairgoer an intangible commodity outside the franchise of the church and beyond the jurisdiction of the city. He was "a spiritual Interloper, that steals a Trade underhand, and by dealing in Prohibited Commodities can undersell, and allow better Bargains of Sins and Absolution, than those that deal fairly and openly can afford."[145] To a sufficiently skeptical eye, he was, like the actor, an "artificial person," a "puppet saint" whose faith was neither a voucher for his authenticity nor a substitute for ecclesiastical authority.

This at least was the way in which James I characterized the Puritans in his *Basilikon Doron* (1599). They showed "contempt of the civill Magistrate," he wrote, "... breathing nothing but sedition and calumnies, aspiring without measure, rayling without reason, and making their owne imaginations (without any warrant of the worde) the square of their conscience."[146] And it was in this vein that Samuel Butler drew his character of the Hypocritical Nonconformist – "an Embassador Extraordinary of his own making, not only from *God Almighty* to his *Church,* but from his Church to him; and pretending to a plenipotentiary Power from both, treats with himself, and makes what Agreement he pleases; and gives himself such Conditions as are conducible to the Advantage of his own Affairs."[147] Looking back from the relative security of the Restoration, Butler put his case against the Puritans baldly and succinctly; for all their cant of precision and purity, the Puritans, in his view, had only obscured the grounds and bounds of representation and authority in English society.

English Puritans had indeed accelerated a process of deritualization, the effect of which was to erase those seasonal boundaries or break points when the incongruities and injustices of the social order could be confronted and in various, albeit symbolic, ways corrected. Such privileged, liminal moments of misrule were no longer tolerable to the new religionists, who saw about them the "spectre of an endless feast of fools." "A Christian hath no solstice," John Donne wrote, "where he may stand still, and go no further."[148] For him as for so many others inside and outside the church, life already seemed a perpetual pilgrimage, a ceaseless, cumulative experience of becoming. Evidence for that conviction appeared in the countless diaries where Puritans recorded their "pilgrim's progress"; it was also visible in the Presbyterians' decision to move their baptismal fonts from the church entrance to the church altar.[149] With this change, the presbyteries openly proclaimed their placelessness, and an elementary rite of religious initiation was translated from a finite territorial passage *into* the church to an endless spiritual journey. A physical threshold had been removed from sight, to be sure, but only to be reinstalled, sub*liminally* as it were, deep within the psyche of the initiate. Puritanism was, in effect, a religion of permanent liminaries, who, despite their repugnance for misrule, were systematically and methodically turning their own world upside down.[150]

In another sense, however, Butler's judgment on the Puritans was misplaced, for the impetus to what he called their mummery and masquerade lay elsewhere than in themselves. It lay rather in the placeless market, whose new forms of exchange were drawing more of England's population, resources, and goods into its embrace while at the same time stripping away the peculiarities of time and place by which they had once been represented. For Puritans to have focused on the expressive signs of belief and grace (as opposed to the "scenical apparatus" of ecclesiastical authority) was for them to have done no more than what popular literature and drama had recommended to counter the diminishing transparency of exchange.[151] After all, why not grant to faith and its simulacra the same general physiognomical properties that society ascribed to other sorts of intention? Why not finally treat *all* representations of experience as more likely to divulge than to display their truths? Why not, in short, regard all expression as disclosure, as a discourse punctuated by its own unwitting and revelatory asides?

I have put here in the form of questions ideas the Puritans ventured chiefly in the form of answers, if only to show how these answers inevitably heightened the very sense of theatricality they were meant to dissolve. But though this paradox was one we have seen the Renaissance handbook refuse to consider, it plagued the conscience of the Puritan bent on searching his or her own life for signs of grace. And it is only in the context of that search that we can fully appreciate the distaste Puritans felt for the daily and deliberately fabricated "conversions" of the common player. No one knew better than the Puritan, after all, the temptations of settling for a *visible* sainthood – no one, that is, save perhaps the actor.

Still, there were those Puritan writers who did reach a tentative accommodation with hypocrisy. To them the unbridled enthusiasms of the antinomian were as repellant as the effrontery of the actor, and both were infinitely more threatening to the moral order than the moderate pretense of the individual covenanter. Discipline itself, John Cotton reminded his followers, could render hypocrites "serviceable and useful in their callings."[152] More than anything else, work promised the ultimate antidote against the theatricality of the placeless market and the placeless church; it cleansed exchange of any taint of promiscuity or imposture by subjecting all relations to the summary judgment of the balance sheet: the world divided neatly by column rules, with receipts balanced against expenditures, good against evil, sin against redemption – the difference being, of course, that each person now drew on his or her own accumulations and not on the church's treasury of grace. Whether it was in their recurrent imagery of spiritual bookkeeping or in the obsessive dichotomies of Ramist logic, Puritan theologians displayed what Walter J. Ong has called "an accountant's approach to knowledge."[153]

Language itself recorded some of the ways in which a concept of material earnings was being made to answer the claims of spiritual yearnings. Take the word "purchase," for example. In its earliest forms, the term had been used to describe acts of hunting, pillage, and robbery and, generally, to a life lived by shifts. In law, the word referred quite broadly to the acquisition of property by any means other than inheritance. Yet by the sixteenth century, "to purchase" could mean, quite specifically, to acquire something by means of a set payment of money. In the seventeenth century, moreover, the word was broadened once again (by Hobbes among others) to refer to acts of acquisition accomplished at the cost of something immaterial: effort or suffering, for example. In this way, a word once freighted with predatory and illicit connotations gradually changed shape and signification and, in the process, signaled the arrival of a new labor standard of value. Yet another example was the word "factory," which underwent a similar metamorphosis within an even briefer compass of time. Introduced in the sixteenth century as a name for the consular outposts of foreign merchants (with all of their extraterritorial immunities), the word became in the seventeenth century a synonym for "manufactory," a theater of production rather than of exchange, a site for the redeeming discipline of labor.[154]

On September 2, 1642, the Long Parliament issued an ordinance suppressing the performance of stage plays throughout the kingdom. "Public sports do not well agree with public calamities," the members declared, "nor public stage plays with the seasons of humiliation." And though an occasional production continued to be staged in noblemen's houses and at such popular sites as the Fortune and the Red Bull, the English theater, its principal playhouses torn down, fell silent until the Restoration.[155]

It would be convenient to point to a corresponding disappearance of the theatrical analogy in English literature after 1642, but commonplaces are by their very nature durable. The emblem of the *theatrum mundi* appeared in Milton (who composed his masque *Comus* of 1634 partly in response to Prynne's claim that Comus was "the God of Wantonesse, and riot") and in John Bunyan.[156] But the usage was far less frequent and differed according to the social character of its audience: more Stoic in the inspirational literature, more histrionic in the courtly drama. Lost was the compact multiplicity and density of the Renaissance emblem, the overdetermined nature of its (and the theater's) meaning. In this respect, the Puritans' project of mortification had been all too successful. The living pattern of mutual reflection and connection within the metaphor had been abruptly severed.

One is forced to look elsewhere – across the Channel – for

echoes of the Renaissance sensibility, to Calderón, for example, or to Joseph De La Vega. The latter was a speculator on the Amsterdam exchange (the new center of international banking) when he wrote his *Confusion de Confusiones* (1688). There he described the stock market as a "Tower of Babel" and at the same time as a drama:

> Among the plays which men perform in taking different parts in this magnificent world theatre, the greatest comedy is played at the Exchange. There, in an inimitable fashion, the speculators excel in tricks, they do business and find excuses wherein hiding-places, concealment of facts, quarrels, provocations, mockery, idle talk, violent desires, collusion, artful deceptions, betrayals, cheatings, and even the tragic end are to be found.... Thus the whole stock exchange is represented in the drama.[157]

De La Vega's imagery recalls that of Dekker, Earle, Jonson, and Shakespeare before him, but it was a vision from which Shakespeare, at least, was already retreating as early as 1600. His tragedies belittled the maneuvers of the courtly marketplace, the "elaborate game of suit and service." According to Anne Righter, the actor became for him "a man who *cheapens* life by the act of dramatizing it."[158] His tone toward the theater and the "idea of the play," she observes, grew almost puritanical in *Troilus and Cressida* (1602). For him, *The Tempest* (1611) portended the end of a theater in which "life had been engulfed by illusion," engulfed, in John Bulwer's words, "in the fluctuation of [man's] bedlamlike phrensye."[159] Regarded in this light, the drowning of Prospero's book at the end of the play appears to be a renunciation of Shakespeare's own theatricality, a preemptive act of self-mortification by the player-playwright.

Was *The Tempest* a rejection of the Jacobean "illusion of power," the elaborate court masque, and, with it, the equally "elaborate game of suit and service?" It is hard to know. But if the play looked back wistfully toward the Elizabethan ideal of a magical political *imperium,* as Frances Yates has suggested, it also resuscitated an even older image of an open stage spread out beneath the fixed and finite canopy of the medieval universe.[160] In this regard, it was less a life "engulfed in illusion" than any life enclosed by man-made means that Shakespeare's last play opposed.

Like Bulwer's *Anthropometamorphosis, The Tempest* appears to be a final gesture proffered against the offensive spectacle of the man-made self and the self-made man. Here, Shakespeare seems to have anticipated the more general alienation from public and private theaters that took hold in London after 1610. Signs of this antagonism were already visible in the voluminous antistage literature of the period, of course, but the changing sentiment could also be seen in such demonstrations as the Shrove Tuesday riot of 1617. In that fracas, a crowd of London apprentices broadened their annual rampage against the city's brothels to include a determined effort to pull down the popular public theater, the Cock-Pit – an ominous portent indeed to those who thought of the 'prentices as their most devoted audience.[161]

But there was also a growing animus against the private theaters during these years as the identification between the crown and the stage grew even more pronounced in the minds of hostile municipal authorities and parliamentary enthusiasts.[162] City magistrates might occasionally commission playwrights to compose extravagant pageants for the annual Lord Mayor's Show, but this tolerance seldom extended to the courtly protection afforded the professional player or, for that matter, to the lavish masques that graced the Jacobean and Caroline courts. These displays served powers other than the aldermen's own, notwithstanding their expressed loyalties to the crown.[163] The theatricality of the Stuart court was a thing too notorious (and too expensive) for a magistracy already deeply conscious of its constituency and its pockets. Commenting on the execution of Charles I in 1649, a Puritan pamphleteer gleefully observed how "remarkable" it was that the king "should end his dayes in a Tragedie at the Banqueting-house, where he had seene, and caused many a Comedy to be acted upon the Lord's Day." Poetic justice, the writer might well have called the episode, had his mind sought any but a providential explanation.[164]

Still, the theatricality of the Stuart court was a far more complex matter than would seem to be the case at first glance. Masques, for example, had allowed England's ruling class to articulate in spectacularly visual ways the very practices of social courtship that were opening their ranks to new forms of wealth. Here, courtly theater would seem to have acknowledged its practical ties to the wider circles of "dealing" around it and, hence, to the growing fluidity of social relations in general. Yet the accent in these interludes invariably fell on the decorous representation of power, not on the instrumental presentation of self. The parts that courtiers enacted were, like those of the moralities, allegorical; they were thus entirely at odds with the concept of role playing simultaneously emerging on the public stage. Roles were ordained in the masque; they were "investments" only in the older, honorific sense, not in the newer, *credit*able sense. Whatever else they were, they were not the negotiable, promissory agreements about identity that so deeply yet obliquely implicated the playhouse audiences in their performance.[165]

Masques were a "magical theater" performed on a talismanic stage for a court already immersed in a "constant atmosphere of make-believe." They offered an epitome or "character" of power in which the court itself could participate; they were, in Jonson's phrase, "Court hieroglyphicks."[166] With their ornate proscenium arches and their elaborate mechanical devices, masques heightened the illusionary aspect of the state in order to appropriate its powers to the political purposes of the court. In doing so, they stimulated, according to Frances Yates, the "first large-scale employment of technical skills, other than for military purposes."[167] Yates's comparison is doubly apt, for the masque offered nothing less than a dramatistic equivalent of war, a symbolic assertion of sovereignty in which the mercenaries had changed from soldiers to players. Spectacular though it was, this courtly effort at persuasion turned progressively inward as time passed, for just as royal progress pageantry disappeared from the streets during the Jacobean and Caroline periods, so it declined (along with chronicle plays) in the drama. And just as civic pageantry shifted to the dramatization of bourgeois rule in the form of the Lord Mayor's Show, so courtly attention focused on the masque until, as Stephen Orgel has shown, the form was reduced to an insulated and solipsistic diorama of Caroline politics.[168] Masquers and players alike felt the burden of growing class tensions, narrowing their sights and their audiences to the dimensions of the royal household.[169]

Where, then, did the professional player figure in a masque dominated by powerful courtiers and ingenious scenery? It is a question that Ben Jonson himself was wont to ask. "Painting and Carpentry are the Soule of Masque," he once complained. "This is the money-gett, Mechanick Age!"[170] What was to become of the player displaced by a figure like Inigo Jones, who would rather build a set than a character? Here was a man – Jonson seemed to be saying of the actor – victimized by a theatricality wrought into architecture and propelled by machines. His lament expressed the anger of a poet and actor expropriated by a species of aesthetic enclosure. In this, however, he was not so wide of the mark as his hyperbole would suggest. The vocabulary of the theater had indeed penetrated the literary vision of nature in much the same way as the language of the market before it. "Scenical," for example, was already used as a synonym for "emotional," and "scenery" would soon come to mean an observed land-scape.[171] The new, architechtonic masque offered the ironic spec-tacle of the actor dispossessed by his own devices, betrayed, as it were, by "another nature."

Actors were not entirely displaced from the masque, of course, and what rhetorical powers they retained were, if anything, en-larged by the addition of elaborately contrived framing devices.[172] Still, Jonson's allusion to the "money-gett" age was as relevant to the player as to the stage craftsman, for the Stuart court held both of them at much the same distance as the actors held their own hirelings (actors who were not sharers in a company). More than anything else, the dramatic conventions of the masque ex-pressed the court's contempt for the players and, by that same measure, the world the players represented. Elite masquers never doubled, nor did they impersonate in any naturalistic sense. From the earliest years of the Tudor masque, courtiers declined to speak their parts, preferring instead to have the masque's important words embroidered on their costumes.[173] Stuart masques did in-troduce dialogue, to be sure, but these speaking portions were called "antimasques" and were reserved exclusively for the professional players. Because acting amounted to a violation of the Christian and Platonic congruence of inward and outward action, decorum required the aristocratic masquers to confine themselves to the dance. As antimasquers, Orgel writes, profes-sional actors "presented a world of disorder or vice, everything that the ideal world of the . . . courtly main masque, was to overcome and supersede."[174] The professional actor was the foil of courtly theater, not its fulfillment.

Like the Puritans, then, the Stuart courtiers were at pains to dissociate themselves from the common player, sealing themselves off via the antimasque from the contagion of the latter's theatricality and the taint of his commerciality. It was one thing, after all, to use the players, quite another to join them. Few men of power – court or country – were prepared to see themselves identified with the "artificial persons" of the professional stage. Here again, the player was reminded of his marginal status. Yet whether he was silenced or merely exiled to the island of the antimasque, the common player was suppressed less because he was common than because he was a player, less because he was of humble estate than because he was estateless, less, in other words, because he was Caliban than because he was Proteus.

4. The spectacle of the market

It is evident then, that as I see nothing but what is far from
being retired, in the forced retreat of an island, the thoughts
being in no composure suitable to a retired condition, no, not
for a great while; so I can affirm, that I enjoy much more
solitude in the middle of the greatest collection of mankind in
the world, I mean at London, while I am writing this, than ever
I could say I enjoyed in eight and twenty years confinement to a
desolate island.

> Daniel Defoe, *Serious Reflections of*
> *Robinson Crusoe* (1719)

Were it possible that a human creature could grow up to
manhood in some solitary place, without any communication
with his own species, he could no more think of his own
character, of the propriety or demerit of his own sentiments and
conduct, of the beauty or deformity of his own face.... Bring
him into society, and he is immediately provided with the
mirror which he wanted before. It is placed in the countenance
and behaviour of those he lives with, which always mark when
they enter into, and when they disapprove of his sentiments.

> Adam Smith, *The Theory of*
> *Moral Sentiments* (1759)

WHEN JOHN WINTHROP COMPOSED his famous lay
sermon, "A Model of Christian Charity," aboard the
Arbella in 1630, he groped for an image to capture the
keen sense of historical self-consciousness surrounding the journey of the Puritan settlers to Massachusetts. Though his gaze
focused on the headland before him, his sermon looked back to
those left behind. How was he to describe the sensation of having
"the eyes of all people...upon us"? Like Shakespeare before
him, he could have borrowed from the example of Elizabeth,
who had once spoken of herself as set on a stage "in the sight
and view of all the world duly observed." The metaphor Winthrop ultimately chose, however, was not one of a theater but
of a "city upon a hill."[1] Of course Boston was quite literally a city
on a hill, and the first century of public life there remained fixed

to the antitheatrical course that Winthrop and his fellow passengers had charted for themselves and their children. No professional theater appeared in Boston before 1792 and none in New England as a whole until 1761, when David Douglass brought his players to Newport to perform "a series of MORAL DIALOGUES" on the "Evil Effects of Jealousy and other Bad Passions" – in other words, *Othello*.[2]

Where colonial drama did make headway against the force of piety and prejudice, it was most often in the form of occasional entertainments by itinerant companies of English actors. Playhouses did spring up in Williamsburg, Charleston, and Annapolis during the eighteenth century, but they were mostly short-lived. The ascetic legacy of the original religious settlements continued to confine those colonists who might have used the drama as a means to display their Cavalier affiliations with British culture; it also constrained those less favorably placed who might otherwise have supported an indigenous drama. Not until 1787 would an American audience see an American drama performed on a professional stage. Even then, the play – Royall Tyler's *The Contrast* – aimed at a British target, turning the conventions of Restoration drama against itself by juxtaposing the homespun honesty of its American characters against the calculating hypocrisy and theatricality of their British counterparts.[3] Only a newly awakened nationalism, it seemed, could successfully lift the burden of Puritanism's moral protectorate from the shoulders of the aspiring American playwright and player.

Isolated from the daily life of American cities by the fundamentally alien and derivative character of its drama, colonial theater furnished an ill-placed mirror for its scattered and occasional audiences. What reflections its spectators found on this stage were of a world some three thousand miles away and, at times, a century removed from their own. Audiences listened in vain for local topics, local idiom, or local inflections from a theater that lived on borrowed lines. Homesickness was the complaint such drama was best equipped to minister to, and wit and nostalgia its favorite remedies. Given the limitations under which the strolling players were compelled to labor, the theater did not and indeed could not operate as it had in England; that is, it could not serve as a crucible wherein new social and cultural forms of exchange could be tested and tempered.

Few other institutions, however, seemed ready to offer themselves in the theater's place. Nowhere does one find among the colonies' secular writers the kind of metaphorical speculation on the market that had so successfully engaged the literary and dramatic authors of Tudor–Stuart England. Even in the colonies' bustling port towns, where the ties with Britain were the strongest, public memory was neither long nor common enough and private patronage neither broad nor deep enough to support the complex, polysemous drama of misrepresentation at which the Renaissance dramatists had excelled. Colonial society was too young and colonial authority too brittle to countenance the collective public dreamwork projected by the Elizabethan and Jacobean theater at the height of its power.

This is not to say that colonists were indifferent to the marketplace questions of identity, transparency, and accountability that had vexed them and their ancestors in Britain. Quite the contrary. The same theocrats who barred players from the enjoyment of Boston's franchise were at first not much more hospitable to the merchants among them. The very historical circumstances that had hardened the hearts of New England settlers against an outcast theater rendered them only grudgingly tolerant of the players' more enterprising neighbors: the commercial middlemen. Trade remained "morally the most dangerous" occupation for seventeenth-century Calvinists, and their first response to early instances of price gouging revealed a distinctly medieval cast of mind. The Reverend John Cotton, for example, composed strict "Rules for Trading," and though these regulations were never actually implemented, the Massachusetts General Court nonetheless assessed "all merchants, shopkeepers, and factors" on their entire "stocke and estate, be it presented to view or not." The practices of regrating, forestalling, and engrossing were widely prohibited, as were direct sales between shipmasters and colonists.[4] Even at this, Boston exercised the least effective regulatory authority over its hawkers and hucksters of all colonial ports before the mid–eighteenth century.[5]

To the colonists' religious and secular leaders, then, trade still suggested disquieting possibilities for the fabrication of impressions as well as goods. But where English city dwellers had (until 1642 at least) countered their market-born doubts and apprehensions with an almost homeopathic indulgence of them on the stage, American colonists systematically repressed their misgivings by suppressing the stage itself – the stage and all of its ambivalent associations. Against the specter of commercial duplicity, indeed against the specter of all duplicity, settlers held up an ideal of single-minded piety. Against the threat of cultural formlessness, colonists replied by enjoining their own continual reformation. Settlers who found themselves torn between the security of a household economy and the risks of a burgeoning agricultural and commercial capitalism were most likely to frame their responses to the market in ascetic and purgative terms. From the witchcraft mania of the seventeenth century through the religious awakenings and nonimportation movements of the mid–eighteenth century, Americans repeatedly resorted to ritual acts of collective mortification in order to draw boundaries around the seemingly infinite appetites and polymorphous forms of their market selves.[6]

Flanked on one side by a staggeringly boundless wilderness and on the other by a similarly boundless world market, colonists sought to reduce their own sense of marginality, of liminality, by sharpening the visible boundaries of their own social and spiritual identities.[7] Here, the early settlers' obsessive disputation of theological matters was of a piece with their equally earnest litigation of economic matters. Both reflexes betokened the settlers' recurrent need to reground, indeed, to recharter their past and future. Churches and courts housed a permanent, if episodic, cultural revolution, of which the events of the 1770s were at once an end and a beginning. In fact, it was only after those events had run their course that markets *and* theaters began to take full root in American soil.[8] What a difference this state of affairs presented to that of late-seventeenth- and early-eighteenth-century Britain!

I

In the years following the civil wars, British society witnessed a recrudescence of mercantile capitalism *and* professional theater.

An officially sanctioned theater was "restored" to London after 1660 and to the provinces a century later, while strolling companies frequented the fairs and innyards of urban and rural Britain throughout the period.[9] Opera, melodrama, political satire, and the comedy of manners emerged as distinct genres, and new periodicals such as *The Tatler, The Review,* and *The Spectator* were introduced in order to monitor their successes and failures. Still, for all these developments, the drama itself remained a largely derivative art, surviving, in Muriel Bradbrook's words, "on scenic tradition and shriveled reproductions of Shakespearean forms."[10] This shrinkage in the imaginative and original qualities of the "dramatic" was countered by, perhaps even invited by, a correspondingly expansive interest in the "theatrical." From *The Rehearsal* (1671) through *The Stage Mutineers* (1733), English theater made itself – its conventions, its politics, its personalities – the subject of its own enactments and hence the object of a continuous public debate.[11] The theatrical effects wrought by actor-managers like Colley Cibber and, to an even greater extent, by David Garrick became common topics of public controversy, literary and painterly emulation, and philosophical rumination.[12]

To compare this popular embrace of the theatrical perspective with its Elizabethan and Jacobean forerunners, however, is to note immediately how much more facile and confident was the eighteenth-century version. Satire remained a fundamentally conservative form, and of the seventy or so plays that took the theater as their subject in the years before the Licensing Act of 1737, none invoked the kind of epistemological or ontological anxiety that Elizabethan tragedy as a whole, and Shakespearean tragedy in particular, had invested in the trope of the *theatrum mundi*.[13] As we have already seen, that tradition had permitted "a quite extraordinarily open interaction of social order and social disintegration," an intermingling where, as Raymond Williams puts it, "questions about the nature of the human order itself were directly enacted."[14] Such radical doubts are not to be found in the heroic and sentimental dramas of the early eighteenth century; none, of course, had been intended. And even had the occasional playwright used the theatrical metaphor to venture such a challenge to public complacency, the experiment could scarcely have survived the obligatory and formulaic fifth-act resolution. John Gay's "tragical-comical-pastoral farce," *The What D'Ye Call It* (1715), for example, mocked every contemporary genre of drama, including the terrifying spectacle of English justice. It failed. Theater could, within limits, be politically skeptical; it could not, in Jonas Barish's phrase, be "ontologically subversive."[15]

How, then, can we explain the peculiar self-consciousness of the Restoration and Hanoverian stage? More precisely, how can we account for the callous and ultimately complacent theatricality of its outlook? For one historical sociologist at least, the phenomenon is best understood as a microcosm of the elaborately coded conversation of dress, gesture, and speech that patrician and plebeian city dwellers carried out in London's squares, streets, and coffeehouses. The eighteenth century, according to Richard Sennett, was the Age of Public Man. In his view, urban life operated along widely shared conventions of public performance that both sanctioned and structured an easy sociability between classes and sexes. Public life flourished in this epoch, he argues, because these conventions kept the introspective demands of an earlier Puritanism and the voyeuristic intimacies of an embryonic romanticism temporarily at bay. Manners were extravagant precisely because they were intended to be taken not as the private symbols of spontaneous personal feelings but as the public signs of obligatory social responses; they were not the *evidence* of attitudes but, quite simply, the attitudes themselves.[16] As such, the stylized gestures of public life formed part of a complex secular ritual peculiar to urban living, a ritual, Sennett notes, in which the capacity to distance oneself from one's social role no longer inspired any deeper doubts about its authority or authenticity. From this perspective, the eighteenth-century theater seems doubly reflexive, for it appears to have enacted an exhibitionist pattern of sociability that was already modeled on the stage.

Sennett paints a detailed and compelling portrait of cosmopolitan fashion in Europe's great cities, but his explanation of the theatricality of Hanoverian London is ultimately less persuasive than his description of it. It is not enough to see the mannerisms of public life as behavioral adaptations to the unique ecology of eighteenth-century London; it is more fruitful, I think, to see them as affective accommodations to the fundamental political, social, and economic settlements of eighteenth-century Britain. In that century, particularly in its early years, Britain's ruling factions assented to new political arrangements aimed at stabilizing the Parliament's relation to the crown, the crown's relation to the church, and the church's relation to the nonconforming sects. As a result, new and more inclusive rules of representation, literal and figurative, were introduced. And though the statutory frame for these accommodations was put into place between 1688 and 1707, it was the "social lubricant of gestures" on the one hand and the material lubricant of "influence" on the other that set the whole structure into a steady, almost inertial motion for the remainder of the century.[17]

That this stability was achieved without the threat of a large standing army or domestic police force may go some way toward explaining the extraordinary weight that all classes came to place on the symbolic dimension of public life: the calculated gestures of civility and incivility. That this stability was secured as well by an intense and protracted negotiation over place, patronage, and power ("influence") may also explain why these gestures took on such a self-conscious, indeed theatrical, appearance. Mindful, perhaps, of the bloody reversals suffered during the seventeenth-century wars, Britain's postrevolutionary rulers sought to enact and to transact – the two impulses were often indistinguishable – a system of paternalism and deference they had neither the means nor the men to enforce on their own. Thus, the gentry mounted its periodic displays of authority – "the ritual of the hunt; the pomp of the assizes (and all the theatrical style of the law courts); the segregated pews, the late entries and early departures, at church" – all of which was met by similarly deliberate demonstrations of popular festiveness and insubordination: the maypole, the anonymous threat, the food riot.[18]

It would be foolish to dismiss these elaborately choreographed contests as empty displays. Judiciously staged spectacles of terror and magnanimity did confer on the social order a legitimacy that a more sustained and methodical exercise of force might otherwise have threatened. Still, the aggressive tenor of this eighteenth-century "theater and counter-theater," as E. P. Thompson describes it, indicates "a more active and reciprocal relationship than the one normally brought to mind under the formula 'paternalism and deference.' "[19] Less and less did this flamboyant protocol assert unquestioned and immemorial rights and obligations; more and more was it seen to rehearse claims on negotiable prerogatives and perquisites. The process of social bargaining was lengthy, complex, and, as historians have noted, extraordinarily stylized, but out of it a consolidated ruling aristocracy of birth and inheritance did eventually reemerge by mid-century.[20] Yet the terms of its victory were now set more firmly than ever before in the market. Where once the personal relations of patronage and paternalism had restricted the scope and regulated the operation of "free" market values, now those same values traveled outward from the marketplace along the same filiations of clientage and custom that had once confined them.

Ironically, the very success of agricultural capitalism in Britain between 1660 and 1760, producing surpluses of goods and labor at the same time, restrained the gentry from adopting laissez-faire ideals. The same process of economic rationalization that made paternalism a delicate, precarious, yet indispensable enterprise for landlords and manufacturers drove both groups toward mercantilist policies in the hope that a balance of trade would settle an increasingly mobile and restive laboring class.[21] Periodic economic depressions put considerably greater pressure on rural elites than on the merchant class, whose assets were far more liquid and whose concern for the docility of the labor force was correspondingly far less pronounced. Despite the ground gained by free-trade advocates during the seventeenth-century debate over economic policy, the loyalty of landed interests to a burgeoning free-trade ideal remained tenuous at best. Thus, when deep commercial crises struck Britain, as happened during the 1690s, the nation's propertied classes were quick to close ranks around a strong mercantilist program.[22] Still, as Joyce Appleby notes, this rapid retreat to a strict protectionist program owed more to the gentry's appreciation of ideological and political necessities than to any abiding sense of class obligation; mercantilism, too, was a compromise, an accommodation cut to fit the shape of a postfeudal society. Britain's ruling classes envisaged a state-monitored economic and social equilibrium, to be sure, but one now markedly free of the traditional providential or sovereign imprimatur.[23]

Even at that, the government of the early 1700s could no longer be said to undergird or, for that matter, to oversee the nation's market activity in the visibly superordinate fashion to which it had once been accustomed. First, the market in land, labor, and goods had grown so expansive and so elusive that it defied the capacity of a local magistracy to render it accountable, much less comprehensible. Bewildered by the intangibility and anonymity of these relations, Britons came to use the term "stock-jobbing" to describe virtually all market transactions.[24] There were more bubbles in the sea of trade, it seemed, than even the most vigilant administrator, armed with the most detailed Book of Orders, could hope to burst. But even more distressing, especially to Britain's oppositional Country party, was the growing suspicion that the state itself had become a willing hostage to the whims of any merchant willing to invest in it. For the government to issue its own notes, as it began to do during the late seventeenth century, was for it to place its relation to the market in an entirely new and disturbing light. And indeed, with the passage of the Million Act of 1693, the establishment of the Bank of England in 1694, and the panic attending the Recoinage Act of 1696, a long and rancorous debate broke out over the issue of public credits.[25] As the national debt grew, swollen in large part by war expenditures, investors began to look on the state as an explicitly speculative venture: a collective representation, so to speak, whose authority or, more precisely, whose credit fluctuated according to the wealth invested in it. And though it was not until the last quarter of the eighteenth century that the specifically commercial connotations of the word "speculation" took root in popular discourse, the conjectural, even visionary, meanings of the term were already present in the arguments advanced for and against the issuance of government stock.[26]

To some observers, at least, it now appeared as if the nation were to be sustained by the image that investors held out to themselves (and to others) of a moment that would never actually arrive – the day of repayment. Deficit financing appeared to put the state in the position of a merchant attempting to convert credibility to credit and credit, in turn, to capital in a perpetually renewable cycle of imaginative projection. To support the principle of a national debt, then, was to endorse a society that maintained itself – in J. G. A. Pocock's words – by "perpetually gambling on its own wish-fulfillments." The financial revolution of the early eighteenth century, he suggests, propelled itself forward by means of an elaborate "exchange of fantasies"; "what one owned was promises, and not merely the functioning but the intelligibility of society depended on the success of a program of reification."[27]

"Reification" and "wish-fulfillment" are obviously twentieth-century terms; they put in abstract and impersonal form a process that contemporaries were more likely to regard as concrete and personal. For Britain's policy makers, the reality conferred on the new government notes more closely resembled the reality conferred on the drama, a reality that Samuel Johnson treated as an artifact of the audience's collective suspension of disbelief. True, Court and Country parties were sharply divided over the usefulness of the repayment fiction, but few ever doubted for a moment that it was a fiction. What the debate over the national debt brought home to these men of power, notwithstanding their internal divisions, was a lesson that the "theater and counter-theater" of paternalism had already disposed them to consider: that security lay as much in the promise of performance as in the performance of promises.[28]

This sly appreciation of the instrumental power of social, political, and economic convention lay at the heart of the eighteenth-century resurrection of the *theatrum mundi* metaphor, particularly in the satire and caricature that distinguished Augustan letters. Men of reputation may well have strutted through the streets and coffeehouses of London, but never were they more methodically stripped of their masks and pretensions than in the pages of Swift and Pope, the plates of Hogarth and Cruikshank, and the broadsides of countless anonymous scribblers, all of whom made generous use of the idiom and iconography of the theater. The analogy of world and stage, Henry Fielding wrote in *Tom Jones* (1749), had "been carried so far, and become so general, that some words proper to the theatre, and which were at first metaphorically applied to the world, are now indiscriminately and literally spoken of both." Thus, he added, "stage and scene are by common use grown as familiar to us when we speak of life in general as when we confine ourselves to dramatic performances; and when we mention transactions behind the curtain, St. James's is more likely to occur to our thoughts than Drury Lane."[29]

Considered from this perspective, the plots of eighteenth-century drama must have paled not only in comparison with those of their seventeenth-century forebears but also in comparison with those that Fielding's own audiences suspected in the world around them. "More than any other period in English history," Gordon Wood has written, "the century or so following the Restoration was the great era of conspiratorial fears and imagined intrigues."[30] French and Irish, Jacobites and Dissenters, Catholics and High Churchmen, Whigs and Tories – all were accused of plots at one time or another. Even the word "cabal" was said at one point to have been conjured out of the first initials of Charles II's five chief privy councilors. Yet it must be added that polemicists exploited such coincidences more as conceits than as convictions; in Charles's case, for example, the accusation of a cabal was a barb aimed at his new and opaque form of political management through cabinet rule.[31] As Wood quite properly reminds us, the fears and imaginings that filled the late-seventeenth- and early-eighteenth-century press are not to be treated as symptoms of some paranoid pathology but rather as evidence of a new, Enlightenment-inspired understanding of social causality. The common suspicion of widespread conspiratorial designs, he argues, indicated a faith in human agency far broader and more inclusive than that of Elizabethan "Machiavellianism." Only when individual intentions were believed to be efficacious in the world could they be seen as requiring masks to conceal their objects.[32]

Wood's concern to place the so-called paranoid style of eighteenth-century Anglo-American politics within the intellectual context of a maturing social thought is well founded, but in a sense it fails to go far enough. The popular preoccupation with ministerial, commercial, and sectarian conspiracies amounted to something more than a makeshift cognitive solution to "Western man's long struggle to comprehend his social reality."[33] It sprang out of that reality itself, out of a social and political stalemate whose prolongation hung on the talents and shrewdness its main actors brought to the waning drama of paternalism and the waxing spectacle of the market. The eighteenth-century revival of the theatrical perspective in Britain is perhaps best understood as a direct response to the overt theatricalization of social relations. The language of "stage and scene" recovered its appeal for the literate classes not because it recalled the ritual entreaty to a divine order but because it implied the conventional fabrication of a secular order. In other words, writers and artists turned to the conventions of the theater because no other analogy seemed so well equipped to capture the radical disjuncture between "gesture" and "influence," between public and private that characterized British life during the eighteenth century and that, at the same time, explained its remarkable stability.

Neither the stability of that society nor the hegemony of its ruling class was to survive the century intact, but the longevity of the Restoration and Hanoverian settlement was exceptional enough to stir numerous writers to ponder its mechanics. Much of eighteenth-century moral philosophy and political economy offered itself, therefore, as an answer to the threefold challenge of seventeenth-century skepticism and atomism. How was a *political* order possible, Hobbes had asked, in the presence of competing individual fears and desires? How, furthermore, was a *social* order possible in the absence of a shared experience of those fears and desires? And, finally, if a political and social order were indeed possible, what was to be the basis on which their isolated subjects represented themselves to and for one another?

In Hobbes's time, these questions, or ones very much like them, had issued out of a general crisis of representation occasioned by the disruption of the governing status order (its land, its labor, its goods, and ultimately its meanings) by the centrifugal tendencies of a placeless market. And as a commonplace image for the hollowness and vanity of all human representations, the *theatrum mundi* had seemed at first a convenient metaphor with which to encapsulate and explain the diminishing transparency of social exchange. But since the *theatrum* itself had changed so markedly during these years, the effect of the stage analogy was to intensify rather than to subdue the simultaneous anxiety and exhilaration that this cultural crisis had inspired. For the Elizabethan and Jacobean theater to explore, as it did, the formal limits of its own polymorphous possibilities was for it to reenact this confusion within its own walls. As we know, it was a venturesomeness for which the stage found itself first supported and then suppressed.

By the eighteenth century, however, the determination to settle these Hobbesian questions of representation in a definitive and authoritative manner was no longer to be denied. So although the theatrical metaphor, like the theater itself, reappeared in literary circles of this epoch, it did so largely to serve poets and philosophers bent on domesticating the somber legacy of its meaning. In their hands, a metaphor long used to question the very foundation of perception came to be incorporated within a general philosophical outlook that, by the latter half of the eighteenth century, could proudly call itself Common Sense. Like so many other aspects of culture in that time, the deconstructive dimension of the theatrical perspective was restrained and recast in a more manageable form; it, too, was "settled," albeit imperfectly and impermanently.

Yet to the extent that the theatrical metaphor survived at all, it was the author rather than the playwright who came to its rescue. Derivative, formulaic, and after 1737, officially censored, London's theater had lost most of its nerve and much of its audience by the middle of the century. What cultural contests continued to be waged shifted their field of action from Drury Lane to Grub Street, where a new reading public eagerly bought up experiments in literary form similar in spirit to the earlier improvisations of Tudor–Stuart playwrights.[34] But where those dramatists had, to a man, focused on the impostures and impersonations of the actor, eighteenth-century authors declared their epoch the age of the Spectator. Few more popular figures are to be found in the literature of that time than that of the detached or impartial observer, but though its champions saw in it (as in the *theatrum mundi*) a foil to the self-interested persona of Hobbes, the figure of the spectator brought with it some of the same paradoxes and perplexities that had once plagued the "artificial person" of the professional actor. Eighteenth-century men of letters may have prided themselves on their scientific observation and systematic categorization of human motives – from man's ineradicable self-interest to his equally irresistible compassion – but the questions to which these motives stood as answers still lingered, concealed within the very figures of speech contrived to resolve them.

II

For the professional and patrician writers of the eighteenth century, the role of the spectator – and it was very much a role – appealed on a number of grounds. First and most broadly, the literary posture of spectatorship conformed to the general neoclassical bent of Augustan letters, particularly to its Stoic ideal of detached and dispassionate contemplation of the world's follies. In this way, one of the ancient meanings of the *theatrum mundi* was carried forward, if somewhat feebly, into the eighteenth century. Second, the model of the impartial or disinterested observer suited the image that Enlightenment scientists and philosophers held of themselves, one they almost invariably contrasted to the blind or distorted vision of the religious and political fanatic. Finally and relatedly, to declare oneself a spectator was to announce, however disingenuously, one's political neutrality – an important signal in an age when political polemic offered both the most lucrative and the most closely watched of literary occupations.[35] Spectatorship was thus a term of art sufficiently adaptive and attractive to be shared by aristocratic moral philosophers and hack political journalists alike.

Among the moral philosophers, Anthony Ashley Cooper, third earl of Shaftesbury, was the first to place the spectator at the center of his ruminations. Ill health had removed him from the cabalistic politics with which his grandfather, the first earl of Shaftesbury, had been popularly associated during the reign of Charles II and consigned him to a literary life. However, the grandson was not much more comfortable in the houses of booksellers and printers than in the House of Commons. Much of his work, in fact, suggests a concerted effort to steer a middle course between the single-mindedness of religious enthusiasm and the double-dealing of literary entrepreneurialism.

In 1711 Shaftesbury drew together his most important and influential essays in a volume entitled *Characteristics of Men, Manners, Opinions, Times*. Like Samuel Butler's unpublished *Characters* (ca. 1669), Shaftesbury's work evinced a strong skepticism toward the claims of pietism, though without the bile that distinguished the Restoration wits. *"Gravity,"* he wrote in "A Letter Concerning Enthusiasm" (1707), was "of the very essence of imposture," except that its victims were as likely to be the enthusiasts themselves as the unregenerate sinners whom they rebuked. Sentiment itself was not to be disparaged; rather, what Shaftesbury sought was a "noble enthusiasm" purged of all false feeling and fanaticism by a systematic application of reason and ridicule.[36] "Defensive raillery," he argued in *"Sensus Communis; An Essay on the Freedom of Wit and Humour"* (1709), was "a more lenitive remedy against vice, and a kind of specific against superstition and melancholy delusion."[37] The moderate and good-natured jest was to be regarded as a prophylactic measure that inhibited the spread of zealotry by opening itself to the very humor it aimed at others. Raillery countered self-deception, Shaftesbury believed, by separating and pitting against one another the parts of the self that enthusiasm deludedly forged into a single and uniform whole.

The remedies Shaftesbury sketched out in his "Letter" of 1707 and in his subsequent "Essay" of 1709 were refined and recast in his celebrated "Treatise" of 1710, *"Soliloquy* or Advice to an Author." There, Shaftesbury wrote at length about a "gymnastic method" that reproduced the workings of conscience without its inquisitorial goads to blind conformity. Soliloquy was for him a "powerful figure of inward rhetoric" whereby "the mind apostrophises its own fancies, raises them in their proper shapes and personages and addresses them familiarly, without the least ceremony or respect." By such means, he assured his readers, "two formed parties" would inevitably "erect themselves within" the individual.[38] If readers still doubted whether anyone could "thus multiply himself into two persons and be his own subject," Shaftesbury urged them to consult the poets. "Nothing," he insisted, was "more common with them, than this sort of soliloquy."

> A person of profound parts, or perhaps of ordinary capacity, happens on some occasion to commit a fault. He is concerned for it. He comes alone upon the stage; looks about him to see if anybody be near; then takes himself to task, without sparing himself in the least. You would wonder to hear how close he pushes matters, and how thoroughly he carries on the business of self-dissection. By virtue of this soliloquy he becomes two persons.[39]

Shaftesbury, then, did not consider soliloquy an extradramatic or extratextual form of address to a visible and acknowledgeable audience. He was, if anything, repelled by those essayists and memoirists who shamelessly and directly unburdened themselves in books.[40] The dialogue he imagined was wholly private, wholly internal; it was, in his words, a form of "mirror writing" or "magical glasses" with which "the parties accustomed to the practice would acquire a peculiar speculative habit, so as virtually to carry with them a sort of pocket-mirror, always ready and in use."[41] Armed with this "dramatic method," individuals could divide themselves "into two different parties" and set about "the work of self-inspection" with some hope of success. Conscience, in this view, was less the cause than the product of reflection.

Shaftesbury's "mirror writing" was deliberately opposed to the Puritan conviction that "one must scrub away his own image from the mirror and replace it with Christ's."[42] Soliloquy had the power to break the embargo that single-mindedness imposed on the free trade in ideas without thereby unleashing anarchy. Liberty permitted men to polish one another and rub off their "corners and rough sides by a sort of amicable collision." Deprived of an internal "inspector or auditor," however, men were at a loss to estimate the value of this commerce.[43] Only by "first taking an inventory of the same kind of goods within ourselves, and surveying our domestic fund," could there be reliable estimates of the "different humours, fancies, passions, and apprehensions of others."[44] Like Hobbes, whom he otherwise rejected, Shaftesbury mistrusted man's capacity to fantasize, since it was in the "mint and foundary of the imagination" that appetites and desires were fabricated and from which they derived "their privilege and currency." Only in the imagination, therefore, could this "false coinage" be suppressed. "Must I busy myself with phantoms?" Shaftesbury asked rhetorically, "fight with apparitions and chimeras?" Of course, he answered. "Either I work upon my fancies, or they upon me. . . . There can be no truce, no suspension of arms between us."[45] Soliloquy was not madness, then, but a measure to forestall madness; a pin to prick the speculative bubbles of the imagination.

Shaftesbury's writings portrayed a self that defied intuition and introspection, a self that had to be represented or performed in order to be recognized. Readers were urged to "personate" themselves that they might find themselves, though there was no assurance that a "real and genuine" self discovered through personation would not be lost, or at least masked, through impersonation.[46] What, after all, was to prevent a method of representation from degenerating into a habit of misrepresentation? Shaftesbury did not answer this question, in part because he was not prepared to raise it directly. For him, the "doctrine of the two persons in one individual self" granted each individual "a certain resolution, by which he shall know where to find himself; be sure of his own meaning and design; and as to all his desires, opinions, and inclinations, be warranted one and the same person to-day as yesterday, and to-morrow as to-day."[47] Though such assurances would scarcely have comforted those not privy to the internal operations of others' soliloquizing, it was precisely the private character of this "warrant," and of the internal theater in which it was issued, that guaranteed its authenticity in Shaftesbury's eyes. However social or theatrical soliloquy appeared to be, it was at bottom a presocial and antitheatrical method in aim; that is to say, it was a "sovereign remedy" to be taken up by the individual *before* his entry into the Babel of society and *against* its impostures.

Small wonder, then, that when questions of misrepresentation (and the market) arose in Shaftesbury's work, they did so in the guise of asides or framing devices introduced to resolve the problematic social relation he felt toward the commodity form of his own text – a printed book – and toward the anonymous readers who purchased it. Ultimately, it was Shaftesbury's own deep ambivalence toward those readers and toward the kind of theater he believed to govern his relation to them that stirred him to expound on the virtues of soliloquy and to replicate its conventions, as far as it was possible to do so, within the covers of a published book. Indeed, one of the most striking aspects of Shaftesbury's writing in moral philosophy was its recurrent impulse to deny the presence of the very readers for whom his thoughts were presumably penned and almost certainly published.

As David Marshall has shown in some detail, Shaftesbury went out of his way to define his works as anything but the books they would have so visibly appeared to be.[48] It was the bookseller,

Shaftesbury explained, who had insisted on labeling his thoughts on enthusiasm a "Treatise," whereas he had first formulated them in a "private letter" that only "by accident... came to be read abroad in copies, and afterward in print."[49] His "essay" on common sense had likewise been offered as "a letter to a Friend." There were doubtless "certain merchant-adventurers in the letter-trade," Shaftesbury wrote in *"Soliloquy,"* who "would be shrewdly disappointed if the public took no notice of their labours," but such notice was of "no concern" to him. "What I write is not worth being made a Mystery," so that "if it be worth any one's purchasing," what value there was fell entirely to the purchaser and to his judgment. Moral philosophy was not and ought not to be a trade. And if its contents happened to circulate in the literary marketplace as the price paid for the special clarity and convenience of a printed text, then it was "a traffic I have no share in, though I accidently furnish the subject matter." For his own part, Shaftesbury claimed, he wrote only for his acquaintances and for his "private entertainment"; to his mind the fact of print changed nothing, though others apparently thought differently.[50] He could not conceive "why a man may not be permitted to write with iron as well as quill... or how a writer changes his capacity by this new dress, any more than by the wear of wove-stockings, after having worn no other manufacture than the knit."[51]

In a sense, the imagery of Shaftesbury's complaint was even more appropriate than he was disposed to acknowledge. Technology, as his comparison suggested, was indeed not the source of the anxieties he brought to writing. True, the press and the loom had revolutionized the means of textual and textile production. Still, Shaftesbury's bewilderment and resentment aimed less at the machines themselves ("that Alphabetic engine called the Press") than at the social and economic relations that had called them forth.[52] It was not so much the shift from quill to type that had changed the conditions of authorship as the shift from the private circulation of handwritten manuscripts within close courtly circles to the public distribution of printed volumes before a new and anonymous readership.[53] In the end, it was the "merchant-adventurers in the letter-trade," far more than the

religious enthusiasts, who inspired Shaftesbury's contempt, not
to mention the extraordinary measures he took to deny the book-
ish properties of his publications.

Shaftesbury knew and named his targets. He mocked those
"philosophers and divines" who were content "to write in learned
Billingsgate to divert the coffee-houses, and entertain the assemblies at booksellers's shops or the more airy stalls of inferior book
retailers!"[54] He condemned the "coquetry" of those writers
"whose epistles dedicatory, prefaces, and addresses to the reader
are so many affected graces, designed to draw the attention from
the subject towards himself, and make it be generally observed,
not so much what he says, as what he appears, or is, and what
figure he already makes, or hopes to make, in the fashionable
world."[55] And he attacked the "common practice among others
to feign a correspondency, and give the title of a private letter
to a piece addressed solely to the public."[56] Pandering, hypocrisy,
impersonation, misrepresentation, false intimacies – here was a
"dramatic method" from which Shaftesbury was at pains to dis-
associate himself, a method by which an author schemed to "purchase" the favor of his readers "by all imaginable compliances
and condescensions."[57] Such theatricality was detestable because
it was abject; it was literary courtship transformed into common
prostitution. "Our modern authors," Shaftesbury wrote, "are
turned and modelled (as themselves confess) by the public relish
and current humour of the times."

> They regulate themselves by the irregular fancy of the world, and
> frankly own they are preposterous and absurd, in order to
> accommodate themselves to the genius of the age. In our days the
> audience makes the poet, and the bookseller the author, with what
> profit to the public, or what prospect of lasting fame and honour
> to the writer, let any one who has judgment imagine.[58]

As a deliberately private exercise, then, soliloquy was not for
Shaftesbury a piece of stage business. It was, if anything, a defense
against the stage of business, against the spectacle of the market.
Nothing was more mortifying to him than those "indecent" essayists and memoirists who spoke out loud, as it were, in a direct address
to their readers, for this was to "exhibit on the stage of the world that
practice which they should have kept to themselves."[59]

Because Shaftesbury believed that true soliloquy deliberately ignored its audience, he contrived an anonymous and conspicuously private epistolary form for his "advice," refusing to "subscribe" his name or that of his addressees to a medium (the printed book) to which his readers might themselves expect to subscribe.[60] "An author who writes in his own person," Shaftesbury warned, "has the advantage of being who or what he pleases. He is no certain man, nor has any certain or genuine character; but suits himself on every occasion to the fancy of his reader, whom, as the fashion is nowadays, he constantly caresses and cajoles." He acts for an audience that, in turn, applauds him. "All turns on their two persons."[61] By dividing or doubling the author, however, soliloquy internalized and thus broke off his relation to the reader. Dialogue dissolved the "I" and "thou" of authorial (or extradramatic) address, for in dialogue "the author is annihilated, and the reader, being no way applied to, stands for nobody."

> The self-interesting parties both vanish at once. The scene presents itself as by chance and undesigned. You are not only left to judge coolly and with indifference of the sense delivered, but of the character, genius, elocution, and manner of the persons who deliver it. These two are mere strangers, in whose favour you are no way engaged.[62]

By thus converting the reader from a willing accessory to an uninvited and unacknowledgeable spectator of the author's thoughts (or his characters' conversations), the epistolary style (like the dialogue) allowed Shaftesbury to imagine himself freed from the corrupt and mercenary pressures of the "letter-trade." Yet the language of his solution, with its references to self-interest, indifference, and strangers, suggests that Shaftesbury may have only deepened the commercial and theatrical properties of authorship he had sought to remove.

Taken together, Shaftesbury's experiments with the character and the conventions of soliloquy disclose his struggle to redefine the role of his readers. (Had he wished to remove them altogether, he would not have published at all.)[63] Those conventions were the fundamental constituents of literary and dramatic realism, which is to say that they effaced the relation of author and reader (actor and spectator) in order to heighten the autonomous and self-sufficient aspect of the drama played out on the page, and on the stage. In effect, the barrier of studied indifference that Shaftesbury sought to erect between himself and his readers stood as the textual equivalent of the fourth wall in drama. Like Garrick at the Drury Lane or Voltaire at the Comédie Française, Shaftesbury yearned to remove the all too palpable presence of those spectators presumptuously seated on the stage of his text and to enforce, by means of his own authorial withdrawal, a collective silence on the rest.[64] Though his method clearly aimed at erasing all taint of theatricality from his text, it actually called for greater rather than lesser collusion from his readers, since they were now expected to assent to the voyeuristic convention of their own invisibility. His readers were to become, more thoroughly than even before, his spectators.

Shaftesbury's *"Soliloquy"* would not compel so much of our attention, however, were it not possible to see in his determination to deny the theatricality of his text an equal resolution to negate the spectacle of the market. The irony of his failure was thus twofold, for not only did his textual strategies further theatricalize his relation to his readers, but they reproduced at the same time the impersonal conventions of social exchange peculiar to the placeless market. Repulsed by the shameless cajolery and "learned Billingsgate" of London's open market in letters, Shaftesbury conjured up in its stead a world of "mere strangers," the delights of which were intended, or so it seemed, for anyone but the reader who paid for them. Despite his many pronouncements on man's natural affections, Shaftesbury left no doubt that, in the end, the reader was to shape his interest to the curve of the author's indifference.[65]

III

As essayists, Joseph Addison and Richard Steele shared the Earl of Shaftesbury's moderate Whiggism, Stoicism, and aestheticism; they also shared his interest in the figure of the spectator. But where Shaftesbury used the literary conventions of spectatorship as a psychic distancing mechanism, Addison and Steele used them to cultivate the very readers whom Shaftesbury affected to despise. As J. H. Plumb has pointed out, their daily magazine, *The*

Spectator (1711–12, 1714), was the first English periodical to discover and exploit the new, leisured middle-class readership of
eighteenth-century London, and their astonishing success in this
effort set the model for a new kind of popular journalism encompassing the arts, manners, morals, as well as politics.[66] In
one sense, Addison and Steele's review formed part of a general
commercialization of leisure during the eighteenth century, a
development that included the explosive growth of newspapers,
prints, penny ballads, chapbooks, partbooks, music, sports, shops,
and consumer products.[67] In another sense, the sense implied in
its name, *The Spectator* took up a position outside this bewildering
array of goods and services in order to offer itself as a judicious,
confident, and charming arbiter of their value; such a role or
persona was new enough in the early 1700s for English writers
to borrow the word "connoisseur" from the French in order to
describe and legitimate it.[68]

The *Spectator* thus staked out a place both inside and outside
this new world of cultural commodities, for its contents – rang-
ing from short reviews to "nugget fiction" – vicariously performed the same acts of consumption on which the publication
ostensibly stood in judgment. The word "taste" ran throughout
the pages of the review and of its sundry imitators as a mark of
their belletristic ambitions, although the term itself had acquired
its association with aesthetic discrimination only after the Restoration. Connotations of savoring still lingered within a word
that writers otherwise sought to empty of its sensuous meanings,
with the result that the act of spectatorship itself became as deeply
implicated in the urge to sample as in the urge to judge the
spectacle of London's leisure market.[69]

Traces of the Stoic spectator survived in Addison's and Steele's
essays, as in their occasional allusion to the ancient trope of the
theatrum mundi. In a contribution entitled "On the Love of Honour and Distinction," for example, Addison, like George Chapman before him, drew on Epictetus's advice to the slave as a
cautionary example to his readers:

> We are . . . as in a Theater, where every one has a Part allotted to
> him. The great Duty which lies upon a Man is to act his Part in
> Perfection. We may indeed say, that our Part does not suit us, and

that we could act another better. But this, says the Philosopher, is not our Business. All that we are concerned in is to excel in the Part which is given us. If it be an improper one, the Fault is not in us, but in Him who has cast our several Parts, and is the great Disposer of the Drama.[70]

Yet the prospect that "in the other World" mankind would be "ranged in different Stations of Superiority and Pre-eminence" could hardly have reassured the "Fraternity of Spectators," as Addison defined them.[71] His "good Brothers and Allies" were not slaves, after all, but men and women "who live in the World without having anything to do in it; and either by the Affluence of their Fortunes, or Laziness of their Dispositions, have no other Business with the rest of Mankind but to look upon them," in short, "every one that considers the World as a Theatre, and desires to form a right Judgment of those who are Actors on it."[72] This jestful piece of flattery to his subscribers reveals the shallowness and ultimate complacency of Addison's Stoicism, for it was not the world but *The Spectator* that was his theater – a theater that could take the time, as in Numbers 445 and 488, to debate with its readers the price of its own commodity.

Addison and Steele considered the free trade of ideas in much the same light as Shaftesbury regarded his own "private" correspondence: as the "liberty of *the club,* and of that sort of freedom which is taken amongst gentlemen and friends who know one another perfectly well."[73] And it was on this plane of familiarity and easy intimacy that the review's anonymous editors addressed their readership on both sides of the Atlantic. Three thousand subscribers, they estimated (in the first recorded calculation of this kind), meant thirty thousand readers, once each copy had circulated sufficiently. And if *The Spectator,* like Shaftesbury's "*Soliloquy,*" happened to reach the "Shopkeeper's Counter," where it was "every day quoted by Persons . . . who when they have got a little *smattering* . . . for the most part employ it to very ill purposes," so be it. Such eventualities were a small price to pay for a commerce that had striven, as Addison put it, to bring Philosophy "out of the Closets and Libraries, Schools and Colleges, to dwell in Clubs and Assemblies, at Tea-Tables and in Coffee-Houses."[74]

A century earlier, the playwright Thomas Dekker had pictured the Elizabethan city dweller as haunting the theaters in order "to furnish the necessity of his bare knowledge to maintain table-talk."[75] The eighteenth-century Londoner, however, needed to look no farther than his or her twopenny edition of *The Spectator*. As the editors themselves suggested, the review was best "looked upon as a Part of the Tea-equipage," a compendium of "Materials for thinking" and "wholesome Sentiments" for those "needy Persons [who] do not know what to talk of, 'till about twelve a Clock in the Morning." Addison and Steele did not think that such "gentle Readers, who have so much Time on their Hands [would] grudge throwing away a Quarter of an Hour in a Day on this Paper, since they may do it without any Hindrance to Business."[76] *The Spectator* did not soliloquize in the Shaftesburian vein, since it directly addressed its readers. But if the review openly recognized its audience, it did so in a fashion that invited readers to recognize themselves in *The Spectator,* indeed *as* the Spectator. In that respect, Shaftesbury's ideal of a "pocket-mirror, always ready and in use," was admirably realized in the review.

Still, the reader's capacity to identify with the persona of Mr. Spectator was by no means a faculty that Addison and Steele took for granted. It was, if anything, an incapacity that the editors sought to overcome. "I have observed," Addison wrote in *The Spectator*'s inaugural issue, "that a Reader seldom peruses a Book with Pleasure 'till he knows whether the Writer of it be a black [dark-complexioned] or a fair Man, of a mild or cholerick Disposition, Married or a Batchelor, with other Particulars of the like nature, that conduce very much to the right Understanding of the Author."[77] To gratify this natural curiosity, he offered a capsule autobiography that stressed his lifelong inclination to remain a silent "Spectator of Mankind." "In short," he concluded, "I have acted in all the Parts of my Life as a Looker-on, which is the Character I intend to preserve in this Paper."[78]

For all its familiar detail, however, Addison's profile of the Spectator revealed an essayist bent, like the reader, on anonymity. Anonymity, Addison insisted, was the mask behind which his candid observations of the fashions and foibles of life could continue undetected; it was the voucher for their authenticity and the vehicle of their power. He did not wish to be drawn out of the obscurity he had enjoyed for so long and to be exposed "in

Public Places to several Salutes and Civilities," which he had always found disagreeable; "the greatest Pain I can suffer," he confessed, "is the being talked to, and being stared at." To escape notice, then, he transformed himself to suit the occasion, becoming what Poe would later call the "Man of the Crowd."

> There is no Place of general Resort, wherein I do not often make my Appearance; sometimes I am seen thrusting my Head into a Round of Politicians at *Will's,* and listning with great Attention to the narratives that are made in those little Circular Audiences. Sometimes I smoak a Pipe at *Child's;* and whilst I seem attentive to nothing but the *Post-Man,* over-hear the Conversation of every Table in the Room. I appear on *Sunday* Nights at St. *James's* Coffee-House, and sometimes join the little Committee of Politicks in the Inner-Room, as one who comes to hear and improve. My Face is likewise very well known at the *Grecian,* the *Cocoa-Tree,* and in the Theaters both of *Drury-Lane,* and the *Hay-Market.* I have been taken for a Merchant upon the *Exchange* for above these ten Years, and sometimes pass for a *Jew* in the Assembly of Stock-Jobbers at *Jonathan's.* In short, where-ever I see a Cluster of People I always mix with them, tho' I never open my Lips but in my own Club.[79]

By these means, the Spectator boasted, he had made himself a "Speculative Statesman, Soldier, Merchant, and Artisan without ever medling with any Practical Part in Life."[80] Yet what could have been more practical than the Spectator's impersonations? Did they not furnish the following morning's commodity as well as the most appropriate "Character" in which to serve it up? The answer seems indisputable. To observe in this fashion was, inescapably, to act, both in the ordinary and in the theatrical sense of the word. Indeed, the Spectator's readers appeared even more deeply implicated in his performance than his informants; the latter actually patronized the clubs and coffeehouses, whereas the former were expected to translate the social conventions of these gatherings to the printed page. It was *The Spectator's* readers who had to accept the pretense that a taciturn author, with "neither Time nor Inclination to communicate the Fulness of my heart in Speech," had resolved on their behalf to put his sentiments into writing and "to Print my self out, if possible, before I die." It was they, in sum, who had to credit the journalistic persona of

Mr. Spectator, a self-avowed bystander whose own camouflage confirmed the opacity of men's minds and characters even as it purportedly drew them out.[81]

Neither Addison nor Steele allowed such paradoxes to disturb the resolutely genial and cosmopolitan style of their review. Theirs was a journalism of aesthetic notes and social vignettes, ill-suited to the darker broodings of a Swift or Pope – though Pope was an occasional contributor. More moralists than moral philosophers, Addison and Steele shared with Shaftesbury a predeliction for the essay. They preferred to gesture at the problems of representation besetting their literary and social milieu rather than to make them the subject of a deliberate and systematic investigation. But as the bubbles of literary and financial speculation expanded during the eighteenth century, with corresponding crises of satirical and pecuniary deflation, new writers and thinkers appeared and, with them, a new determination to theorize solutions to the problematic spectacle of the market. In the years between 1725 and 1775, roughly speaking, a number of writers took up the challenges of atomism, materialism, and skepticism posed by Hobbes, Mandeville, and Hume – took them up, that is, in order to put them to rest. Among these thinkers, we may include Joseph Butler, Francis Hutcheson, Adam Ferguson, Thomas Reid, Lord Kames, and Adam Smith, all of whom looked back, to a greater or lesser degree, to Shaftesbury's confident pronouncements on man's natural sociability and moral sensibility. By the end of the eighteenth century, the result of these men's labor was a school of thought that styled itself Common Sense and that, in keeping with its name, assured its many academic and popular adherents of the adequacy of man's senses, the efficacy of his intuitions, the rationality of his judgments, the immediacy of his sympathies, and the mutuality of his relations with others.[82] This was the house that the spirit of the Scottish Enlightenment built, and it was in this house (with its Utilitarian additions) that the Georgian and Victorian bourgeoisie contented itself to dwell.

Within this overarching ideological structure, Common Sense writers erected a partition between the claims of propriety – with its representations of truth and beauty – and the claims of property – with its representations of authority and value – assigning the former to the care of moral aestheticians and the latter to the care of political economists. In these two distinct lines of inquiry lay the dichotomy between culture and society (or economy) that the High Victorians would later enthrone and that continues to obscure the understanding of the market's meanings in our own time. For the eighteenth-century reader, however, propriety and property were less easily distinguished. It was not just the fact of their common etymological roots, nor that such roots preserved the long-standing association of honor and decorum with ancient and prescriptive rights in the land. It was that the concepts of propriety and property were themselves changing to fit, in J. G. A. Pocock's phrase, "a world of moving objects."[83]

In drama as in life, honor was increasingly understood to be a particularly stable and solid form of credit, whereas land was coming to be seen as an especially illiquid form of capital.[84] When, for example, wartime losses slowed England's trade at sea during the mid-1690s, one newspaper noted that "few that had Money were willing it should be idle, and a great many that wanted Employments studied how to dispose of their Money, that they might be able to command it whensoever they had occasion, which they found they could more easily do in Joint-Stock, than in laying out the same in Land, Houses, or Commodities."[85] As the eighteenth century advanced, propriety and property came to be conceived less as the timeless prerogatives of rank than as the timely prerequisites of trade: a social and economic form of capital sufficiently liquid to meet and defeat the vicissitudes of a placeless market. Indeed, Shaftesbury and Addison were but the first of a distinguished body of eighteenth-century commentators to see in commerce – the world of moving objects – a powerful incentive toward propriety, toward sociability and *politesse*. Merchants, Mr. Spectator observed, "knit Mankind together in a mutual Intercourse of good Offices"; theirs was a "grand Scene of Business" because the necessities of trade impelled men of widely differing interests and backgrounds to diplomatic measures. "Factors in the Trading World," he concluded, "are what Ambassadors are in the Politick World."[86]

Addison's analogy between commerce and diplomacy did little to soften Hobbes's and Mandeville's skeptical views on man's natural benevolence toward his fellow beings; if anything, it implied a tactical rather than a natural interest in the welfare of humanity, an interest perhaps best represented in the opening pages of Adam Smith's *Wealth of Nations* (1776). "It is not from the benevolence of the butcher, the brewer, or the baker, that we expect our dinner, but from their regard to their own interest," he wrote. "We address ourselves, not to their humanity but to their self-love, and never talk to them of our own necessities but of their advantages."[87] Nor was it out of our own concern for the public welfare, he added, that we were led to serve it, but rather by the "invisible hand" of the market that we were induced to promote an end that was otherwise no part of our intention.[88] Many writers had prepared the way for these particular observations, as Joyce Appleby has shown, but it was Smith who transformed their scattered thoughts into a full-blown theory of a market process removed from the Procrustean grip of its society's moral, religious, and aesthetic code.[89] The effect of Smith's reasoning was to subordinate the domain of what would later be called culture to the immediate and ineluctable imperatives of trade – in short, to treat propriety as the unintended effect or function of property. Man was social, it seemed, despite, against, and, at the same time, because of his worst intentions.

For these reasons, the anatomy of human motivation was peripheral to Smith's inquiry into the wealth of nations.[90] Having offered his initial and somewhat desultory reference to man's "propensity to truck, barter, and exchange," he laid the question of motives to the side for the remainder of the work – understandably so, since, as I have suggested, he wished to detach private fears and desires from any direct or intentional relation to their collective effects. And though this functionalist "economic" approach to human behavior ran against the conspiratorial and personalist currents of popular discourse, the deliberately restricted scope of economics' jurisdiction as a science left the sphere of private religious and ethical sentiment open to the scrutiny and judgment of philosophers and moralists. The ideological division of labor that Smith and his successors thereby fostered allowed the tensions between (and within) the new political economy and the new moral philosophy to go largely unexamined by those who embraced the Scottish Enlightenment and its Com-

mon Sense wisdom. Only when one takes up Smith's single
venture into moral philosophy, *The Theory of Moral Sentiments*,
do those tensions emerge into plain, or at least plainer, view.

IV

So different and opposed do *The Theory of Moral Sentiments* (1759)
and *The Wealth of Nations* (1776) appear at first glance that for
some years scholars referred to the task of their reconciliation as
the "Adam Smith problem."[91] From the very first pages of the
Theory, in a section titled "Of the Sense of Propriety" and subtitled "Of Sympathy," Smith seemed determined to single out
the social affections and compassionate instincts of mankind.
"How selfish soever man may be supposed," the opening par-
agraph began, "there are evidently some principles in nature,
which interest him in the fortune of others, and render their
happiness necessary to him, though he derives nothing from it
except the pleasure of seeing it." Even the "greatest ruffian, the
most hardened violator of the laws of society," Smith argued,
was not altogether without this pity or compassion.[92]

Moreover, pity and compassion were but part of man's general
capacity for sympathy, which Smith took care to define as "our
fellow-feeling with any passion whatever."[93] The "attentive spectator" was no less moved by the sight of a delighted and relieved
victor than by the sight of a suffering and dejected victim. "Our
joy for the deliverance of those heroes of tragedy and romance
who interest us," Smith observed, "is as sincere as our grief for
their distress, and our fellow-feeling with their misery is not more
real than with their happiness."[94] But even more real and compelling than man's disposition to sympathize with others was his
need to win their sympathy for himself, for man was endowed
by nature "with an original desire to please, and an original
aversion to offend his brethren."[95] Furthermore, it was out of
these desires and dispositions that the rules of moral and aesthetic
propriety originally arose, and though it required reason to formulate and articulate them as rules, only sentiment itself could
press reason into such service. "If virtue . . . necessarily pleases
for its own sake, and if vice as certainly displeases the mind,"
Smith argued, "it cannot be reason, but immediate sense and

feeling, which, in this manner, reconciles us to one, and alienates us from the other."[96] Smith sought nothing less than to show how the need and gift for sympathy that the "Author of nature" had implanted within man could generate, in their turn, the entire structure of his moral and aesthetic judgment.

Sympathy, sentiment, society – Smith's characteristic reliance on these terms would seem to place his *Theory of Moral Sentiments* squarely within the tradition of moral thought that Shaftesbury and the Latitudinarian writers had inaugurated and that Smith's mentor, Francis Hutcheson, had carried forward in his *Inquiry into the Original of Our Ideas of Beauty and Virtue* (1725).[97] There, Hutcheson had joined Lockean psychology to Shaftesburian philosophy in order to give the latter's concept of "moral sense" the status of a human faculty. Hence, by substituting his theory of moral *sentiments* for Hutcheson's concept of moral *sense* and by situating those sentiments within the framework of a social rather than an individual psychology, Smith appeared to deepen the sentimentalist and anti-Hobbesian animus of Scottish moralism. But the case was quite different than it appeared, owing in large part to Smith's peculiar view of sympathy and of the world of spectators in which he understood it to operate.

For Smith, sympathy invariably implied the presence of a witness or spectator because fellow-feeling was, more than anything else, a mark of the immense distance that separated individual minds rather than a sign of their commonality, as most moralists believed. Smith had no use whatsoever for the traditional definition of sympathy as an almost magical confluence of sentiment or emotional contagion. "As we have no immediate experience of what other men feel," he reminded his readers, "we can form no idea of the manner in which they are affected, but by conceiving what we ourselves should feel in the like situation."[98] Sympathy was not for him a sentiment but an agreement between sentiments, not an emotional identification with another's passion but an *imaginative* identification with the situation occasioning the passion. Only by means of a deliberate act of the imagination, he argued, could we form a conception of another's sensations, and even then the "copy" would be of "the impressions of our own senses, not those of his."[99] Sympathy thus offered a route, perhaps the only route, out of man's affective solipsism, a route which that very solipsism impelled him to take, if only to learn how to obtain the sympathies of others in return. Mutual sympathy thus sprang, paradoxically, out of the realization of mutual inaccessibility.

Smith's theory presupposed a society, in contrast to a community, of sympathizers. Though he conceded that man's sympathies diminished as he moved outside the circle of his immediate household, Smith rejected any suggestion that within that circle sympathy operated according to primal or elemental bonds of sentiment. "The force of blood," he noted sardonically, "exists no-where but in tragedies and romances."[100] Where tribalism survived, as in the Scottish Highlands for example, it was a defensive tactic rather than a communal expression. Smith was certain, in fact, that sympathy withered in primitive and "Barbarous" communities and thrived in "civilised" society because it was only with man's release from the immediate exigencies of survival that he became free to extend and expect sympathy. "Before we can feel much for others," he concluded, "we must in some measure be at ease ourselves."[101] Once man had physically distanced himself from the demands of material necessity, he was in a position to appreciate and to overcome the emotional distance that still separated him from his brethren. "Our imagination," he wrote, "which in pain and sorrow seems to be confined and cooped up within our own persons, in times of ease and prosperity expands itself to every thing around us."[102] By virtue of its opulence and (though Smith makes no mention of it) its division of labor, a commodity economy would inevitably bring forth a world of spectators and, in this way, increase the supply of sympathy.[103]

But if affluence enlarged man's capacity for sympathy, as Smith insisted, it did not thereby remove the obstacles in the way of its exercise. The problem of man's affective isolation and estrangement, for which prosperity was presumed to offer relief, was at the same time the problem it threw into relief. Indeed, one can scarcely imagine a more formidable and intimidating prospect than Smith's image of a society composed of detached and casual spectators, unbound by ritual, communal, or tribal loyalties.[104] Yet this image was precisely the one that Smith intended, for the difficulties that beset the act of sympathy were just those that, in his view, ensured the practical and moral regulation of society. Seen in this light, *The Theory of Moral Sentiments* appears to be a long set of stipulations and qualifications on the supposed largesse of man's sympathetic imagination.

A sympathy founded on discrete acts of imaginative representation and identification was, according to Smith, a sympathy that inevitably fell short of the sentiments experienced by its object:

> Mankind, though naturally sympathetic, never conceive, for what has befallen another, that degree of passion which naturally animates the person principally concerned. That imaginary change of situation, upon which their sympathy is founded, is but momentary. The thought of their own safety, the thought that they themselves are not really the sufferers, continually intrudes itself upon them; and though it does not hinder them from conceiving a passion somewhat analogous to what is felt by the sufferer, hinders them from conceiving any thing that approaches the same degree of violence.[105]

In life as in theater, then, the spectator (and the sufferer) was aware from the outset that the fate of the sufferer was not his own and that knowledge further diluted the compassion that imagination provoked. Moreover, as Smith remarked, man's propensity to sympathize with joy was "much stronger" than his propensity to sympathize with sorrow; consequently, sympathy, like riches and rank, was unequally distributed in society.[106] Those blessed with "ease and prosperity" were not only more sympathetically disposed toward others; they were more sympathetically regarded by others. Their words, gestures, and actions were "observed by all the world," in stark contrast to the poor, who came and went unnoticed. In the midst of a crowd, the pauper found himself "in the same obscurity as if shut up in his own hovel."

> The poor man . . . is ashamed of his poverty. He feels that it either places him out of the sight of mankind, or, that if they take notice of him, they have, however, scarce any fellow-feeling with the misery and distress which he suffers. He is mortified upon both accounts.[107]

As death was the price of crime, so mortification was the price of poverty. To be thrust outside the sympathy of a society of spectators by the spectacle of one's own destitution was to suffer the peculiarly social death of an internal exile or excommunicant. Yet it was just this "dread of death" – "the great poison to the happiness, but the great restraint upon the injustice of mankind" – that Smith believed protected, regulated, and advanced society.[108] Because nothing was so mortifying as being forced to expose one's afflictions to an unsympathetic public, men devoted themselves to "the pursuit of wealth, of power, and preeminence." As a goad to industry, material comfort hardly compared to "this regard to the sentiments of mankind," this overriding compulsion to become or to remain "the object of attention and approbation."[109] *The Theory of Moral Sentiments* thus offered a distinctively social motive for the wealth of nations; one became a Public Man out of horror of one's own isolation.

Still, it was not Smith's precocious social psychology that set him apart or against the individualism and materialism of Hobbes and Mandeville. On the contrary, Smith's account of the inadequacies of the sympathetic imagination and of the corresponding fears of indifference and mortification suggest his strong affinities with the Hobbesian tradition, affinities he shared, in more or less subterranean fashion, with many of his contemporaries.[110] Just as surely as the specter of social and economic death haunted Smith's moral philosophy, so it remained a felt presence in the plays of George Lillo, the novels of Daniel Defoe, and the "progresses" of William Hogarth. In all of these works, the niggardliness of nature found its counterpart in the niggardliness of nurture; theirs was a drama in which bankruptcy and ostracism waited patiently in the wings. Yet of all these men, it was Smith alone who forged out of these sundry impressions a theory of society founded on the frailty rather than the force of sympathy.

The Theory of Moral Sentiments sought to portray individuals as driven by their need for that minimal measure of attention on which sympathy and its corollary, approbation, were founded. The convergence of these needs transformed attention itself into a limited commodity for which isolated individuals competed.[111] Honor in this context, as in that of Restoration comedy, amounted to a bottomless line of credit, a claim or protection against the contingencies of the social marketplace where reputations fluctuated like so much stock.[112] Hence, kings remained the proper subjects of tragedy not because of their monopoly of virtue or passion but because "of the easy price at which they may acquire the public admiration." In this instance as in earlier ones, the language is Smith's, but it could as well have been Hobbes's.[113]

This is not to say that Adam Smith was an unreconstructed Hobbesian. He was not. But to the extent that he openly differed with Hobbes, it was to propose, or at least to imply, a view of the self far more theatrical than any Hobbes might have imagined and, by extension, far more subversive than any the sentimentalist philosophers may have suspected. Hobbes, it should be recalled, had borrowed from the idiom of the theater to frame solutions to the problem of political and commercial representation in a contractual society, where impersonality and impersonation threatened older forms of authority and exchange. Smith, too, looked to the theater for a vocabulary adequate to the market spectacle of sympathy and therefore sprinkled his text with allusions to acts, parts, spectators, applause, and censure. But the effect of these references was, if anything, to obscure still further the content and boundaries of the self Smith placed at the center of his theater of moral sentiments. As with Shaftesbury and Addison before him, Smith's attachment to the "impartial spectator" raised the same Protean confusions as Hobbes's embrace of the "artificial person" of the player a century earlier. The self thus constituted – whether spectator or actor – seemed always in danger of slipping away.

Never was the Smithian "self" more elusive, ironically, than in Smith's rejoinder to the Hobbesian and Mandevillian argument that all sympathy was reducible to self-love. Smith insisted that sympathy was *not* a case of putting oneself in another's situation and imagining what one would feel under similar circumstances; "though sympathy is very properly said to arise from an imaginary change of situations with the person principally concerned, yet this imaginary change is not supposed to happen to me in my own person and character, but in that of the person with whom I sympathize."

> When I condole with you for the loss of your only son, in order
> to enter into your grief I do not consider what I, a person of such
> a character and profession should suffer, if I had a son, and if that

son was unfortunately to die: but I consider what I should suffer if I was really you, and I not only change circumstances with you, but I change persons and characters.[114]

In other words, the situation into which the spectator's sympathy imaginatively projected him included the very *self* of the sufferer into whose sentiments he was attempting to enter. Sympathy thus required the spectator to impersonate the sufferer within the theater of his own mind. To be a spectator in this sense was to be an actor, and to be an actor in this sense was to risk the loss of the self whose sympathy was at stake.

Such trials, however, were infinitely more bearable in Smith's view than those undergone by the sufferer in his endless quest for the relief that only sympathy could bring. Here, Smith argued, mankind's "dull insensibility to the afflictions of others" compelled the sufferer to take the part of his spectators toward himself, since it was only by such measures that the sufferer could discover at what level he needed to cast the expression of his own feelings to win their sympathy. Though such sympathy offered him "his sole consolation," the sufferer could "only hope to obtain this by lowering his passion to that pitch" which his spectators found tolerable. He had to "flatten," in Smith's words, "the sharpness of its natural tone, in order to reduce it to harmony and concord with the emotions" of those about him.[115] Fearing the exhibitionist impression that a direct appeal to his spectators might produce, the sufferer turned instead to a more deeply theatrical and collusive set of relations with his audience. For even as he took their place in his mind, he ignored their existence in his "acts." Their presence obliged him, in effect, to pretend their absence, to appropriate as his own "fourth wall" the barrier of their natural indifference to his plight. His self-command was the mirror and measure of their "dull insensibility" – an odd relation, to be sure, but the only one, Smith implied, through which the supply and demand for sympathy and approbation could enter into equilibrium.[116]

The particular expressive conventions through which this sympathetic equilibrium was achieved at any given time constituted Smith's definition of moral and aesthetic propriety. Even though the discipline required to conform to those conventions divided and doubled the selves of both sufferers and spectators in an almost infinite regress of reflection and representation, it nonetheless ordered and regulated the larger social drama.[117] Out of the "exchange of fantasies" within and between actors and spectators came the exchange of sympathy, and out of the exchange of sympathy sprang the whole complex pattern of material and social exchange that created civilizations. Societies were founded on a dramaturgical rather than a categorical imperative. "We do not originally approve or condemn particular actions," Smith wrote, "because, upon examination, they appear to be agreeable or inconsistent with a certain general rule. The general rule, on the contrary, is formed, by finding from experience, that all actions of a certain kind, or circumstanced in a certain manner, are approved of or disapproved of." Roles, not rules, socialized mankind.[118]

Smith's understanding of the way in which man internalized the values of his society was not entirely behavioral or other-directed, to be sure. Looking back, perhaps, to Butler's notion of conscience, Shaftesbury's method of soliloquy, and Addison's image of the "indifferent spectator," Smith devised his own theory of internalization in the form of an "impartial spectator," a hypothetical third party generated out of the habit of sympathetic identification and residing within the breast of each man. It was this "great arbiter of his conduct," Smith held, that impelled man not just to seek praise but to be, in act and thought, praiseworthy.[119] Even here, however, Smith conceded that "the abstract and ideal spectator of our sentiments and conduct, requires often to be awakened and put in mind of his duty, by the presence of the real spectator: and it is always from that spectator, from whom we can expect the least sympathy and indulgence, that we are likely to learn the most complete lesson of self-command."[120] For all his faith in the workings of sympathy, Smith could never long forbear from returning to the hard facts of its limited supply and its limitless demand.

We can see now how *The Theory of Moral Sentiments* foreshadowed the functionalist and materialist approach to eighteenth-century society that Smith would take up in *The Wealth of Nations,* though it is perhaps more helpful to think of the *Theory*'s operative principle as an "invisible eye" rather than an "invisible hand."[121] The resemblance between the two works is worth noting if only because Smith himself took such pains to distinguish the propriety of a civilization founded on sympathy from that of a purely commercial society. The latter, he speculated, might "subsist among different men, as among different merchants, from a sense of its utility, without any mutual love or affection; and though no man in it should owe any obligation, or be bound in gratitude to any other, it may still be upheld by a mercenary exchange of good offices according to an agreed valuation." But, he added, "the prevalence of injustice" would eventually destroy such an enterprise, since there was nothing beyond utility to hold it together.[122]

Yet how different, finally, was this dismal prospect from the bleak and uncertain future toward which Smith's anxious sufferers looked? What did injustice or inequity mean for them if not the very deficiency of sympathy that drove them to scramble for the attention and applause of indifferent and disinterested spectators, while at the same time dissembling over the depth of their need? What was sympathy in this context but an ultimate commodity: a universal equivalent into which all other goods could be converted? And what was the self in this context but a speculative fiction of joint manufacture: a venture, a text, a performance in which all spectators, investors, and consumers were invited, albeit obliquely, to subscribe? What indeed was Smith's theater of moral sentiments but a placeless market in which the peculiarly tacit conventions of dramatic realism were called on to conceal the character of the negotiation from the parties themselves?

Insofar as *The Theory of Moral Sentiments* can be said to raise these questions, it did not raise them for the eighteenth-century reader. Of course the work did not exactly open itself to questions of this or any kind. The title itself signaled Smith's determination to offer a systematic scheme of explanation in contrast to the more discursive essays and inquiries of the "sentimentalist" tradition. Smith still shared with Shaftesbury and the editors of *The Spectator* a modest yet assured authorial voice. But even more important, he made it a point to share that modest confidence with his readers. Like the ideal sufferer of his theory, Smith used the editorial "we" throughout the work to invoke the presumptive authority of common experience, thereby denying or, again, dissembling the emotional isolation that lay at the heart of his system. "Even the superficial and careless Reader," an early reviewer noted, "will be pleased with his agreeable manner of illustrating his argument, by the frequent appeals to fact and experience"; Smith's language, Edmund Burke exclaimed, was "rather painting than writing."[123] The book was a success because, as one scholar remarked, "Adam Smith was probably more successful than most philosophers of his time in giving it the image it hoped to receive."[124] That the image was touched with shadows of envy, emulation, and indifference as well as the lights of commiseration, love, and affection only added to its credibility. Though Smith's writings never approached the transatlantic popularity of *The Spectator* in his own century, they were nonetheless widely read and respected.[125] Even the scrupulous John Adams did not hesitate to appropriate (as his own) long passages from *The Theory of Moral Sentiments* for his *Discourses on Davila* (1791). This was fellow-feeling of a special kind.[126]

Taken together, the "spectatorial" writers of the early eighteenth century may well have acquired their popularity *because* of the contradictions and paradoxes they so gracefully embodied rather than in spite of them.[127] Like its philosophical forerunners, *The Theory of Moral Sentiments* marked out a separate social and psychological realm where the cultivation and direction of man's moral and affective life was subject to its own laws and limits. At the same time, Smith insinuated within this separate world an economy of attention and affection that bore an uncanny, if implicit, resemblance to the market imperatives from which it presumably stood apart. If the histrionic calculus of the *Theory* seemed to deal in anxieties foreign to the hedonistic calculus of the *Wealth of Nations,* the two works nevertheless assumed a common performance principle at work in history: a common presupposition about people's need to reckon returns in their relation with others. But where *The Wealth of Nations* confined this reckoning to the interests of a given self, *The Theory of Moral Sentiments* applied its calculus to the conditions and conventions by which any self was given; that is, to the kinds of imaginative enactments and exchanges that engendered and sustained a credible or estimable social self in the marketplace of human sympathy. Without this concept of a figured and figurable self, Smith would most likely have been less drawn than he was to the image of the spectator, indeed, to the whole subversive dialectic of the theatrical metaphor. Yet without that metaphor, our own sense of the work's contradictions would be far less pronounced than it is, for it was a feature of Smith's and his fellow sentimentalists' work that it plunged more deeply into the theatricality it reviled with every effort to break free.

Nowhere was this predicament more poignant than in the fate of the moral sentiments Smith had so earnestly extracted from the catchpenny world of the primary senses. Part of that earnestness was evidenced in his repudiation of "those whining and melancholy moralists" who bade their readers work up "an artificial commiseration" for the afflictions of mankind in general. This was not true affect, Smith protested, but affectation, not true sentiment, but sentimentality, and he condemned the effects as "hypocritical."[128] Yet it was just this sentiment of sentiment, this view of feeling as an object, good, or property in itself, that bourgeois popular culture embraced in the late eighteenth and nineteenth centuries and in which Smith himself may be said to have figured, even if it was against his will. In drama, in painting, in prints, in sculpture, and in romance, what Ann Douglas has called "the commercialization of the inner life" went on apace during this epoch.

> Sentimentalism [as Douglas defines it] is a cluster of ostensibly private feelings which always attain public and conspicuous expression. Privacy functions in the rituals of sentimentalism only for the sake of titillation, as a convention to be violated. Involved as it is with the exhibition and commercialization of the self, sentimentalism cannot exist without an audience.[129]

Given the overriding masculinist and Stoical cast of his thought, Smith would surely have recoiled at the suggestion that his own work might have abetted the sentimentalist ethos that flourished after his death. Nevertheless, the constituents of sentimentalism – its interplay of privacy and publicity, its voyeurism, its sense of sympathy as an article of trade – were all present in the moral philosophy of the spectatorial writers, and they were present in the philosophy because they were also present in the culture whose contradictions philosophy was trying to resolve.

It is worth recalling here that the political and religious settlement of postrevolutionary Britain had restored and stabilized the nation's social order but that it had done so within forms and according to terms that had converted rank itself to a negotiable asset. In accordance with this widespread awareness of social bargaining, public and private life assumed an extraordinarily theatrical style as classes, factions, and individuals maneuvered for position on a cultural terrain that years of violent upheaval and slow economic change had steadily defamiliarized. Popular consciousness was adapting, to recur to Pocock's phrase, "to a world of moving objects" and, we might add, to an increasingly detached and mobile population.

Among the age's countless itinerants were the writers and thinkers of the Scottish Enlightenment, provincial emigrés to the metropolis who took it upon themselves to refamiliarize their adopted landscape by bringing its boisterous and stylized social relations within the comforting compass of Common Sense. And with the notable exception of David Hume, they rose enthusiastically to their task: purifying the meanings that the market had so promiscuously mixed together by assigning them, in effect, to the respective domains of political economy and moral aestheticism. By thus dividing the world into the discrete and opposed spheres of utility and propriety – market and culture – economists and belletrists succeeded in suppressing a more direct popular recognition of the solvent and subversive dynamic of *market culture,* the same dynamic or dialectic that the theatrical perspective had for two centuries captured and reproduced. But that suppression, as the example of both the Puritans and Common Sense writers suggests, was neither complete nor permanent. A market or theater thus domesticated was, more often than not, a market or theater whose contradictions had merely been brought home to roost.

To the extent that the paradoxical aspects of market relations found explicit formal expression during the eighteenth century, however, it was not in the epoch's increasingly moralistic and sentimental melodrama but rather in an entirely new cultural form: the novel. Urbanism, consumerism, and censorship had all contributed to the formation of a reading public far broader and potentially far more profitable than the audiences attending the metropolitan and provincial theaters, and authors were quick to respond to this shift in fortunes. Henry Fielding was only one of several writers to make the leap from plays to novels, a leap made all the easier by the hazy lines that separated one genre from another. Yet the ease of movement between genres did not remove the need to legitimate one's final choice of expressive form. Since novels themselves had emerged out of what Lennard Davis has called the "undifferentiated matrix" of journalism, history, and exotic tale telling, they were almost always accompanied and, Davis argues, distinguished by elaborate framing devices (similar in spirit to the Elizabethan induction) that both asserted and subverted the authenticity of their narratives, and their narrators.[130] "The world is so taken up of late with novels and romances," Daniel Defoe wrote in his anonymous preface to *Moll Flanders* (1722), "that it will be hard for a private history to be taken for genuine, where the names and other circumstances of the person are concealed, and, on this account we must be content to leave the reader to pass his own opinion upon the ensuing sheets, and take it just as he pleases."[131] *Caveat emptor,* the anonymous author seemed to be saying, in a distant echo of the Scrivener of Jonson's *Bartholomew Fair.*

The resemblance of Defoe's novel to Jonson's play was at once closer and more remote than that – closer in the sense that the world or underworld projected within *Moll Flanders* resembled a pure market setting in which everyone was engaged in the sale and appropriation of commodities, including themselves; more remote in the sense that Defoe's market was placeless and deritualized, bereft of any redemptive ceremony or conversion whose authenticity might withstand the encompassing cynicism of London's grim and endless Feast of Fools.[132]

Unlike Shaftesbury, who had insisted that the "new dress" of print had left his relation to the reader unchanged, Defoe made imposture the central theme of his novel, thereby implicating his own literary persona with those of his characters and both, in turn, with the wary and diffident reader. For just as Defoe had Moll, his pseudonymous protagonist, impersonate all classes and sexes in her effort to market the commodity of her self, so Defoe (anonymously) admitted to clothing *his* commodity, Moll's alleged confession, in a "dress fit to be seen," leaving his reader to pass his opinion "upon the ensuing sheets." Though Defoe's novels were devoid of sentimentality, they too relied on the simultaneous invention and violation of conventions of privacy. Other, more sentimentalist writers would later resort to Shaftesbury's epistolary strategy to win a sympathy that Defoe seemed happy to leave on guard. But whatever the strategy at issue, the novel remained for the eighteenth-century reader one of the few cultural forms in which the spectacle of the market was formally, as well as substantively, explored. Perhaps this was because the novel's dubious status as a "factual fiction" reproduced the peculiarly ambiguous or transitional position, between ritual and entertainment, that the Elizabethan and Jacobean drama had once occupied. Once again a liminoid genre was enacting the liminal experience of the boundaryless market.[133]

In this context, it is interesting to note how quickly Adam Smith's "whining and melancholy moralists" shifted the burden of their literary censure from the drama to the novel – so quickly, in fact, that Defoe found himself drawing on earlier defenses of the stage to justify his rogue's narrative.[134] Of course the attack on the theater had not halted with the Restoration. Jeremy Collier's *Short View of the Immorality and Profaneness of the English Stage* was only one of some thirty forays against the theater between 1698 and 1747.[135] But the last major offensive of this kind came not from Britain, as it turned out, but from France, and it came from one of the most celebrated puritans *and* sentimentalists of his age: Jean-Jacques Rousseau.

Acting, Rousseau declared in his famous *Lettre à M. D'Alembert* (1758), was a market phenomenon, a "traffic of oneself," a travesty of preaching and oratory where "the man and the role" were the same. "What is the talent of the actor?" he asked.

> It is the art of counterfeiting himself, of putting on another character than his own, of appearing different than he is, of becoming passionate in cold blood, of saying what he does not think as naturally as if he really did think it and, finally, of forgetting his own place by dint of taking another's.[136]

It is known that Rousseau had read Book X (and, one suspects, Book III) of Plato's *Republic* in preparation for his "letter," but his words rang with the intonations of Stephen Gosson and William Prynne. Plato's antipathy toward the Protean in life, his fear that the actor would become irrevocably the evil he personated replicated themselves in Rousseau's text as they had in the Puritan tracts.[137] But where Plato had argued that the sympathy stirred up by the tragic stage would unleash similarly "womanish" sentiments in real life, Rousseau held that it hardened the hearts of spectators toward the misfortunes of others. Where Plato had wished, above all, to avoid the impersonation of corruption, Rousseau saw corruption inherent in the very act of impersonation. Where Plato's objections sprang largely from his view of theater as a gratuitous mimetic form thrice removed from reality, Rousseau's antagonism grew out of his view of acting as a practice already deeply and disturbingly implicated in reality.

Rousseau need not have consulted Prynne's *Histrio-Mastix*, however, for he had to go no farther than John Witherspoon's *Serious Enquiry into the Nature and Effects of the Stage*, published the year before. Witherspoon, then a Presbyterian minister at Beith, Scotland, had inveighed against the stage as inconsistent with the Christian principle of "self-denial and mortification." Like Rousseau, he saw the stage as an "unprofitable consumption of time," a dangerous stimulus to the passions, an incitement to the vanity of women, and an institution which by familiarity bred indifference to "the most terrible objects" of existence.[138] And like Rousseau, he conjured up a picture of the actor as a mobile, characterless social being. "What then is the life of a player?" Witherspoon asked in a question as rhetorical as Rousseau's.

> It is wholly spent in endeavouring to express the language and exhibit a perfect picture of the passions of vidious men. . . . How strange a character does it make for one to live, in a manner, perpetually in a mask, to be much oftener in a personated than in a real character. And yet this is the case with all players.[139]

Compared with Witherspoon's *Enquiry*, Rousseau's "letter" seems mild: Rousseau wanted to purge the theater of its "realism" in order to offer it, in the form of a festival, as a salve to those who craved a "sweeter" station; the fundamentally private pleasures of the new theater would no longer compete with the conviviality of the social circles Rousseau saw being supplanted and destroyed by such periodicals as *The Spectator*.[140] Witherspoon, on the other hand, regarded all recreation as an "intermission of duty" – like sleep, a sign of man's weakness.[141]

By its juxtaposition with Rousseau's strictures against the stage, Witherspoon's tract reveals the remarkable tenacity of the Puritan response to theatricality. The numerous ways in which theatricalism and the *theatrum mundi* had resurfaced in eighteenth-century Britain, within the context of a widening sphere of market activity, seemed to have passed Witherspoon by, or perhaps to have strengthened his resolution to resist; his tract against the stage showed even less imagination, if that was possible, than Prynne's. What makes Witherspoon significant for our purposes, however, is not simply the fact that Americans took his attack on the stage, and not Rousseau's, as their model. It is that with his acceptance of the presidency of Princeton in 1768, Witherspoon became the single most influential disseminator of Common Sense philosophy in the colonies, a philosophy that set the conditions for most moral and literary discourse in the first half of the nineteenth century as well.[142] Witherspoon's passage to America recapitulated John Winthrop's journey nearly a century and a half before, for Common Sense philosophy reproduced the Puritan, or more precisely the Ramist, segregation and subordination of the persuasive and performative to the logical dimensions of discourse.[143] However much Jonathan Edwards may have worked to oppose this antirhetorical bias of Puritanism, he died before he could assume the presidency of Princeton; Witherspoon lived to instruct many of the nation's first-generation elite there.

Puritanism thus prepared the ground for the ideological harvest that Common Sense moralists eventually reaped in the northern colonies. Yet Common Sense would never have acquired the hegemony it enjoyed throughout the colonies – and states – had social and economic conditions existed to challenge its claims regarding the transparency and reciprocity of market exchange. To be sure, "free" markets (and theaters) did develop in the colonies before 1750, but even after the Revolution they preserved much of their occasional and local character, in some areas long into the nineteenth century.[144] Despite the inroads made by long-distance trade and commerical agriculture along the seaboard and inland frontiers, the colonial economies remained tied, by and large, to a household mode of production – family or slave. Only in the aftermath of the Revolution and of *its* social, political, and religious settlement did Americans begin to take notice, affirmative and critical, of an expansive and placeless market process.[145]

It was no coincidence that, at the moment Americans began to respond to the prospect of a "free" market, that response found voice in new secular forms of popular literature and entertainment. Much as American market activity had lagged behind British initiatives by as much as a century, so the forms of its documentary culture imitated British models introduced a hundred years before. The commercialization of leisure, which J. H. Plumb dates to the 1720s and 1730s in Britain, did not truly take hold in America before the 1820s, 1830s, and after. Melodrama, magazines, satire, romances, and novels were largely products of the early nineteenth century, though products marked as much by their dialogue with (and against) their British ancestors as by their interest in American themes. Even the *Autobiography* of Benjamin Franklin fell into this mold, the self-deprecating theatricality of its central persona owing much, as Franklin himself acknowledged, to the literary examples of Shaftesbury, Defoe, Addison, and Steele.[146] Begun in 1771 but not published till 1818, the *Autobiography* presented a version of common sense far more liberal and whimsical than that which was then tightening its philosophical grip on American pulpits, podiums, and presses.

Conceived in the womb of Scottish Presbyterianism and nurtured in the bosom of American Presbyterianism, Common Sense philosophy offered an authoritative denial of the market's contradictions, indeed of all contradictions other than those concealed within the heart of the unregenerate sinner. Denial was, in a sense, the classic Common Sense response to the suggestion that the self and its relations might not be or, under certain circumstances, could not be as they were represented to be; denial was the form that its methodological nominalism took and the form that its ethical prescriptions embraced. Common Sense was thus as much a discipline as a discourse, a discipline that bound Winthrop and Witherspoon together despite the generations that separated them.

One need not invoke the shade of Max Weber to see in this

theological and philosophical continuity a testament to the vigor of the Protestant ethic, though it is equally possible to see that ethic, in turn, as an instance of a much older and deeper "antitheatrical prejudice," an abiding fear of all change and instability of form.[147] Yet however universal such fears may be, they were mobilized and channeled in unprecedented ways in the English-speaking world of the sixteenth, seventeenth, and eighteenth centuries. In this study, I have argued that the immediate occasion of that mobilization was the threat posed to Anglo-American society and culture by the peculiarly boundless features of the "free" market.

Some historians have seen the Protestant ethic, including its antitheatrical prejudice, as the disciplinary force at work within the "spirit of capitalism." But if it was a worldly asceticism that lay at the heart of early industrial capitalism, then it was a heart prepared, ironically, *against* the opportunities and importunities of a placeless market. Understood in this way, antitheatrical asceticism appears to have been not simply an economic strategy for ordering a class of workers set in motion *by* the market but a cultural strategy for ordering a mass of meanings set in motion *within* the market. Given such a highly symbolic theater of conflict, the actor was a logical, if unfortunate, target for the ambivalences and anxieties that surrounded the emergence of commercial relations in Britain and America. There were more stages in the development of capitalism, it seems, than we have been prepared to acknowledge.

Epilogue: Confidence and culture

When the shades of night gather around our floating hotel, we all flock to the spacious public saloon, some eighty feet long, tastily furnished, well lighted with blazing fires, &c., &c. Newspapers, books and religious tracts are scattered round by some friendly passengers, for the mutual benefit of the whole. Some read, some talk, some sit in perfect silence, apparently buried deep in thought, while others amuse themselves with a game of chance.

> Philo Tower, *Slavery Unmasked, Being a Truthful Narrative of a Three Years' Residence and Journeying in Eleven Southern States* (1856)

Stools, settees, sofas, divans, ottomans; occupying them are clusters of men, old and young, wise and simple; in their hands are cards spotted with diamonds, spades, clubs, hearts; the favorite games are whist, cribbage, and brag. Lounging in armchairs or sauntering among the marble-topped tables, amused with the scene, are the comparatively few, who, instead of having their hands in the games, for the most part keep their hands in their pockets. These may be the philosophers.

> Herman Melville, *The Confidence-Man: His Masquerade* (1857)

IN 1857, EXACTLY A CENTURY after John Witherspoon's indignant attack on the perils of the theater, Herman Melville published what was to be the most theatrical of his novels – also his last. At the very height of Victorian ideological complacency, a moment for which Witherspoon and other Common Sense writers had long prepared, Melville threw out his final, desperate challenge to the smug assurances of his age. The result was a novel more deeply and bleakly skeptical than anything he had theretofore written. Indeed, few novels before or since have gone farther than *The Confidence-Man* in questioning man's consistency, transparency, individuality, and mutuality. But though the novel stood stubbornly apart from all contemporary works in the depth and breadth of its skepticism, Melville achieved his

195

effects by seeming to adopt, formally and thematically, the principles by which Adam Smith and his American disciples had warranted the bourgeois world to be knowable, reliable, and workable, namely, the transactional or "performance" principles of commercial capitalism. Within the novel, nothing is allowed to escape their rule; every character, every relation, and every form of discourse eventually succumbs to the moral and epistemological ambiguities of a permanent theater and a placeless market. Theatricality and commerciality are so deeply interwoven as to confer on all forms of exchange – real and fictive – a problematic and deeply disquieting character. Accordingly, Melville subtitled his novel *His Masquerade*.

Appropriately, the story is set along that peculiar social and cultural margin of antebellum America traced out by the maunderings of the Mississippi River. Like so much else in the novel, this marginality and aimlessness seem deliberate, for in keeping with the classical dramatic unities, Melville confines the whole of his narrative's action to the span of a single day (April Fools' Day) and the space of a single ship (the steamboat *Fidèle*) as it makes its slow and stately pilgrimage to New Orleans. The ship and the waters it navigates constitute for Melville, as for his contemporaries, a picturesque extraterritorial zone – a world apart – a liminal locale where the conventional reciprocities of life have been momentarily suspended in favor of a feverish process of negotiation.[1] A quarter of a century later, Mark Twain would recast this same literary journey as an engaging and ultimately affirmative rite of passage, but for Melville in 1857, the odyssey served as a far more sinister synecdoche: not a part *of* the whole but rather a part *for* the whole, a passage or metamorphosis that no rite could ever complete. The *Fidèle* is a floating liberty, an amoral suburb beyond the jurisdiction of local authorities, beyond the pale of respectable society, and, not least of all, beyond the reach of those "psychological" novelists for whom Melville had so much contempt.

Some seven years before the publication of *The Confidence-Man*, Ralph Waldo Emerson had paid a visit to these same environs. There, at Cairo, Illinois, he came upon an old steamboat filled with "amiable gentlemen who professed to be entire strangers to each other" and who beckoned to him to try his hand at cards.[2] In similar fashion, Melville makes the *Fidèle* a "ship of fools," a vessel "always full of strangers" who exchange themselves at every stop "with strangers more strange." These strangers are, in turn, the victims and victimizers of the novel's central character, the confidence man or "Cosmopolitan," as Melville calls him, a stranger "in the extremest sense of the word." The latter's arrival is first announced in a warning circular posted outside the captain's office, around which crowds gather "as if it had been a theatre bill." But the crowds themselves are preoccupied.

> Merchants on 'change seem the passengers that buzz on her decks, while from quarters unseen, comes a murmur as of bees in the comb. Fine promenades, domed saloons, long galleries, sunny balconies, confidential passages, bridal chambers, staterooms plenty as pigeon-holes, and out-of-the-way retreats like the secret drawers in an escritoire, present like facilities for publicity or privacy. Auctioneer or coiner, with equal ease, might somewhere drive his trade.[3]

Again and again Melville joins the imagery of stage and marketplace to create a fictive world where all common-sense assumptions founder on the snags and shallows of his characters' misrepresentations. The effect is one of deep "ontological mistrust."[4]

With its labyrinthine corridors and its "shop-like windowed spaces," the design of Melville's "deadal boat" hints at the complexity of his design in the novel. His plot, for example, wanders in a manner that mimics the calculated aimlessness of its central character, the confidence man. Episodes do not build on one another so much as they refer to one another, an allusiveness that only adds to the elusiveness of the narrative as a whole. Most of the chapters are keyed to the successive guises of the confidence man and, as such, offer themselves up as an elaborate literary acrostic that dares the reader to decode it. But is it some kind of hermetical wisdom that lies concealed therein or merely that "which may pass for whatever it may prove to be worth" to "those to whom it may prove worth considering"?[5] *Caveat emptor*. Nothing on the steamer can be taken at face value, yet all that Melville presents to view are faces, or rather masks: biblical masks, Miltonic masks, even Hindu masks. "Does all the world act?" the confidence man asks of one of his deck companions at one point. "Am *I*, for instance, an actor? Is my reverend friend here, too, a performer?" "Yes," the companion replies in a Shakespearean vein, "don't you both perform acts? To do, is to act; so all doers are actors."[6] At this, the confidence man chides his companion for trifling with him, but it is of course not the companion alone who trifles; the confidence man has already chosen his "reverend friend" as his next victim. The play, or rather the negotiation, goes on.

Like the bemused passengers aboard the *Fidèle*, the reader soon learns to distrust all voices within the novel. Even the genial authorial voice that periodically interrupts the narrative to philosophize on fiction and reality speaks in a deliberately veiled and contradictory manner.[7] Its studied detachment echoes the casual tone of the confidence man and thereby strengthens the reader's suspicion toward the work as a whole. Because the novel's many hints and clues lead everywhere and nowhere, its psychological interior remains as opaque to the reader as the characters do to one another. In true Jonsonian fashion, Melville mocks the literary contract or indenture between author and reader, taking special aim at the convention of a narrator's omniscience. If there is an Invisible Eye aboard the ship, it is closed in a broad wink. If there is an Invisible Hand, it is doubtless picking the pockets of the passengers and the readers alike. The *Fidèle* is a Barnum's museum of transparent fraud, and like Barnum, Melville guilefully propels his narrative forward along the same currents of diffidence and disbelief that his central character so insistently condemns.[8]

To bring off this trick, Melville borrows alternately from the Socratic and the tall-tale traditions of discourse, but only to subordinate both forms of dialogue to one even more ancient: the bargain. As the passengers negligently circle one another in arcs of apparent indifference, Melville sketches their movements in a style that is suitably neutral and cryptic. By means of intricate qualifying phrases and countless double-negative formulations, the narrator's insidiously dialectical manner eventually converts all his declarative statements to their opposites, where it does not render them altogether senseless. Indeed, Melville so encumbers his prose with various ambiguous codicils and self-canceling clauses that, from a contractualist point of view, the narrative seems written entirely in small print. The reader is both taken in and taken aback.

Here, Melville carefully fits the contradictions of his novel's form to those of its content, allowing each aspect of the work to pun or play on the other.[9] When, for example, the Cosmopolitan asks his "boon companion," Charlie Noble (Melville's caricature of Thoreau), for a loan, Charlie immediately declines, insisting that loans are "unfriendly accommodations" more appropriate to banks than to companions. "An *unfriendly accommodation?*" the confidence man asks in mock surprise and hurt. "Do these words go together handsomely?" Yes, Charlie replies, for "the emnity lies couched in the friendship, just as the ruin in the relief."[10] Noble's oxymoron captures perfectly the paradox that Melville lodges at the center of the novel's innumerable transactions, including those arising between author and reader. Like the Vice figure of the confidence man, Melville simultaneously invites and denies his audience access to his meanings. The novel abounds with references to the popular events and figures of the day, but these commonplaces undergo a radical defamiliarization in Melville's hands. Nothing is what it seems in the placeless market and theater of the *Fidèle.*

In this respect *The Confidence-Man* stands as one of the most extraordinary contributions to that long, imaginative tradition of reflection on the "free" market with which this study has been occupied. What makes it even more striking are the clear indications that Melville appropriated and telescoped this tradition within the novel itself. There is thus nothing accidental about his reference to the *Fidèle* as a ship of fools, for the novel repeatedly evokes the themes of the late medieval and early modern literature of estates and characters – that sardonic and progressively sociological canon of complaint with which this inquiry began. Virtually every rank and type of midcentury American society is brought aboard the *Fidèle* to have its respective defects and deceits methodically exposed. Chaucer's pilgrims mingle with Awdeley's rogues, Shakespeare's knaves, Jonson's tricksters, Bulwer's changelings, and Bunyan's fairgoers. These are the cunning men, whipjacks, and fraters of the nineteenth century.

Natives of all sorts, and foreigners; men of business and men of pleasure; parlor-men and back-woodsmen; farm-hunters and fame-hunters; heiress-hunters, gold-hunters, buffalo-hunters, bee-hunters, happiness-hunters, truth-hunters, and still keener hunters after all these hunters. Fine ladies in slippers and moccasined squaws; Northern speculators and Eastern philosophers; English, Irish, German, Scotch, Danes; Santa Fe traders in striped blankets, and Broadway bucks in cravats of cloth of gold; fine-looking Kentucky boatmen and Japanese-looking Mississippi cotton-planters; Quakers in full drab, and United States soldiers in full regimentals; slaves, black, mulatto, quadroon; modish young Spanish Creoles, and old-fashioned French Jews; Mormons and Papists; Dives and Lazarus; jesters and mourners, teetotalers and convivialists, deacons and blacklegs; hard-shell Baptists and clay-eaters; grinning negroes and Sioux chiefs solemn as high-priests. In short, a piebald parliament, an Anarcharsis Cloots congress of all kinds of that multiform pilgrim species, man.[11]

Regarded in the light of this motley taxonomy of types, the novel's episodic and ambiguous form seems of a piece with the carnivalesque character of its content. *The Confidence-Man* resembles nothing so much as a visit to Bartholomew Fair.

Yet if the world of the *Fidèle* is a carnival, it is a curiously bodiless and bloodless affair. None of the earthy or bawdy elements that Bakhtin defines as the essence of the carnivalesque appear in the novel. The narrative teems with characters but not with passions. Far from overflowing its bounds, sentiment shrinks to fill the narrower dimensions of private obsession. But even these motives are left for the reader to infer, since the novel is as spare in its emotional description as it is in its physical description. In fact, if there is any underlying need or impulse at work in the story, it is the characters' overriding compulsion to know, to be sure, to be, in short, confident. Few incidents in Melville's fiction are more pregnant with evil than the arrival of the Cosmopolitan – precisely midway through the novel – his jovial slap on the back of one of the passengers, and his greeting in a voice "sweet as a seraph's: 'A penny for your thoughts, my fine fellow.' "[12]

For Melville, confidence, credibility, and credit are not the unconditional bases for social transactions, as evangelical faith and political economy would have it, but rather the unattainable objects of those transactions, for it is those same transactions, he implies, that place the ideal of mutual transparency farther out of reach. Melville's literary carnival adamantly refuses either to reveal or to redeem the world it turns upside down. Instead, it leaves its characters and its readers where it finds them, in limbo – betwixt and between. In this, the novel is far removed from the satirical tradition of ecclesiastical complaint and festive mockery. The laughter aboard the *Fidèle* is neither festive nor remissive.

Thus Janus-like, *The Confidence-Man* points in two directions at once: backward, toward an ancient tradition of corrective criticism, and at the same time forward, toward the modernist's stance of indeterminacy. The novel deploys the ambiguities and contradictions of market exchange to deconstruct Common Sense, the conventional novel, and, in the end, Melville's own relation to his reader. Words are the current coin of this relation (indeed, of all relations within the narrative), and like coin they are so frequently exchanged against one another as to lose any stable connection with reality or, more precisely, with an operative order of signification. The characters and the reader are thus left the hapless victims of their own circulating medium. "In its echoes and cross-references, its mutations and repetitions," Waichee Dimock has written, the "lexical universe [of *The Confidence-Man*] constitutes an oddly uncommunicative world." As she puts it, "We see a limited stock of words in close circulation, miraculously perpetrating their lives, passing from one character to another without much regard to who these characters really are. Words like 'confidence,' 'nature,' 'invention,' and 'original genius' trace a lineage more enduring and more important to the book than the life of any single character, with the possible exception of the confidence man." But he too, she adds, is "merely a figure of words."[13]

Money, then, is more than a figure *of* speech for Melville; it is a figure *for* speech as well. Conversely, Melville treats the Protean language of *The Confidence-Man* as a transfiguration of money, a literary expression of the abstract power of commensurability embodied in coin. Such generic metaphorical power, he appears to suggest, invites Americans to treat money as "the sole motive to pains and hazards, deception and deviltry," even in instances where motives would seem inappropriate or irrelevant attributions. Thus, Melville has one of the *Fidèle's* passengers confess that he mistrusts nature because she once "embezzled" ten-thousand dollars worth of "natural scenery" through flood damage.[14] The man can understand the unexpected movements of the Mississippi only through what Marx would call the "language of commodities." Money's arithmetical precision gives a sense of order "to the sudden shiftings of the banks" while preserving the element of arbitrariness common to the commercial and natural worlds.[15] But though the price form thereby promises to render both worlds calculable, it does so only by rendering them correspondingly calculating: theatrical, masklike, opaque. As a result, whatever questions of motive the form of money may seem to answer, the *formlessness* of money – its "infinite purposiveness" in Simmel's phrase – only deepens. There are no pennies for nature's thoughts, nor for the market's.

At the heart of the many difficulties that beset *The Confidence-Man* as an intelligible literary work, then, lies the fundamental problematic of a placeless market: the problems of identity, intentionality, accountability, transparency, and reciprocity that the pursuit of commensurability invariably introduces into that universe of particulate human meanings we call culture. In this context, the characteristic forms of theatricality (and of the theatrical perspective) that we have seen accompanying the spread of a "free" market in Anglo-American society can best be understood as a recurrent response, at once accommodative and critical, to the threat and the promise of an embryonic market culture.

By 1857 such culture was, of course, no longer embryonic. Melville knew this, as did his contemporary, Marx. As a matter of fact, it was in 1857 that Marx began the first of his notebooks that would crystallize a decade later as the opening volume of *Capital:* the first systematic study of capitalism to begin by analyzing the mystifying properties of the commodity form. Couched in the familiar terms of contemporary political economy, Marx's message, however radical, won for itself a transatlantic readership. Not so with *The Confidence-Man.* It was Marx's challenge to Adam Smith, not Melville's, that found an audience. The reasons for this are many, but among them we should include Melville's resolute refusal to issue a manifesto, to promise a revelation, or to forecast an apocalypse. Melville explicitly excluded himself from the ranks of those writers, from psychological novelists to political economists, who claimed to penetrate the mysteries of the mind and society. Like the skeptic David Hume before him, Melville revived the epistemological anxieties of the medieval *theatrum mundi* without offering the corresponding consolations of otherworldliness or utopia. Only darkness lay beyond the multiplicity, the liquidity of his many meanings – a "waning light" sustainable, perhaps, only through his narrator's final and equivocal pledge that "something further may follow of this Masquerade."[16]

Not surprisingly, Herman Melville's last novel suffered the same immediate fate as Hume's *Treatise of Human Nature*, falling "dead-born from the press." Though its title page listed Melville as the "Author of 'Piazza Tales,' 'Omoo,' 'Typee,' " only a few hundred readers saw fit to purchase the first edition on the basis of Melville's reputation. And those who did were puzzled. "When we meet with a book written by Herman Melville," one critic wrote, "we take up the work with as much confidence in its worth, as we should feel in the possession of a checque drawn by a well-known capitalist. So much greater is the disappointment," he concluded, "when we find the book does not come up to our mark." Published on April Fool's Day, *The Confidence-Man* gathered dust on the shelves of American bookstores until, a month later, its publisher went bankrupt.[17] As it happened, nothing further did follow of Melville's masquerade – no sequel, indeed no other novel in his lifetime. Yet as to the larger theater that *The Confidence-Man* evoked – the theater of a market society – its curtain has yet to be rung down, even if its history remains, mystifyingly, unwritten.

Notes

PROLOGUE: COMMERCE AND CULTURE

1 Two works that attempt a phenomenology of the market world are those of Georg Simmel, *The Philosophy of Money*, Tom Bottomore and David Frisby, trs. (Boston, 1978), and Alfred Sohn-Rethel, *Intellectual and Manual Labor: A Critique of Epistemology*, Martin Sohn-Rethel, tr. (London, 1978). Simmel's treatise abstracts from history, however, whereas Sohn-Rethel's is only tenuously connected to it. Among authors who consider the relation between economic and literary form are Marc Shell, *The Economy of Literature* (Baltimore, 1978); Shell, *Money, Language, and Thought: Literary and Philosophical Economies from the Medieval to the Modern Era* (Berkeley, 1982); Kurt Heinzelman, *The Economics of the Imagination* (Amherst, Mass., 1980); Lewis Hyde, *The Gift: Imagination and the Erotic Life of Property* (New York, 1983). Insights into market culture are scattered throughout Max Weber, *Economy and Society* (New York, 1968) and Marx's early manuscripts; the brief section in the first volume of *Capital,* Frederick Engels, ed., Samuel Moore and Edward Aveling, trs., 3 vols. (New York, 1967) on the "fetishism of commodities" furnishes one of the theoretical points of departure for the present study, as does the anthropological perspective offered in Michael Taussig, *The Devil and Commodity Fetishism in South America* (Chapel Hill, N.C., 1980).

2 Bernard Barber, "Absolutization of the Market: Some Notes on How We Got from There to Here," in *Markets and Morals,* Gerald Dworkin, Gordon Bermant, and Peter G. Brown, eds. (New York, 1977), 18; see also Cyril Belshaw, *Traditional Exchange and Modern Markets* (Englewood Cliffs, N.J., 1965), 79.

3 One of the earliest anthropological formulations of this neoclassical, or "formalist," approach to exchange is that of Melville J. Herskovitz, *Economic Anthropology* (New York, 1952). For more recent applications, see Samuel L. Popkin, *The Rational Peasant* (Berkeley, 1979); Richard A. Posner, "A Theory of Primitive Society with Special Reference to Law," *Journal of Law and Economics,* 23 (April 1980), 1–54. The "substantivist" critique of this position can be found in *Trade and Market in Early Empires,* Karl Polanyi, Conrad Arensberg, and Harry Pearson, eds. (New York, 1957); *Primitive, Archaic and Modern Economies: Essays of Karl Polanyi,* George Dalton, ed. (Boston, 1968); James C. Scott, *The Moral Economy of the Peasant* (New Haven, Conn., 1976). The debate between formalist and substantivist schools is recapitulated in Edward E. LeClair, Jr., and Harold

Schneider, eds., *Economic Anthropology* (New York, 1968), but see also S. C. Humphreys, "History, Economics, and Anthropology: The Work of Karl Polanyi," *History and Theory*, 8 (1969), 165–212; Douglas C. North, "Markets and Other Allocation Systems in History: The Challenge of Karl Polanyi," *Journal of European Economic History*, 6 (Winter 1977), 703–16; Michael Hechter, "Karl Polanyi's Social Theory: A Critique," *Politics & Society*, 10 (1981), 399–427; J. I. Prattis, "Synthesis, or a New Problematic in Economic Anthropology," *Theory and Society*, 11 (March 1982), 205–29.

4 Joyce Oldham Appleby, *Economic Thought and Ideology in Seventeenth-Century England* (Princeton, N.J., 1978), 93–4; see also G. L. S. Shackle, *Epistemics & Economics: A Critique of Economic Doctrines* (Cambridge, Eng., 1972), 98–104.

5 On the collapse of social, political, and economic "process" into its outcome in the social sciences, see Laurence H. Tribe, "Policy Science: Analysis or Ideology?" *Philosophy & Public Affairs*, 2 (Fall 1972), 66–110.

6 Karl Polanyi, "The Economy as an Instituted Process," in *Trade and Market*, Polanyi, Arensberg, and Pearson, eds., 255.

7 Simmel, *Philosophy of Money*, 477.

8 See, for example, Karl Brunner and Alan H. Meltzer, "The Uses of Money: Money in the Theory of an Exchange Economy," *American Economic Review*, 61 (December 1971), 784–805.

9 Simmel, *Philosophy of Money*, 213.

10 My approach to the structuring of motives (or reasons) in specific social contexts is indebted to Kenneth Burke, *A Grammar of Motives* (1945; reprint Berkeley and Los Angeles, 1969), and to C. Wright Mills, "Situated Actions and Vocabularies of Motive," in *Power, Politics and People*, Irving Louis Horowitz, ed. (New York, 1963), 439–52.

11 See Marshall Sahlins, "The Original Affluent Society," in *Stone Age Economics* (Chicago, 1972), 1–39; Edmund S. Morgan, *American Slavery, American Freedom: The Ordeal of Colonial Virginia* (New York, 1975), ch. 3.

12 See Appleby, *Economic Thought*, passim; Albert O. Hirschman, *The Passions and the Interests: Political Arguments for Capitalism before Its Triumph* (Princeton, N.J., 1977); Ian Watt, *The Rise of the Novel: Studies in Defoe, Richardson and Fielding* (Berkeley and Los Angeles, 1957); Joan Webber, *The Eloquent "I": Style and Self in Seventeenth-Century Prose* (Madison, Wis., 1968); Arnold Weinstein, *Fictions of the Self: 1550–1800* (Princeton, N.J., 1981); Stephen Greenblatt, *Renaissance Self-Fashioning: From More to Shakespeare* (Chicago, 1982).

13 Mills, "Situated Actions," 441–3.

14 See Raymond Williams, *Culture and Society, 1780–1950* (New York, 1958), ch. 6.

15 Immanuel Wallerstein, *The Modern World-System: Capitalist Agriculture and the Origins of the European World-Economy in the Sixteenth Century* (New York, 1976), ch. 2.

16 See, for example, E. P. Thompson, "The Crime of Anonymity," in *Al-*

bion's Fatal Tree: Crime and Society in Eighteenth-Century England, Douglas Hay, Peter Linebaugh, John G. Rule, E. P. Thompson, and Cal Winslow, eds. (New York, 1975), 255–308.

17 See E. P. Thompson, "Exploitation," in *The Making of the English Working Class* (New York, 1963), 189–212.

18 See Ruth Mohl, *The Three Estates in Medieval and Renaissance Literature* (New York, 1933); Georges Duby, *The Three Orders: Feudal Society Imagined,* Arthur Goldhammer, tr. (Chicago, 1980).

19 The phrase is taken from Bruce Wilshire, who uses it for different purposes in *Role Playing and Identity: The Limits of Theatre as Metaphor* (Bloomington, Ind., 1982), 94.

20 On the theater's confrontation with its own theatricality, see ibid., 60–75; Anne Righter, *Shakespeare and the Idea of the Play* (London, 1962).

21 See, for example, Trevor Aston, ed., *Crisis in Europe 1560–1660* (London, 1965).

22 On the theatricality of eighteenth-century urban life, see Richard Sennett, *The Fall of Public Man* (New York, 1977), 45–106. Sennett stresses the therapeutic and harmonizing (rather than the problematic) aspects of self-presentation in eighteenth-century public life.

23 On the theatricality of the early novel, see David Marshall, *The Figure of Theater: Shaftesbury, Defoe, Adam Smith and George Eliot* (New York, 1986); John Preston, *The Created Self: The Reader's Role in Eighteenth-Century Fiction* (London, 1970); Wolfgang Iser, *The Implied Reader: Patterns of Communication from Bunyan to Beckett* (Baltimore, 1975); Robert Alter, *Partial Magic: The Novel as a Self-Conscious Genre* (Berkeley and Los Angeles, 1975).

24 For more extended treatments of the *theatrum mundi* theme, see Ernst Robert Curtius, *European Literature and the Latin Middle Ages,* Willard Trask, tr. (New York, 1953), 138–44; Richard Bernheimer, "Theatrum Mundi," *Art Bulletin,* 38 (1956), 225–47; Jean Jacquot, " 'Le Théâtre du Monde' de Shakespeare à Calderon," *Revue de littérature comparée,* 31 (July–September 1957), 341–72; Herbert Weisinger, "Theatrum Mundi: Illusion as Reality," *The Agony and the Triumph: Papers on the Use and Abuse of Myth* (East Lansing, Mich., 1964), 58–70; Harriett Bloker Hawkins, " 'All the World's a Stage,' Some Illustrations of the Theatrum Mundi," *Shakespeare Quarterly,* 17 (Spring 1966), 174–8; Frances Yates, *The Art of Memory* (Chicago, 1966), chs. 6, 15, and 16; *The Theatre of the World* (Chicago, 1969); Frank W. Warnke, "The World as Theatre," in *Versions of the Baroque: European Literature in the Seventeenth Century* (New Haven, Conn., 1972), 66–89; Jackson I. Cope, *The Theater and the Dream: From Metaphor to Form in Renaissance Drama* (Baltimore, 1973), 20–2, 242–4, and passim; Righter, *Idea of the Play,* 64–86; Thomas B. Stroup, *Microcosmos: The Shape of the Elizabethan Play* (Lexington, Ky., 1965), ch. 1; Elizabeth Burns, *Theatricality: A Study of Convention in the Theatre and in Social Life* (New York, 1972), 8–11.

25 Jacquot, " 'Le Théâtre du Monde,' " 352–4; Stroup, *Microcosmos,* 13; Cope, *Theater and Dream,* passim; Burns, *Theatricality,* 8–9.

26 Curtius, *European Literature*, 139–40; " 'Le Théâtre du Monde,' " 354–5.
27 Mohl, *Three Estates*, 7; J. Huizinga, *The Waning of the Middle Ages* (New York, 1949), ch.2.
28 Yates, *Art of Memory*, ch. 6; Jacquot, " 'Le Théâtre du Monde,' " 347, 366; Arthur O. Lovejoy, *The Great Chain of Being: A Study of the History of an Idea* (Cambridge, Mass., 1936), 24–6.
29 Jonas Barish's *The Antitheatrical Prejudice* (Berkeley and Los Angeles, 1981) is easily the most comprehensive and astute survey of the perceived problem of theatricality, but his inclination is to treat its timeless aspect. "The antitheatrical prejudice," he concludes, "seems too deep-rooted, too widespread, too resistant to changes of place and time to be ascribed entirely, or even mainly, to social, political, or even economic factors" (116–17). I shall be stressing just such factors.
30 Two of the most accessible examples of this genre of sociological explanation are Erving Goffman, *The Presentation of Self in Everyday Life* (Garden City, N.Y., 1959), and Stanford M. Lyman and Marvin B. Scott, *The Drama of Social Reality* (New York, 1975), but see also the idiosyncratic Nicolas Evreinoff, *The Theatre in Life*, Alexander I. Nazaroff, tr. (1927; reprint New York, 1970).

1. THE THRESHOLD OF EXCHANGE

1 See, for example, E. A. J. Johnson, *The Organization of Space in Developing Countries* (Cambridge, Mass., 1970); Stuart Plattner, "Rural Market Towns," *Scientific American*, 232 (May 1975), 66–79. Central-place theory was introduced in the 1930s by the German economic geographers Walter Christaller and August Losch.
2 On the use of the natural and human environment as a mnemonic device, see Francis Harwood, "Myth, Memory, and the Oral Tradition: Cicero in the Trobriands," *American Anthropologist*, 76 (December 1976), 783–96; Walter Ong, "Memory as Art," in *Rhetoric, Romance, and Technology* (Ithaca, N.Y., 1971), 104–12; and Frances A. Yates, *The Art of Memory* (Chicago, 1966).
3 Karl Polanyi, "Aristotle Discovers the Economy," in *Trade and Market in the Early Empires*, Karl Polanyi, Conrad M. Arensberg, and Harry W. Pearson, eds. (New York, 1957), 64–94; Kurt Singer, "Oikonomia: An Inquiry into the Beginnings of Economic Thought and Language," *Kyklos*, 11 (1958), 29–57; Hannah Arendt, *The Human Condition* (Chicago, 1958), 28–33; Karl Marx, *Capital*, Frederick Engels, ed., Samuel Moore and Edward Aveling, trs., 3 vols. (New York, 1967), 1:59–60; M. I. Finley, "Aristotle and Economic Analysis," *Past and Present*, 47 (May 1970), 3–23; Finley, *The Ancient Economy* (Berkeley, 1973), 17–22.
4 H. Knorringa, *Emporos: Data on Trade and Trader in Greek Literature from Homer to Aristotle* (Amsterdam, 1926), 2, 7, 16–18; Singer, "Oikonomia,"

39–40; M. I. Finley, *The World of Odysseus* (1954; rev. ed. New York, 1965), 66–70; Robert M. Adams, "Anthropological Perspectives on Ancient Trade," *Current Anthropology*, 15 (September 1974), 242; S. C. Humphreys, "Homo Politicus and Homo Economicus: War and Trade in the Economy of Ancient Greece," in *Anthropology and the Greeks* (London, 1978), 168–72.

5 Alvin W. Gouldner, "The Norm of Reciprocity," *For Sociology* (Harmondsworth, Eng., 1973), 251–3; Knorringa, *Emporos*, 5; Marcel Mauss, *The Gift: Forms and Functions of Exchange in Archaic Society*, Ian Cunnison, tr. (New York, 1967), 61–2, 127 n. 101; F. G. Bailey, "Gifts and Poison," in *Gifts and Poison: The Politics of Reputation*, G. Bailey, ed. (New York, 1971), 1–25; Emile Benveniste, *Problèmes de linguistique générale* (Paris, 1966), 315–26; J. Huizinga, *Homo Ludens: A Study of the Play Element in Culture* (1950; reprint Boston, 1955), 46–76.

6 Barry Schwartz, "The Social Psychology of the Gift," *American Journal of Sociology*, 73 (July 1967), 1–11; Basil Sansom, "A Signal Transaction and Its Currency," in *Transaction and Meaning: Directions in the Anthropology of Exchange and Symbolic Behavior*, Bruce Kapferer, ed. (Philadelphia, 1976), 143–61; Adams, "Anthropological Perspectives," 249. On the place of envy and jealousy in archaic or "primitive" societies, see Svend Ranulf, *The Jealousy of the Gods and the Criminal Law at Athens*, 2 vols. (London, 1933–4); E. R. Dodds, *The Greeks and the Irrational* (Berkeley, 1951), 29–31, 48, 62 n. 108; Helmut Schoeck, *Envy: A Theory of Social Behavior*, Michael Glenny and Betty Ross, trs. (New York, 1966), 46–61; George M. Foster, "The Anatomy of Envy: A Study in Symbolic Behavior," *Current Anthropology*, 13 (April 1972), 165–202.

7 George Thomson, *Studies in Ancient Greek Society*, 2 vols. (London, 1949–55), 1:356; Marx, *Capital*, 1:88; Maurice Dobb, ed., *A Contribution to the Critique of Political Economy* (New York, 1970), 50; P. J. H. Grierson, *The Silent Trade* (Edinburgh, 1903), 56; Joseph Campbell, *The Hero with a Thousand Faces* (New York, 1956), 77–89; Knorringa, *Emporos*, 27; Arendt, *Human Condition*, 28; Arnold van Gennep, *The Rites of Passage*, Monika B. Vizedom and Gabrielle L. Caffee, trs. (Chicago, 1960), 18; Johannes Hasebroek, *Trade and Politics in Ancient Greece*, L. M. Fraser and D. C. Macgregor, trs. (London, 1933), 128.

8 Norman O. Brown, *Hermes the Thief* (Madison, Wis., 1947), 6–35, 39–41; Grierson, *Silent Trade*, 42; Knorringa, *Emporos*, 26–7; A. Hingston Quiggin, *A Survey of Primitive Money* (London, 1949), 11–12; E. T. Elworthy, *The Evil Eye* (London, 1895), 1–3, 13–15; Schoeck, *Envy*, 49–51; Edward S. Gifford, Jr., *The Evil Eye: Studies in the Folklore of Vision* (New York, 1958), 5–7, 50–1; John M. Roberts, "Belief in the Evil Eye in World Perspective," in *The Evil Eye*, Clarence Maloney, ed. (New York, 1976), 223–78; Humphreys, "Economy and Society in Classical Athens," in *Anthropology and the Greeks*, 148. Although I am aware that different modes of production coexisted and overlapped in antiquity, I shall be focusing on the movement out of the domestic or household mode of production.

For a discussion of these categories, see Marshall Sahlins, "The Domestic Mode of Production, I and II," in *Stone Age Economics* (Chicago, 1972), 41–148; Kevin D. Kelly, "The Independent Mode of Production," *Review of Radical Political Economy*, 11 (Spring 1979), 38–48.

9 Brown, *Hermes the Thief*, 8–13, 36–45, 78, 85, 108; M. I. Finley, "The Alienability of Land in Ancient Greece: A Point of View," *Eirene*, 7 (1968), 25–32.

10 Finley, *World of Odysseus*, 68; Josué V. Harari and David F. Bell, Introduction to Michel Serres, *Hermes: Literature, Science, Philosophy* (Baltimore, 1982), xxx–xxxi.

11 Brown, *Hermes the Thief*, 44–5; Knorringa, *Emporos*, 57.

12 Chester G. Starr, *The Economic and Social Growth of Early Greece 800–500 B.C.* (New York, 1977), 97, 112; Hasebroek, *Trade and Politics*, 70–1; Humphreys, "Homo Politicus," 168–74; Paul Einzig, *Primitive Money* (London, 1949), 228–34.

13 Xenophon, *Cyropaedia*, 1.2.3; Herodotus quoted in Finley, "Aristotle and Economic Analysis," 21.

14 See Aristotle's discussions in Book 5 of the *Nichomachean Ethics* and Book 1 of the *Politics*. See also Singer, "Oikonomia," 39–40; Finley, "Aristotle and Economic Analysis," 3–23; Joseph J. Spengler, "Aristotle on Economic Imputation and Related Matters," *Southern Economic Journal*, 21 (April 1955), 371–89; S. Todd Lowry, "Aristotle's 'Natural Limit' and the Economics of Price Regulation," *Greek, Roman and Byzantine Studies*, 15 (Spring 1974), 57–63; Thomas J. Lewis, "Acquisition and Anxiety: Aristotle's Case Against the Market," *Canadian Journal of Economics*, 11 (February, 1978), 69–90; Warren R. Brown, "Aristotle's Art of Acquisition and the Conquest of Nature," *Interpretation*, 10 (May–September, 1982), 159–95.

15 Humphreys, "Economy and Society," 136.

16 J. G. A. Pocock, "The Mobility of Property and the Rise of Eighteenth-Century Sociology," in *Theories of Property: Aristotle to the Present*, Anthony Parel and Thomas Flanagan, eds. (Waterloo, Ont., 1979), 162.

17 Brown, *Hermes the Thief*, 44; Finley, "Aristotle and Economic Analysis," 22–4; Finley, *Ancient Economy*, 35–61; Gustave Glotz, *Ancient Greece at Work*, M. R. Dobie, tr. (London, 1926), ch. 4; Karl Marx, *Grundrisse*, Martin Nicolaus, tr. (New York, 1973), 148–9.

18 See Jan Pečírka, "A Note on Aristotle's Conception of Citizenship and the Role of Foreigners in Fourth Century Athens," *Eirene*, 6 (1967), 23–6.

19 Van Gennep, *Rites of Passage*, 19–22, 26, 192; H. Clay Trumbull, *The Threshold Covenant* (New York, 1896), 5–23, 97, 194; Victor Turner, *The Ritual Process* (1969; 2nd ed. Ithaca, N.Y., 1977), 94–108; Turner, "Pilgrimages as Social Processes," in *Dramas, Fields, and Metaphors* (Ithaca, N.Y., 1974), 166–230.

20 Victor Turner, "Passages, Margins, and Poverty," in *Dramas, Fields, and Metaphors*, 231–71; Georg Simmel, *The Philosophy of Money*, Tom Bottomore and David Frisby, trs. (London, 1978), 98–9; Mary Douglas, *Purity and Danger* (London, 1966), 94–7, 117; van Gennep, *Rites of Passage*, 11–

12, 26; Terence S. Turner, "Transformation, Hierarchy and Transcendence: A Reformulation of van Gennep's Model of the Structure of Rites of Passage," in *Secular Ritual,* Sally F. Moore and Barbara G. Meyerhoff, eds. (Assen-Amsterdam, 1977), 53–70, esp. 56–7.

21 Victor Turner, "Variations on a Theme of Liminality," in *Secular Ritual,* Moore and Meyerhoff, eds., 37.

22 See Plato's discussion of the actor-poet in Book 10 of the *Republic;* see also Jonas Barish's analysis of this passage in *The Antitheatrical Prejudice* (Berkeley, 1981), 5–37.

23 Sahlins, "On the Sociology of Primitive Exchange," in *Stone Age Economics,* 201; Hasebroek, *Trade and Commerce,* 88; F. Roy Willis, *Western Civilization: An Urban Perspective,* 3 vols. (Lexington, Mass., 1973), 1:33.

24 See Colin Renfrew, "Trade as Action at a Distance: Questions of Integration and Communication," *Ancient Civilization and Trade,* Jeremy A. Sabloff and C.C. Lamberg-Karlovsky, eds. (Albuquerque, N.M., 1975), 3–59; Sidney W. Mintz, "Internal Market Systems as Mechanisms of Social Articulation," *Proceedings of the American Ethnological Society* (Seattle, Wash., 1959), 20–30.

25 Fritz Pringsheim, *The Greek Law of Sale* (Weimar, 1950), 23–4, 26, 43–6, 68, 85, 90–1; Joseph Plescia, *The Oath and Perjury in Ancient Greece* (Tallahassee, Fla., 1970), 1–2, 11, 80–2; Barry Gordon, *Economic Analysis Before Adam Smith: Hesiod to Lessius* (London, 1975), 44–5; Pocock, "Mobility of Property," 142; see also Jan Pečírka, "The Crisis of the Athenian Polis in the Fourth Century B.C.," *Eirene,* 14 (1976), 5–29, esp. 20–4.

26 Humphreys, "Economy and Society," 147.

27 Ibid. Victor Turner restricts the use of the term "liminal" to "ritual proper in tribal and agrarian societies or to those special sectors of complex, industrial societies that are still communitarian enough over a long run of time to have or generate true rituals with a rite de passage initiation structure." He reserves "liminoid" for "modern symbolic inversions and expressions of disorder" that split off from communal ritual and develop into autonomous genres or commodities in industrial society. See "Comment," in *The Reversible World: Symbolic Inversion in Art and Society,* Barbara A. Babcock, ed., (Ithaca, N.Y., 1978), 286–7; see also Turner's "Liminal to Liminoid, in Play, Flow, and Ritual: An Essay in Comparative Symbology," *Rice University Studies,* 60 (Summer 1974), 53–92.

28 For two non-Marxist critiques of the mystifying powers of money and the spurious epistemological clarity of neoclassical economics, see Einzig, *Primitive Money,* 454–5, and G. L. S. Shackle, *Epistemics & Economics: A Critique of Economic Doctrines* (Cambridge, Eng., 1972), 359–61 and passim.

29 Historians anxious to preserve the applicability of the neoclassical model of motivation to England's manorial economy (for example) have had to explain away an apparent seigneurial indifference to transactional economies in terms of the lord's individual preference for the satisfactions of authority as a "consumption good." See Stefaneo Fenoaltea, "Authority, Efficiency, and Agricultural Organization in Medieval England and Be-

yond: A Hypothesis," *Journal of Economic History*, 35 (December 1975), 693–718, esp. 698, 714–15.

30 W. Cunningham, *The Growth of English Industry and Commerce During the Early Middle Ages*, 2 vols. (London, 1890–2), 1:76; T. F. G. Dexter, *The Pagan Origin of Fairs* (Cornwall, 1930), 24–5; Maurice Beresford, *New Towns of the Middle Ages* (New York, 1967), 59, 133–41, 396–8; R. H. Britnell, "The Proliferation of Markets in England 1200–1349," *Economic History Review*, 2nd ser., 34 (May 1981), 213.

31 Alan Everitt, "The Marketing of Agricultural Produce," in *The Agrarian History of England and Wales, 1500–1640*, Joan Thirsk, ed. (Cambridge, Eng., 1967), 467–9, 481, 497. See also Margaret T. Hodgen, "Fairs of Elizabethan England," *Economic Geography*, 18 (October 1942), 399; R. H. Britnell, "English Markets and Royal Administration before 1200," *Economic History Review*, 2nd ser., 31 (May 1978), 183–96; Britnell, "King John's Early Grants of Markets and Fairs," *English Historical Review*, 94 (January 1979), 90–6; R. H. Hilton, "Lords, Burgesses and Hucksters," *Past and Present*, 97 (November 1982), 3–15; cf. Robert Latouche, *The Birth of Western Economy: Economic Aspects of the Dark Ages*, E. M. Wilkinson, tr. (New York, 1961), 240–4.

32 Britnell, "Proliferation of Markets," 215–21; Everitt, "Marketing," 467–9. On the commercial revolution, see Robert Lopez, *The Commercial Revolution of the Middle Ages, 950–1350* (1971; reprint Cambridge, Eng., 1976).

33 Everitt, "Marketing," 468–75; L. F. Salzman, *English Trade in the Middle Ages* (Oxford, 1931), 9–11, 35–6, 101–17. On the treatment of foreign traders and brokers in general, see Alice Beardwood, *Alien Merchants in England, 1350–1377* (Cambridge, Mass., 1931); T. H. Lloyd, *Alien Merchants in England in the High Middle Ages* (New York, 1982), esp. chs. 1 and 2.

34 J. L. Bolton, *The Medieval English Economy, 1150–1500* (London, 1980), 119, 286.

35 Martin Holmes, *Elizabethan London* (New York, 1969), 31–4.

36 K. L. McCutcheon, *Yorkshire Fairs and Markets to the End of the Eighteenth Century*, Publications of the Thoresby Society, vol. 39 (Leeds, 1939), 47; N. S. B. Gras, *The Evolution of the English Corn Market from the Twelfth to the Eighteenth Century* (Cambridge, Mass., 1915), 32–3; E. Lipson, *An Introduction to the Economic History of England*, 3 vols. (London, 1915), 1:199–200; A. V. Judges, ed., *The Elizabethan Underworld* (London, 1930), liv; cf. Latouche, *Birth of Western Economy*, 162.

37 Abbott Payson Usher, *The Early History of Deposit Banking in Mediterranean Europe*, 2 vols. (Cambridge, Mass., 1943), 1:28, 53–4; Salzman, *English Trade*, 166, 176; McCutcheon, *Yorkshire Fairs*, 157; Britnell, "English Markets," 187; "Proliferation of Markets," 214; Lipson, *Economic History*, 1:199–200; M. T. Clanchy, *From Memory to Written Record, England, 1066–1307* (Cambridge, Mass., 1979), 205, 208, 210, 231–57.

38 Quoted in Clanchy, *From Memory*, 202.

39 Usher, *Deposit Banking*, 1:24, 72, 107; Herman Van der Wee, "Monetary,

Credit and Banking Systems," in *Cambridge Economic History of Europe*, E. E. Rich and C. H. Wilson, eds. 7 vols. (Cambridge, Eng., 1941–8), 5:329.

40 J. R. Lander, *Conflict and Stability in Fifteenth-Century England* (London, 1969), 40; Everitt, "Marketing," 565–6.

41 On the zero-sum approach to peasant marketing, see George M. Foster, "Peasant Society and the Image of Limited Good," *American Anthropologist*, 67 (April 1965), 293–315. On the bodily representation of honor, see Julian Pitt-Rivers, "Honour and Social Status," in *Honour and Shame: the Values of Mediterranean Society*, J. G. Peristiany, ed. (Chicago, 1966), 26. On the persistence of personal and familial networks of credit, see Everitt, "Marketing," 567–8. On churchyard and sabbath marketing, see McCutcheon, *Yorkshire Fairs*, 25–7; Lipson, *Economic History*, 1:204–7; Salzman, *English Trade*, 123–5; Gras, *English Corn Market*, 32; Hilton, "Lords, Burgesses and Hucksters," 6; Beresford, *New Towns*, 106.

42 On the familial and household "subsumption" of identity in early modern England, see Peter Laslett, *The World We Have Lost*, 2nd ed. (New York, 1971), 20–1.

43 McCutcheon, *Yorkshire Fairs*, 123–4; Paul S. Clarkson and Clyde T. Warren, *The Law of Property in Shakespeare and the Elizabethan Drama* (Baltimore, 1942), 185–6; Gras, *English Corn Market*, ch. 3; R. B. Westerfield, *Middlemen in English Business, 1660–1760* (New Haven, Conn., 1915), ch. 2; S. Thrupp, "The Grocers of London: A Study of Distributive Trade," in *Studies in English Trade in the Fifteenth Century*, Eileen Power and M. M. Postan, eds. (New York, 1966), 278, 283–4; Maurice Dobb, *Studies in the Development of Capitalism* (1947; rev. ed. New York, 1963), 90–1; R. W. Dobson, "Admissions to the Freedom of the City of York in the Later Middle Ages," *Economic History Review*, 2nd ser., 26 (February 1973), 15, 18, 20–1; D. M. Palliser, "The Trade Guilds of Tudor York," in *Crisis and Order in English Towns 1500–1700*, Peter Clark and Paul Slack, eds. (London, 1972), 93.

44 Everitt, "Marketing," 456; Hilton, "Lords, Burgesses and Hucksters," 7–10; Dorothy Davis, *A History of Shopping* (London, 1966), 3–24. *Forestallers* bought outside or before the market in order to sell at retail within it; *regraters* bought and sold speculatively within the same market; *engrossers* sought to "corner" supplies in a commodity in order to raise its price.

45 Everitt, "Marketing," 496–562; Hodgen, "Fairs," 397–8; Lipson, *Economic History*, 1:211–12; Britnell, "King John's Early Grants," 93–4; cf. Georges Duby, *Rural Economy and Country Life in the Medieval West*, Cynthia Postan, tr. (Columbia, S. C., 1968), 130–4.

46 See John Merrington, "Town and Country in the Transition to Capitalism," in *The Transition from Feudalism to Capitalism*, Rodney Hilton, ed. (London, 1976), 170–95; Philip Abrams, "Towns and Economic Growth: Some Theories and Problems," in *Towns in Society*, Philip Abrams and E. A. Wrigley, eds. (Cambridge, Eng., 1978), 9–33; Raymond Williams, *The Country and the City* (New York, 1973).

47 Rodney Hilton, *Bond Men Made Free: Medieval Peasant Movements and the*

English Rising of 1381 (London, 1973), 21, 174–5, 193–5, 226–30; Dobb, *Studies in Capitalism,* 82; cf. Dobson, "Admissions to Freedom," 13.

48 Quoted in Hilton, *Bond Men,* 230.

49 Ibid., 230; see generally, Rodney Hilton, *The English Peasantry in the Later Middle Ages* (Oxford, 1975).

50 Hilton, *Bond Men,* 138–9, 189. On Southwark and Smithfield markets, see Cornelius Walford, *Fairs, Past and Present* (London, 1883), 164–5; W. J. Passingham, *London's Markets* (London, 1935), 105–6.

51 Glynne Wickham, *Early English Stages, 1300–1660,* 3 vols. (London, 1959–81), 1:122, 130–3; Wickham, *The Medieval Theatre* (London, 1974), 20–60; William Tydeman, *The Theatre in the Middle Ages* (Cambridge, 1978), 39, 127–31, 182–7; V. A. Kolve, *The Play Called Corpus Christi* (Stanford, Calif., 1966), 19, 47–9. For an alternative view of Corpus Christi origins, see Alan H. Nelson, *The Medieval English Stage: Corpus Christi Pageants* (Chicago, 1974), 1–14.

52 Wickham, *Medieval Theatre,* 59–60; Kolve, *Corpus Christi,* 102–4; Mikhail Bakhtin, *Rabelais and His World,* Hélène Iswolsky, tr. (Cambridge, Mass., 1968), 8–9.

53 Violence could and occasionally did break out among guilds over the order of procession. See Nelson, *Medieval English Stage,* 13; Palliser, "Trade Guilds," 106.

54 Alan Brody, *The English Mummers and Their Plays* (Philadelphia, 1970), 120; cf. Theodor H. Gaster, *Thespis* (New York, 1961), 17; Campbell, *Hero,* 383–4; Mervyn James, "Ritual, Drama and Social Body in the Late Medieval Town," *Past and Present,* 98 (February 1983), 3–29.

55 Wickham, *Medieval Theatre,* 76.

56 Charles Phythian-Adams, "Ceremony and the Citizen: The Communal Year at Coventry 1450–1550," in *Crisis and Order,* Clark and Slack, eds., 64, 72, 78.

57 Victor Turner has described some carnival celebrations as liminoid rather than liminal phenomena because they are voluntary rather than obligatory festivities. Though medieval festivals did not (and could not logistically) encompass whole cities, they were nonetheless obligatory for a large and significant proportion of the populace. As such, they bisected the movement out of serious, liminal observances into "leisurely," liminoid genres. See Turner, "Liminal to Liminoid," 73–5; see also Richard Schechner, "From Ritual to Theatre and Back: The Structure/Process of the Efficacy-Entertainment Dyad," in *Essays on Performance Theory 1970–1976* (New York, 1977), 76–9.

58 On the extraterritorial dimension of carnival, see Bakhtin, *Rabelais,* 154.

59 For various views on and examples of carnival ritual, see Natalie Zemon Davis, "The Reasons of Misrule" and "Women on Top," in *Society and Culture in Early Modern France* (Stanford, Calif., 1975), chs. 4 and 5; Peter Burke, *Popular Culture in Early Modern Europe* (New York, 1978), ch. 7; E. Le Roy Ladurie, *Carnival in Romans,* Mary Feeney, tr. (New York, 1979).

60 Wickham, *Medieval Theatre,* 5–8, 45; Margery M. Morgan, "'High Fraud':

Paradox and Double-Plot in the English Shepherds' Play," *Speculum* 39 (October 1964), 678.

61 On rituals of inversion, see Davis, "Reasons of Misrule" and "Women on Top"; E. K. Chambers, *The Medieval Stage* (1903; rev. ed. Oxford, 1943), vol. 1, chs. 13–15; and Phythian-Adams, "Ceremony and Citizen," 68–9; but see also Kolve, *Corpus Christi*, ch. 6. On the "boundless" body of carnival versus the self-contained body *(homo clausus)* implied by the six-teenth- and seventeenth-century rules of civility, see Bakhtin, *Rabelais*, 27–9; Norbert Elias, *The Civilizing Process*, Edmund Jephcott, tr., 2nd ed., vol. 1, *The History of Manners* (New York, 1982), 69–70, 245–263.

62 See Davis, "The Reasons of Misrule"; Pitt-Rivers, "Honour and Status," 25–6. On the relation of identity and honor to bodily boundaries, see Helen Merrell Lynd, *Shame and the Search for Identity* (New York, 1958), 136–7 and passim; Carl D. Schneider, *Shame, Exposure, and Privacy* (Boston, 1977), 18–55, 125–9.

63 See Davis, "Women on Top," 136–42, 147–50; Burke, *Popular Culture*, 183.

64 Bakhtin, *Rabelais*, esp. 153–5.

65 Ibid., 160, 186.

66 Ibid., 234, 165. For a useful assessment of Bakhtin's treatment of carnival, see Dominick LaCapra, "Bakhtin, Marxism, and the Carnivalesque," in *Rethinking Intellectual History: Texts, Contexts, Language* (Ithaca, N.Y., 1983), 291–324.

67 Hilton, *English Peasantry*, 51.

68 On the ambiguities and "misrecognitions" involved in ritual reciprocity, see Pierre Bourdieu, *Outline of a Theory of Practice*, Richard Nice, ed. (Cambridge, Eng., 1977), 3–9, 171–183; Sahlins, "Sociology of Primitive Exchange," 192–4. For a general overview of reciprocity and social ex-change, see Gouldner, "Norm of Reciprocity" and "The Importance of Something for Nothing," in *For Sociology*, chs. 8 and 9; Peter P. Ekeh, *Social Exchange Theory: The Two Traditions* (Cambridge, Mass., 1974); Anthony Heath, *Rational Choice and Social Exchange: A Critique of Exchange Theory* (Cambridge, Eng., 1976); Jack N. Mitchell, *Social Exchange, Dramaturgy and Ethnomethodology* (New York, 1978).

69 On market tricksterism (and its corresponding personalism and clientalism) as a defensive response to broader market relationships, see John A. Mariono, "Economic Idylls and Pastoral Realities: The 'Trickster Economy' in the Kingdom of Naples," *Comparative Studies in Society and History*, 24 (April 1982), 211–34; Sidney W. Mintz, "Peasant Markets," *Scientific American*, 203 (August 1960), 112–22; Cyril S. Belshaw, *Traditional Exchange and Modern Markets* (Englewood Cliffs, N.J., 1965), 58–80; Shepard Forman and Joyce F. Rieglehaupt, "Market Place and Marketing System: Toward a Theory of Peasant Economic Integration," *Comparative Studies in Society and History*, 12 (April 1970), 188–212, esp. 202; William G. Davis, *Social Relations in a Philippine Market* (Berkeley, 1973), 211–887; Clifford Geertz, "Suq: The Bazaar Economy in Sefrou," in *Meaning and Order in Moroccan*

Society, Clifford Geertz, Hildred Geertz, and Lawrence Rosen, eds. (Cambridge, Eng., 1979), 123–313.

70 On scholastic views of justice in exchange, see Bernard Dempsey, *Interest and Usury* (Washington, D.C., 1943), 114–85; John T. Noonan, Jr., *The Scholastic Analysis of Usury* (Cambridge, Mass., 1957), 30–1, 251, 296–9; Gordon, *Economic Analysis,* ch. 6, esp. 177–83.

71 *Oxford English Dictionary;* Kenneth Dennis, *'Competition' in the History of Economic Thought* (New York, 1977), 13–17; Bernard W. Dempsey, "Just Price in a Functional Economy," *American Economic Review,* 25 (September 1935), 479; Raymond de Roover, "The Concept of the Just Price: Theory and Economic Policy," *Journal of Economic History,* 18 (December 1958), 425.

72 See the contributions by Ruth Kenyon and Lewis Watt to *The Just Price,* V. A. Demant, ed. (London, 1930), 23–45, 60–75; Dempsey, "Just Price"; Noonan, *Scholastic Analysis,* 82–99; John W. Baldwin, *The Medieval Theories of the Just Price: Romanists, Canonists, and Theologians in the Twelfth and Thirteenth Centuries,* Transactions of the American Philosophical Society, new ser., vol. 49, pt. 4 (Philadelphia, 1959); Samuel Hollander, "On the Interpretation of Just Price," *Kyklos,* 18 (1965), 615–34; Gordon, *Economic Analysis,* 130–3, 142–4, 174–5, 227–62.

73 E. P. Thompson, "The Moral Economy of the English Crowd in the Eighteenth Century," *Past and Present,* 50 (February 1971), 78–9, 83, 98.

74 See Elizabeth Fox-Genovese, "The Many Faces of Moral Economy," *Past and Present,* 58 (February 1973), 161–8.

75 See Hilton, *English Peasantry,* passim; Robert Brenner, "Agrarian Class Structure and Economic Development in Pre-Industrial Europe," *Past and Present,* no. 70 (February 1976), 30–75, and no. 97 (November 1982), 16–113, as well as contributions to an extended discussion of Brenner's work in *Past and Present* by M. M. Postan and J. Hatcher, P. Cloot and D. Parker, H. Wunder (no. 78, February 1978), E. Le Roy Ladurie, G. Bois (no. 79, May 1978), R. H. Hilton, J. Cooper (no. 80, August 1979). See also Maurice Dobb, *Studies in Capitalism,* 33–82; Robert Du Plessis and Martha Howell, "Reconsidering the Early Modern Urban Community: The Cases of Leiden and Lille," *Past and Present,* 94 (February 1982), 49–84.

76 Wickham, *Early English Stages,* 1:51–5. Hugutius, Bishop of Ferrara (1190–1210), compared the *scaena,* or stage platform, to a "little shelter, actually a hidden place in the theatre and concealed by curtains just like merchants' stalls covered with poles and hangings," but Tydeman disputes such analogies (*Theatre,* 48); cf. Richard Southern, *The Open Stage* (London, 1963), 16.

77 R. H. Tawney, *The Agrarian Problem in the Sixteenth Century* (1912; reprint New York, 1961), 332; Wickham, *Early English Stages,* 2:66–7.

78 Tydeman, *Theatre,* 46; cf. Maurice Godelier, "Fetishism, Religion and Marx's General Theories Concerning Ideology," in *Perspectives in Marxist Anthropoloyg,* Robert Brain, tr. (Cambridge, Eng., 1977), esp. 176–85; Clifford Geertz, *Negara: The Theatre State in Nineteenth-Century Bali* (Princeton, N.J., 1980), ch. 4.

79 On the two traditions, see Chapters 2 and 3 as well as Stephen Greenblatt, *Renaissance Self-Fashioning: From More to Shakespeare* (Chicago, 1980), and Russell Fraser, *The War Against Poetry* (Princeton, N.J., 1970).

80 "There are also idols formed by the intercourse and association of men with each other, which I call Idols of the Market Place on account of the commerce and consort of men there. For it is by discourse that men associate, and words are imposed according to the apprehension of the vulgar. And therefore the ill and unfit choice of words wonderfully obstructs the understanding" (*Novum Organum* [1620], 43).

81 The following discussion draws on listings in the *Oxford English Dictionary* and on Norman Davis, "The Proximate Etymology of Market," *Modern Language Review*, 47 (April 1952), 152–5.

82 Marx, *Grundrisse*, 141–7.

83 Marx, *Capital*, 1:113, 115, 116, 154; see also Margaret Gay Davies, *The Enforcement of English Apprenticeship: A Study in Applied Mercantilism, 1563–1642* (Cambridge, Mass., 1956), 98.

84 Gordon, *Economic Analysis*, 170–1.

85 Karl Brunner and Allan H. Meltzer, "The Uses of Money: Money in the Theory of an Exchange Economy," *American Economic Review*, 61 (December 1971), 799–800; cf. Forman and Riegelhaupt, "Market Place," 205.

86 Joan Thirsk, *Economic Policy and Projects: The Development of a Consumer Society in Early Modern England* (Oxford, 1978), 119.

87 Marx, *Capital*, 1:79; Thompson, "Moral Economy," 85, 93; Fernand Braudel, *Afterthoughts on Material Civilization and Capitalism*, Patricia Ranum, tr. (Baltimore, 1977), 49–50; *The Wheels of Commerce*, Siân Reynolds, tr. (New York, 1979), 412–13; Joyce Oldham Appleby, *Economic Thought and Ideology in Seventeenth-Century England* (Princeton, N.J., 1978), 20.

88 Marx, *Grundrisse*, 148.

89 Shackle, *Epistemics & Economics*, n.p., 160; cf. L. M. Fraser, *Economic Thought and Language: A Critique of Some Fundamental Economic Concepts* (London, 1937), 68–70, 270–5, 283–7.

90 See, for example, M. M. Postan, *Medieval Trade and Finance* (Cambridge, Eng., 1973), 1–64; "The Rise of a Money Economy," *Economic History Review*, 2nd ser., 14 (1944), 123–34; Alan Macfarlane, *The Origins of English Individualism: The Family, Property and Social Transition* (London, 1978). Postan differs from Macfarlane in seeing early commercialization (via markets and money) as entirely compatible with the strengthening of feudal ties and exactions. See also Robert Brenner, "The Origins of Capitalist Development: A Critique of Neo-Smithian Marxism," *New Left Review*, 104 (July–August 1977), 25–93; Rodney Hilton, "Individualism and the English Peasantry," *New Left Review*, 120 (March–April 1980), 109–111; Stephen D. White and Richard T. Vann, "The Invention of English Individualism: Alan Macfarlane and the Modernization of Pre-modern England," *Social History*, 8 (October 1983), 345–63.

91 On the lack of synchronicity in money uses, see Fernand Braudel, "Prices in Europe from 1450 to 1750," *Cambridge Economic History*, Rich and Wil-

son, eds., 4:378; Usher, *Deposit Banking*, 201–12; B. E. Supple, "Currency
and Commerce in the Early Seventeenth Century," *Economic History Review*, 2nd ser., 10 (1957), 239–55; Supple, *Commercial Crisis and Change in
England, 1600–1642* (Cambridge, Eng., 1959), 73. But see also Postan,
"Rise of Money Economy," 126–7. The quarrel over the definition of
money persists among academic as well as popular thinkers. See, for example, Jacques Melitz, "The Polanyi School of Anthropology: An Economist's View," *American Anthropologist*, 72 (October 1970), 1020–40; Winston
Williams, "Marketing Money, Not Crops: 'Commodity' Is Redefined"
and H. Erich Heinemann, "Money: Definition and Control," *New York
Times*, December 30, 1982; Thomas Crump, *The Phenomenon of Money*
(London, 1981), ch. 3.

92 Noonan, *Scholastic Analysis*, 53–7, 110–12, 139–51, 251–5, 358, 394–6;
Thomas F. Divine, *Interest* (Milwaukee, Wis., 1959), 70; Gordon, *Economic
Analysis*, 160–79. According to the *Oxford English Dictionary*, "asset" displays a similar change in meaning.

93 Henri Pirenne, *Economic and Social History of Medieval Europe*, I. E. Clegg,
tr. (New York, 1936), 118; Noonan, *Scholastic Analysis*, 12, 53–7, 126–8,
253–6; E. Cannan, W. D. Ross, J. Bonar, and P. H. Wicksteed, "Who
Said 'Barren Metal'?" *Economica*, 5 (June 1922), 105–11; cf. Michael Taussig, *The Devil and Commodity Fetishism in South America* (Chapel Hill, N.C.,
1980), 98.

94 J. Gilchrist, *The Church and Economic Activity in the Middle Ages* (London,
1969), 112.

95 Bolton, *Medieval English Economy*, 342–4; Noonan, *Scholastic Analysis*, 92–
8, 100–53, 177–8, 202–48; Postan, *Medieval Trade*, 13–16; Usher, *Deposit
Banking*, 138–9; Pirenne, *Medieval Europe*, 119; Gilchrist, *Church and Economic Activity*, 48, 108. See also the interesting connection drawn by Lester
K. Little between the mendicant movements and commerce in *Religious
Poverty and the Profit Economy in Medieval Europe* (Ithaca, N.Y., 1978).

96 Usher, *Deposit Banking*, 6–8, 72–108; Van der Wee, "Banking Systems,"
329–30; Bolton, *Medieval English Economy*, 344; Salzman, *English Trade*,
20–1, 106–17; Postan, *Medieval Trade*, 16, 42.

97 Noonan, *Scholastic Analysis*, 109–28, 184–9, 249–67, 328–31, 349–52, 367–
8; Baldwin, *Medieval Theories*, 282–6; Divine, *Interest*, 53–5; Gordon, *Economic Analysis*, 195–204; Appleby, *Economic Thought*, 68; Thomas Nashe,
Christs Teares over Ievrsalem (1593), in *The Works of Thomas Nashe*, Ronald
B. McKerrow, ed., 5 vols., (London, 1904–10), 2:105.

98 Everitt, "Marketing," 531–43; Hodgen, "Fairs," 389–400; Walford, *Fairs*,
141; Pirenne, *Medieval Europe*, 96–102, 209–10; Salzman, *English Trade*,
156–7; Lipson, *Economic History*, I:196–237; Lopez, *Commercial Revolution*,
87–91.

99 Britnell, "King John's Early Grants," 91; McCutcheon, *Yorkshire Fairs*, 1–
9; Salzman, *English Trade*, 142–60; Dexter, *Pagan Origins*, passim.

100 Walford, *Fairs*, 164–9, 242; Davis, *History of Shopping*, 25–48. The Smithfield market was made permanent in 1614. See Henry Morley, *Memoirs of*

Bartholomew Fair (London, 1880); A. B. Robertson, "The Smithfield Cattle Market," *East London Papers,* 4 (October 1961), 80–7.

101 Pirenne, *Economic History,* 97–9; Divine, *Interest,* 40n; Marx, *Grundrisse,* 148.

102 On the changing character of land tenure, see Brenner, "Agrarian Class Structure"; Tawney, *The Agrarian Problem,* pt. 2; Margaret Spufford, *Contrasting Communities: English Villagers in the Sixteenth and Seventeenth Centuries* (Cambridge, Eng., 1974), ch. 2. On private marketing, see Everitt, "Marketing," 506–63; Dobb, *Studies in Capitalism,* 101; F. J. Fisher, "The Development of the London Food Market, 1540–1640," *Economic History Review,* 2nd ser., 5 (April 1935), 46–64.

103 Thirsk, *Economic Policy,* 7–8, 170–1.

104 Ibid., 150–5; Dobb, *Studies in Capitalism,* 100–1; Davies, *English Apprenticeship,* 95–6.

105 Thirsk, *Economic Policy,* 64, 117–18; Supple, *Commercial Crisis,* 147–59.

106 Everitt, "Marketing," 572–3; Drapers quoted in Supple, *Commercial Crisis,* 59.

107 Arthur Eli Monroe, *Monetary Theory Before Adam Smith* (Cambridge, Mass., 1923), 45–80; E. A. J. Johnson, *Predecessors of Adam Smith: The Growth of British Economic Thought* (New York, 1937), chs. 2 and 3.

108 Salzman, *English Trade,* 154; Bolton, *Medieval English Economy,* 303; Usher, *Deposit Banking,* ch. 4.

109 Usher, *Deposit Banking,* 4–8, 103–8; Van der Wee, "Banking Systems," 315–35; Richard Ehrenberg, *Capital and Finance in the Age of the Renaissance,* H. M. Lucas, tr. (New York, 1928), 233–53; D. C. Coleman, *The Economy of England, 1450–1750* (London, 1977), 51; see also Raymond de Roover, "Le Marché monetaire au Moyen Age et au début des temps modernes," *Revue historique,* 244 (1970), 4–44.

110 Quoted in Dobb, *Studies in Capitalism,* 93; Braudel, *Afterthoughts,* 52.

111 Everitt, "Marketing," 506–63; Everitt, "The English Urban Inn, 1560–1760," in *Perspectives in English Urban History,* Alan Everitt, ed. (London, 1973), 91–137; Thirsk, *Economic Policy,* 133–4; Alice Clark, *The Working Life of Women in the Seventeenth Century* (New York, 1920), 202.

112 Peter Aykroyd, *Evil London* (London, 1973), 70–1; Holmes, *Elizabethan London,* 75–92; Dobb, *Studies in Capitalism,* 118; Carl Bridenbaugh, *Vexed and Troubled Englishmen, 1590–1642* (Oxford, 1967), 170–1, 221–4; Paul A. Slack, "Vagrants and Vagrancy in England, 1598–1664," *Economic History Review,* 2nd ser., 34 (August 1974), 374–6.

113 Davies, *English Apprenticeship,* 98; John Walter and Keith Wrightson, "Dearth and the Social Order in Early Modern England," *Past and Present,* 71 (May 1976), 27; Andrew B. Appleby, *Famine in Tudor and Stuart England* (Stanford, Calif., 1978), 155–93; "Grain Prices and Subsistence Crises in England and France, 1590–1740," *Journal of Economic History,* 39 (December 1979), 865–88; Buchanan Sharp, *In Contempt of All Authority: Rural Artisans and Riot in the West of England, 1586–1660* (Berkeley and Los Angeles, 1980), 156–74; R. B. Outhwaite, "Dearth and Government Intervention in Eng-

lish Grain Markets, 1590–1700," *Economic History Review,* 2nd ser., 34 (August 1981), 397, 401–2; T. S. Ashton, *Economic Fluctuations in England 1700–1800* (Oxford, 1959), 34–48; Lopez, *Commercial Revolution,* 162.

114 Sharp, *Contempt of All Authority,* 10–42, esp. 41. On the guilds, see T. H. Marshall, "Capitalism and the Decline of the English Guilds," *Cambridge Historical Journal,* 3 (1929), 23–33; J. R. Kellet, "The Breakdown of Guild and Corporation Control over the Handicraft and Retail Trade in London," *Economic History Review,* 2nd ser., 10 (1958), 381–94.

115 Sharp, *Contempt of All Authority,* ch. 3; John Walter, "Grain Riots and Popular Attitudes to the Law: Maldon and the Crisis of 1629," in *An Ungovernable People: The English and Their Law in the Seventeenth and Eighteenth Centuries,* John Brewer and John Styles, eds. (New Brunswick, N. J., 1980), 47–84. See also the discussion of eighteenth-century responses to riot and theft in E. P. Thompson, "Patrician Society, Plebeian Culture," *Journal of Social History,* 7 (Summer 1974), 382–405; Douglas Hay, "Property, Authority and the Criminal Law," in *Albion's Fatal Tree: Crime and Society in Eighteenth-Century England,* Douglas Hay, Peter Linebaugh, John G. Rule, E. P. Thompson, and Cal Winslow, eds. (New York, 1975), 17–64.

116 E. M. Leonard, *The Early History of English Poor Relief* (1900; reprint London, 1965), 142–83; Everitt, "Marketing," 575–86; Gras, *English Corn Market,* 221–50; Outhwaite, "Dearth," 394, 400–1; N. J. Williams, ed., *Tradesmen in Early-Stuart Wiltshire* (Devizes, Eng., 1960), viii, xx; Vincent Ponko, Jr., "N.S.B. Gras and Elizabethan Corn Policy: A Re-examination of the Problem," *Economic History Review,* 2nd ser., 17 (August 1964), 37.

117 George Rudé, *Ideology and Popular Protest* (New York, 1980), 136–8; Sharp, *Contempt of All Authority,* 32–4; Thompson, "Moral Economy." For a critique of the applicability of the "moral economy" concept to the late-eighteenth-century food riot, see Dale Edward Williams, "Morals, Markets and the English Crowd in 1766," *Past and Present,* 104 (August 1984), 56–73.

118 Tawney, *Agrarian Problem,* 287–310; Spufford, *Contrasting Communities,* 49–50; Lander, *Conflict and Stability,* 26–7; Lawrence Stone, "Social Mobility in England, 1500–1700," in *Society in an Age of Revolution,* Paul S. Seaver, ed. (New York, 1976), 42–3, 51–2.

119 D. C. Coleman, "Labour in the English Economy of the Seventeenth Century," *Society in an Age of Revolution,* Seaver, ed., 112–38, esp. 116; C. B. Macpherson, *The Political Theory of Possessive Individualism: Hobbes to Locke* (Oxford, 1962), 107–36, 144–6, 181–2, 282–6; Christopher Hill, "Pottage for Freeborn Englishmen: Attitudes to Wage Labour in the Sixteenth and Seventeenth Centuries," in *Socialism, Capitalism and Economic Growth,* C. H. Feinstein, ed. (Cambridge, Eng., 1967), 338–50, esp. 342; Braudel, *Wheels of Commerce,* 307–11. On geographic mobility, see Stone, "Social Mobility," 35–6, 39; Lander, *Conflict and Stability,* 47; John Patten, "Rural–Urban Migration in Pre-Industrial England," *Research Papers,* no. 6, School of Geography, Oxford (May 1973).

120 Marx, *Capital,* 1:112. On the liminal status of peasant proletarians, see Taussig, *Devil and Commodity Fetishism,* 103–4.

121 Robert Reyce, quoted in Everitt, "Marketing," 568.
122 Marx, Grundrisse, 221; Dirk J. Struik, ed., The Economic and Philosophic Manuscripts of 1844 (New York, 1964), 169. On the popularity of Protean imagery in this epoch, see Joan Webber, The Eloquent "I": Style and Self in Seventeenth-Century Prose (Madison, Wis., 1968), 112.
123 Supple, Commercial Crisis, 8–14.
124 Edwin Cannan, "Early History of the Term Capital," Quarterly Journal of Economics, 35 (May 1921), 478–81; R. D. Richards, "Early History of the Term Capital," ibid., 40 (February 1926), 329–38; Henry Rand Hatfield, "The Earliest Use of the Term Capital," ibid., (May 1926), 547–8; W. Stark, The History of Economics in its Relation to Social Development (New York, 1944), 30–2.
125 Valerie Pearl, London and the Outbreak of the Puritan Revolution: City Government and National Politics, 1625–43 (Oxford, 1961), 14–51; Fernand Braudel, Capitalism and Material Life 1400–1800, Miriam Kochan, tr. (New York, 1973), 391–2; David J. Johnson, Southwark and the City (Oxford, 1969), chs. 3, 5, and 6; Mary Boast, The Mayflower and Pilgrim Story: Chapters from Rotherhithe and Southwark (London, 1970); Nashe, "Christs Teares," 148.
126 J. D. Gould, "The Trade Crisis of the Early 1620s and English Economic Thought," Journal of Economic History, 15 (1955), 121–33. See also Appleby, Economic Thought, chs. 2 and 3; Paschal Larkin, Property in the Eighteenth Century (1930; reprint Port Washington, N.Y., 1969), 31–2.

2. ANOTHER NATURE

1 See, for example, Bronislaw Malinowski, Magic, Science and Religion (Garden City, N.Y., 1954), 69–111.
2 The City Madam, act 3, sc. 3, lines 35–40, in The Plays and Poems of Philip Massinger, Philip Edwards and Colin Gibson, eds., 4 vols. (Oxford, 1976), 4:64.
3 See listings under "copy" in the Oxford English Dictionary; see also Peter S. Clarkson and Clyde T. Warren, The Law of Property in Shakespeare and the Elizabethan Drama (Baltimore, 1942), 42–3.
4 See G. R. Owst, Literature and Pulpit in Medieval England, 2nd ed. (Oxford, 1961), 287–374; John Peter, Complaint and Satire in Early English Literature (Oxford, 1956), chs. 5–9.
5 Mikhail Bakhtin, Rabelais and His World, Hélène Iswolsky, tr. (Cambridge, Mass., 1968), 53, 106.
6 Ibid., 40.
7 See Christopher Hill, Economic Problems of the Church, From Archbishop Whitgift to the Long Parliament (Oxford, 1956), 184–5, 346–8; Hill, Society and Puritanism in Pre-Revolutionary England (New York, 1964), 397–417; George L. Mosse, The Holy Pretence (Oxford, 1957), 55; Keith Thomas, Religion and the Decline of Magic (New York, 1971), 67–8; Morton J. Hor-

witz, "The Triumph of Contract," in *The Transformation of American Law 1780–1860* (Cambridge, Mass., 1977), 160–210.

8 Ruth Mohl, *The Three Estates in Medieval and Renaissance Literature* (New York, 1933), chs. 4 and 5.

9 Ibid., 7; Owst, *Literature and Pulpit*, 68, 69n, 76.

10 Mohl, *Three Estates*, 143–4. For a genealogy of Barclay's work, see Aurelius Pompen, *The English Versions of the Ship of Fools* (1925; reprint New York, 1967), 311.

11 Alexander Barclay, *The Ship of Fools*, Jamison edition, 2 vols. (New York, 1874), 2:268.

12 Ibid., 2:268.

13 Ibid., 2:314.

14 Ibid., 2:315. See listings under "utterance" in the *Oxford English Dictionary*. On the imagery of the mouth as a mint of words, see Raymond Southall, *Literature and the Rise of Capitalism* (London, 1973), 50–1.

15 On the decline of estates literature, see Mohl, *Three Estates*, 9, 243–4; Benjamin Boyce, *The Theophrastan Character in England to 1642* (Cambridge, Mass., 1947), 57–9.

16 Michel Foucault, *Madness and Civilization: A History of Insanity in the Age of Reason*, Richard Howard, tr. (New York, 1965), 16; for the full discussion, see 3–37.

17 Barclay, *Ship of Fools*, 2:270.

18 Frank Wadleigh Chandler, *The Literature of Roguery*, 2 vols. (Boston, 1907), 1:25–6, 75–6; Frank Aydelotte, *Elizabethan Rogues and Vagabonds* (1913; reprint New York, 1967), 115–16; Louis B. Wright, *Middle-Class Culture in Elizabethan England* (Chapel Hill, N.C., 1935), 439–42.

19 There were also Spanish antecedents; see Chandler, *Literature of Roguery*, vol. 1, ch. 1.

20 Ibid., 1:4, 27–8; D. B. Thomas, ed., Preface to *The Book of Vagabonds and Beggars with a Vocabulary of Their Language and a Preface by Martin Luther*, J. C. Hotten, tr. (London, 1932), xi.

21 *Albumazar: A Comedy*, Hugh Dick, ed., University of California Publications in English, vol. 13 (Berkeley and Los Angeles, 1944), act 1, sc. 1, lines 56–9; Edward Viles and F. J. Furnivall, eds., Preface to *The Rogues and Vagabonds of Shakespeare's Youth: Awdeley's 'Fraternitye of Vacabondes,' and Harman's 'Caveat'* (New York, 1907), ii–iv, xiv–xvi, xx. Edwin Havilland Miller, *The Professional Writer in Elizabethan England* (Cambridge, Mass., 1959), 231–41.

22 Aydelotte, *Elizabethan Rogues*, 52; John Pound, *Poverty and Vagrancy in Tudor England* (London, 1971), 3; J. S. Cockburn, "The Nature and Incidence of Crime in England 1559–1625," in *Crime in England 1550–1800*, J. S. Cockburn, ed. (Princeton, N.J., 1977), 61.

23 Peter Clark, "The Migrant in Kentish Towns 1580–1640," in *Crisis and Order in English Towns 1500–1700*, Peter Clark and Paul Slack, eds. (London, 1972), 117–63; Helen C. White, *Social Criticism in Popular Religious Literature of the Sixteenth Century* (New York, 1944), 13–14; Chandler,

Literature of Roguery, vol. 1, ch. 3; J. J. Jusserand, *English Wayfaring Life in the Middle Ages*, Lucy Toulmin Smith, tr., 4th ed. (London, 1950), 95–119.

24 A. V. Judges, ed., *The Elizabethan Underworld* (London, 1930), plate 6.

25 Margaret Gay Davies, *The Enforcement of English Apprenticeship: A Study in Applied Mercantilism, 1563–1642* (Cambridge, Mass., 1956), 7; M. C. Bradbrook, *The Rise of the Common Player* (Cambridge, Mass., 1962), 34–7; Aydelotte, *Elizabethan Rogues*, 68; Charles W. Camp, *The Artisan in Elizabethan Literature* (New York, 1923), 85, 92; Owst, *Literature and Pulpit*, 353–7; Mohl, *Three Estates*, 355–6.

26 See Normand Berlin, *The Base String: The Underworld in Elizabethan Drama* (Rutherford, N.J., 1968), 90–1, 115.

27 Peter Burke, *Popular Culture in Early Modern Europe* (New York, 1978), 71; Bakhtin, *Rabelais*, 105; Chandler, *Literature of Roguery*, 1:119–23.

28 See listings under "Billingsgate" in the *Oxford English Dictionary* and in Eric Partridge, *A Dictionary of Slang and Unconventional English* (London, 1937).

29 Bakhtin, *Rabelais*, 105–6.

30 Philip H. Wicksteed, *The Common Sense of Political Economy* (London, 1910), 174; see also F. H. Knight, *The Ethics of Competition* (New York, 1935), 282.

31 See listings under "altruism" and "egoism" in the *Oxford English Dictionary;* Benjamin N. Nelson, *The Idea of Usury: From Tribal Brotherhood to Universal Otherhood* (Princeton, N.J., 1949).

32 Christopher Hill, "Protestantism and the Rise of Capitalism," in *Change and Continuity in Seventeenth-Century England* (London, 1974), 84–6; R. H. Tawney, *Religion and the Rise of Capitalism*, rev. ed. (New York, 1926), 96–9.

33 For a general discussion of monastic charity and monastic dissolution, see Brian Tierney, *Medieval Poor Law: A Sketch of Canonical Theory and Its Application to England* (Berkeley and Los Angeles, 1959); G. W. C. Woodward, *The Dissolution of the Monasteries* (London, 1966); Lester K. Little, *Religious Poverty and the Profit Economy in Medieval Europe* (Ithaca, N.Y., 1978). On the growth of poor relief and secular charity, see E. M. Leonard, *The Early History of English Poor Relief* (1900; reprint London, 1965), chs. 1–3; W. K. Jordan, *Philanthropy in England, 1400–1660* (London, 1959), 83–103. Jordan's evidence for the "outward swelling" of generosity in the late sixteenth and early seventeenth centuries has been challenged on the grounds that it fails to take inflation into account; see William G. Bittle and R. Todd Lane, "Inflation and Philanthropy in England: A Re-Assessment of W. K. Jordan's Data," *Economic History Review*, 2nd ser., 29 (May 1976), 203–10. One might also suggest that charitable trusts provided a way of legitimately mobilizing nonventure capital and protecting it from the divisive tendencies of family enterprise. Moreover, even in the Middle Ages, as Sylvia Thrupp has pointed out, charity had the "magic virtue" of cleansing the gains of commerce from suspected usury (*The Merchant Class of Medieval London* [Ann Arbor, Mich., 1948], 177).

34 On vagabonds and social control, see John Walter and Keith Wrightson, "Dearth and the Social Order in Early Modern England," *Past and Present,* 71 (May 1976), 22–42; A. L. Beier, "Vagrants and the Social Order in Elizabethan England," *Past and Present,* 64 (August 1974), 3–29, and a rejoinder by J. F. Pound in ibid., 71 (May 1976), 126–9; Paul A. Slack, "Vagrants and Vagrancy in England, 1598–1664," *Economic History Review,* 2nd ser., 27 (August 1974), 360–79. See also Christopher Hill, *Puritanism and Revolution* (London, 1964), ch. 1; Karl Marx, *Capital,* Frederick Engels, ed., Samuel Moore and Edward Aveling, trs., 3 vols. (New York, 1967), vol. 1, chs. 27 and 28; William Lazonick, "Karl Marx and Enclosures in England," *Review of Radical Political Economics,* 6 (Summer 1974), 8–17. For a general legislative history, see C. J. Ribton-Turner, *A History of Vagrants and Vagrancy and Beggars and Begging* (1887; reprint Montclair, N.J., 1972).

35 William Perkins quoted in Jordan, *Philanthropy,* 152–3.

36 Thomas Jacomb quoted in ibid., 201.

37 Gerard de Malynes quoted in White, *Social Criticism,* 79; see also listings under "policy" in the *Oxford English Dictionary.*

38 Thomas Wilson, *A Discourse Upon Usury* (1572; reprint London, 1925), 366.

39 Ibid., 271; Mohl, *Three Estates,* 147; J. Huizinga, *The Waning of the Middle Ages* (Garden City, N.Y., 1954), chs. 5 and 6. For biographical information see A. J. Schmidt, "Thomas Wilson, Tudor Scholar-Statesman," *Huntington Library Quarterly,* 20 (May 1957), 205–18; Schmidt, "Thomas Wilson and the Tudor Commonwealth: An Essay in Civic Humanism," ibid., 23 (November 1959), 49–60.

40 Huizinga, *Waning of the Middle Ages,* 28.

41 Wilson, *Discourse Upon Usury,* 305, 313; cf. Fernand Braudel, *The Wheels of Commerce,* Siân Reynolds, tr. (New York, 1982), 201. On "dry exchange," or *cambio sicco,* see Raymond de Roover, "What Is Dry Exchange? A Contribution to the Study of English Mercantilism," *Journal of Political Economy,* 52 (September 1944), 250–66.

42 *A Cure for a Cuckold,* act 2, sc. 1, lines 86–89, in *The Complete Works of John Webster,* F. L. Lucas, ed., 4 vols. (London, 1927), 3:46.

43 Francis Bacon, "Of Usury," in *The Works of Francis Bacon,* James Spedding, Robert L. Ellis, and Douglas D. Heath, eds., 14 vols. (London, 1857–74), 6:473–4.

44 William Shakespeare, *Timon of Athens,* act 4, sc. 3, lines 386–9. On the association of alchemy with commercial fraud, see Thomas Dekker, *Old Fortunatus,* act 1, sc. 1, lines 289–92, in *The Dramatic Works of Thomas Dekker,* Fredson Bowers, ed., 4 vols. (Cambridge, Eng., 1953), 1:124; Ben Jonson, *The Alchemist,* passim; Tomkis, *Albumazar,* passim. See also L. C. Knights, *Drama and Society in the Age of Jonson* (London, 1937), 124.

45 See De Winter's introduction to Ben Jonson, *The Staple of News* (New York, 1905), xx–xxi; Louise George Clubb, *Giambattista Della Porta, Dramatist* (Princeton, N.J., 1965), 288. See also Sombart, *The Quintessence of Capitalism,* M. Epstein, tr. (1915; reprint New York, 1967), 35.

46 Hardin Craig, *The Enchanted Glass: The Elizabethan Mind in Literature* (Oxford, 1952), 204; Ruth Kelso, *The Institution of the Gentleman in English Literature of the Sixteenth Century* (Urbana, Ill., 1923), 20–1. On the interpenetration of the merchant class and gentry and the appropriation of symbolic codes of heraldry, see Thrupp, *Merchant Class,* 249, 318; Lawrence Stone, *The Crisis of the Aristocracy, 1558–1641* (Oxford, 1965), 65–218; A. L. Rowse, *The Elizabethan Renaissance: The Life of the Society* (London, 1971), 74–6, 109–11. On the boundary functions of magic, see Mary Douglas, *Natural Symbols: Explorations in Cosmology* (New York, 1973), 178–80.

47 Philip Stubbes, *The Anatomie of Abuses* (1558; facs. reprint New York, 1973), sig. C y^v.

48 Mohl, *Three Estates,* 243; Boyce, *Theophrastan Character,* 59–63.

49 Sir Thomas Overbury, *The Overburian Characters,* W. J. Paylor, ed. (Oxford, 1936), 92. Wendell Clausen disputes Casaubon's importance, preferring instead to see Ben Jonson as the literary mediator between the Theophrastan tradition and the vogue of English character writing ("The Beginnings of English Character Writing in the Early Seventeenth Century," *Philological Quarterly,* 25 [May 1946], 32–45).

50 See Paylor's introduction to *Overburian Characters,* viii–ix; Boyce, *Theophrastan Character,* 129–50, 159–60. For a bibliography of "characters" published between 1608 and 1700, see Gwendolyn Murphy, *A Cabinet of Characters* (London, 1925).

51 Boyce, *Theophrastan Character,* 136; Paylor, Introduction to *Overburian Characters,* xxi; Thomas B. Stroup, *Microcosmos: The Shape of the Elizabethan Play* (Lexington, Ky., 1965), ch. 5; Peter, *Complaint and Satire,* ch. 5.

52 Wayne A. Rebhorn, *Courtly Performances: Masking and Festivity in Castiglione's Book of the Courtier* (Detroit, 1978), esp. chs. 1 and 5; Kenneth Burke, *A Rhetoric of Motives* (Berkeley and Los Angeles, 1969), 221–33.

53 On the aesthetics of self-fashioning, see Thomas Greene, "The Flexibility of Self in Renaissance Literature," and A. Bartlett Giamatti, "Proteus Unbound: Some Versions of the Sea God in the Renaissance," both in *The Disciplines of Criticism: Essays in Literary Theory, Interpretation, and History,* Peter Demetz, Thomas Greene, and Lowry Nelson, Jr., eds. (New Haven, Conn., 1968), 241–64 and 437–76. For a more extensive literary and historical discussion of these issues, see Stephen J. Greenblatt, *Sir Walter Ralegh: The Renaissance Man and His Roles* (New Haven, Conn., 1973); Greenblatt, *Renaissance Self-Fashioning: From More to Shakespeare* (Chicago, 1980).

54 F. O. Mathiessen, *Translation: An Elizabethan Art* (Cambridge, Mass., 1931), 47–9.

55 Rebhorn, *Courtly Performances,* 173.

56 Sir Thomas Hoby, tr., *The Courtyer of Count Baldessar Castilio* (1561; reprint New York, 1967), 132; cf. Baldesar Castiglione, *The Book of the Courtier,* Charles S. Singleton, tr. (Garden City, N.Y., 1959), 119.

57 Mario Praz, *Machiavelli and the Elizabethans* (London, 1928), 2.

58 Ibid., 8–13; E. A. J. Johnson, *Predecessors of Adam Smith: The Growth of*

British Economic Thought (New York, 1937), ch. 13; see also Clarence Valentine Boyer, *The Villain as Hero in Elizabethan Tragedy* (London, 1914).

59 Edward Meyer, *Machiavelli and the Elizabethan Drama* (Weimar, 1897), 62–3, 66–7, 122, 134. On Machiavelli's antipathy toward the mercantile class, see Alfred Von Martin, *Sociology of the Renaissance* (New York, 1944), 65–70.

60 Thomas Heywood, *Machiavel. As He lately appeared to his deare Sons, the Moderne Proiectors* (London, 1641), sigs. B3–B4; see also Boyce, *Theophrastan Character*, 316.

61 William Sprigge quoted in Felix Raab, *The English Face of Machiavelli* (London, 1965), 209. Machiavelli has been described as the first writer to depict the "theatricalization of politics" (Stanley Cavell, *The World Viewed: Reflections on the Ontology of Film* [New York, 1971], 93). See also Burke, *Rhetoric of Motives*, 158–66; Stanford M. Lyman and Marvin B. Scott, *The Drama of Social Reality* (New York, 1975), 9, 22–25, and passim.

62 On the inability to conceptualize political realism in England, see Raab, *Machiavelli*, 26–8, 51, 103–5; cf. Von Martin, *Sociology of Renaissance*, 5–24, and, generally, J. G. A. Pocock, *The Machiavellian Moment: Florentine Political Thought and the Atlantic Tradition* (Princeton, N.J., 1975), esp. vii–ix.

63 Wright, *Middle-Class Culture*, 124–6.

64 Steeuen Guazzo, *The Civile Conversation*, George Pettie, tr., 2 vols. (London, 1581), 2: sig. 5ᵛ.

65 Ibid., 2: sig. 6; 1: sig. 47; emphasis added.

66 Caroll Camden, "The Mind's Construction in the Face," *Philological Quarterly*, 20 (July 1941), 400–1, 412; Bacon, *The Advancement of Learning*, in *Works*, 3:456. See listings under "sympathy" in the *Oxford English Dictionary*.

67 Thomas Hill quoted in Camden, "Mind's Construction," 400–1; Wright, *Middle-Class Culture*, 570–1.

68 Thomas Wright, *The Passions of the Minde in Generall*, 2nd ed. (1604; facs. reprint Urbana, Ill., 1971), 1–2. On the Loyolan exercises, see Thomas O. Sloane's introduction to ibid., xl–xliii; George T. Tade, "Rhetorical Aspects of the *Spiritual Exercises* in the Medieval Tradition of Preaching," *Quarterly Journal of Speech*, 51 (December 1965), 409–18; "The Spiritual Exercises: A Method of Self-Persuasion," ibid., 43 (December 1957), 383–9; Francis Fergusson, *The Idea of a Theatre* (Princeton, N.J., 1944), 238.

69 Wright, *Passions of the Minde*, 136.

70 Bacon, "Of Simulation and Dissimulation," in *Works*, 6:388.

71 See Wright, *Passions of the Minde*, lx, lxiii.

72 Bacon, *Advancement of Learning*, in *Works*, 3:456–7; Boyce, *Theophrastan Character*, 159, 173–85.

73 Bacon, "Of Riches," in *Works*, 6:461; William Scott, *An Essay of Drapery*, Sylvia Thrupp, ed. (Boston, 1953), 9, 29. On the problematic status of merchants, see Lawrence Stone, "Social Mobility in England 1500–1700," in *Society in an Age of Revolution*, Paul S. Seaver, ed. (New York, 1976), 29.

74 Scott, *Essay of Drapery*, 17, 19, 20; Bacon, "Of Simulation," 387.

75 Scott, *Essay of Drapery*, 35.

76 Ibid., 36–6, 47.

77 I(ohn) B(rowne), *The Marchants Avizo*, Patrick McGrath, ed. (Boston, 1957), 9, 10.

78 Scott, *Essay of Drapery*, 34; Bacon, "Of Marriage and Single Life," in *Works*, 6:391.

79 John Earle, *Micro-cosmographie. Or, A Peece of the World Discovered; In Essayes and Characters*, 2nd ed. (London, 1628), sigs. C13ᵛ–D2; cf. Samuel Butler's character of the Hypocrite in *Characters*, Charles W. Daves, ed. (Cleveland, 1970), 219.

80 Scott, *Essay of Drapery*, 28.

81 Daniel Defoe, *The Complete English Tradesman*, 5th ed., 2 vols. (London, 1745), 1:255.

82 Wright, *Passions of the Minde*, 292; Scott, *Essay of Drapery*, 28.

83 See listings under "deal" in the *Oxford English Dictionary*.

84 See Horwitz, "Triumph of Contract," 173–86; but see also the critique of A. W. B. Simpson, who places the changes in contractual law earlier, in the sixteenth century ("The Horwitz Thesis and the History of Contracts," *University of Chicago Law Review*, 46 [Spring 1979], 542–7).

85 See, in this connection, Erich Kahler, *The Inward Turn of Narrative*, Richard and Clara Winston, trs. (Princeton, N.J., 1973); Arnold Weinstein, *Fictions of the Self: 1550–1800* (Princeton, N.J., 1981).

86 Browne, *Marchants Avizo*, 57.

87 Scott, *Essay of Drapery*, 34.

88 Bacon, "Of Negociating," in *Works*, 6:493–4; Bacon, *Advancement of Learning*, in *Works*, 3:368.

89 The word "costume" was in fact derived from "custom"; see also the listings under "habit" in the *Oxford English Dictionary*. On the abolition of sumptuary laws, see Frances Elizabeth Baldwin, *Sumptuary Legislation and Personal Regulation in England* (Baltimore, 1926), 249.

90 Bacon, *Advancement of Learning*, in *Works*, 3:439.

91 Ibid., 409–10.

92 Ibid., 440–2.

93 Ibid., 447.

94 Wright, *Passions of the Minde*, 77.

95 Bacon, *Advancement of Learning*, in *Works*, 3:430; Raab, *Machiavelli*, 74–6.

96 Bacon, *Advancement of Learning*, in *Works*, 3:437, 434. For an interesting discussion of the impact of market relations on "cognitive style" and, in particular, on "recipe knowledge," see Thomas L. Haskell, "Capitalism and the Origins of the Humanitarian Sensibility," *American Historical Review*, 90 (April 1985), 339–61 and (June 1985), 547–66.

97 Thomas Dekker quoted in Aydelotte, *Elizabethan Rogues*, 85; see also Martin Holmes, *Elizabethan London* (New York, 1969), 41.

98 Thomas Dekker, *The Gulls Horn-Book*, in *The Non-Dramatic Works of Thomas Dekker*, Alexander B. Grosart, ed., 5 vols. (1885; reprint New York, 1963), 2:230.

99 Earle, *Micro-cosmographie*, sigs. I11–I12ᵛ.

100 John Bulwer, *Chirologia: or the Naturall Language of the Hand* . . . (London, 1644), 100, 105; Thomas Diconson's dedicatory poem declared:

> All Tribes shall now each other understand
> Which (though not of one lip) are of one *Hand*.
> Chirologie redeemes from *Babels* doome,
> And is the universall Idiome.

For more information on Bulwer, see James W. Cleary, "John Bulwer, Renaissance Communicationist," *Quarterly Journal of Speech*, 45 (December 1959), 391–8; James R. Knowlson, "The Idea of Gesture as a Universal Language in the XVIIth and XVIIIth Centuries," *Journal of the History of Ideas*, 26 (October – December 1965), 496–7; *Dictionary of National Biography* (London, 1949–50), 3:262–3.

101 Bulwer, *Chirologia*, 108.

102 Ibid., 110, 111.

103 Raymond Williams, *The Country and the City* (New York, 1973), 24.

104 John Wheeler, *A Treatise of Commerce* (1601; facs. reprint New York, 1931), 2–3. Wheeler's treatise, unlike Smith's, opposed free trade.

105 Bulwer, *Chirologia*, sig. a4ᵛ.

106 Ibid., sigs. A–Aᵛ; cf. Bacon, *Advancement of Learning*, in *Works*, 3:368.

107 Bacon, *Advancement of Learning*, in *Works*, 3:399; Bulwer, *Chirologia*, 3–4.

108 John Bulwer, *Pathomyotomia, Or a Dissection of the Significative Muscles of the Affections of the Minde* (London, 1649), sigs. aᵛ–a2.

109 Bulwer, *Chirologia*, 2, 15; *Chironomia: Or, The Art of Manuall Rhetorique. With the Canons, Lawes, Rites, Ordinances, and Institutes of Rhetoricians, both Ancient and Moderne, Touching the artificiall managing of the HAND in Speaking* (London, 1644), 9.

110 Bulwer, *Pathomyotomia*, sigs. A3, A2ᵛ.

111 Ibid., 1–4, 40.

112 Thomas Hobbes, *Leviathan. Or the Matter, Forme and Power of a Commonwealth Ecclesiastical and Civil*, Michael Oakeshott, ed. (New York, 1962), 19.

113 Bulwer, *Pathomyotomia*, sig. A10.

114 Ibid., 30, 36, 34.

115 John Bulwer, *Anthropometamorphosis – Man Transform'd: Or, Artificial Changeling* (London, 1653), sig. *2.

116 Ibid., sig. B3.

117 See, for example, Castiglione, *The Courtyer* (Hoby's translation), 348–9; Guazzo, *Civile Conversation* (Pettie's translation), 2:13; Wright, *Passions of the Minde*, 30, 174–5; Bulwer, *Chirologia*, 23, 110, 157; *Chironomia*, 4, 23, 142. See also discussions in Rosamond Tuve, *Elizabethan and Metaphysical Imagery* (Chicago, 1947), ch. 9; T. McAlindon, *Shakespeare and Decorum* (London, 1973), 1–13; B. L. Joseph, *Elizabethan Acting*, rev. ed. (London, 1954), 8–10, ch. 3.

118 See Cicero, *De Officiis*, 1, 120.

119 Bulwer, *Chironomia*, 24, 143; *Chirologia*, 14, 23; see also H. B. Gardiner, Ruth C. Metcalf, and John G. Beebe-Center, *Feeling and Emotion: A History of Theories* (1937; reprint, Westport, Conn., 1970), 135.

120 Walter J. Ong considers Bacon's *Advancement of Learning*, with its identification of the structure of understanding with that of rhetoric, to be still rooted in oral/aural culture (*The Presence of the Word: Some Prologomena for Cultural and Religious History* [New Haven, Conn., 1967], 237).

121 Wright, *Passions of the Minde*, 29; Bacon, *Advancement of Learning*, in *Works*, 3:279–80.

122 Bulwer, *Chironomia*, 99; Bacon, *Advancement of Learning*, in *Works*, 3:402; Clubb, *Della Porta*, 13–25, 30; Gardiner et. al., *Feeling and Emotion*, 139–40; Frances Yates, *The Art of Memory* (Chicago, 1966), 205–6; Francesco Grillo, *Tommaso Campanella in America* (New York, 1954), 47; Bernadino M. Bonansea, *Tommaso Campanella: Renaissance Pioneer of Modern Thought* (Washington, D.C., 1969), 26–7.

123 James Gaffarel, *Unheard-of Curiosities*, Edmund Chilmead, tr. (London, 1650), 174–6. The account is reproduced by Dugald Stewart in a note to his *Elements of the Philosophy of the Human Mind*, 3 vols. (Philadelphia, 1827), 3:319–20. Another version, taken from *Recherches curieuses d'antiquité* (Lyon, 1683), 358, a work by Jacob Spon, who traveled to Italy on an archeological expedition in 1675–6, is paraphrased by Edmund Burke in *A Philosophical Enquiry into the Origin of Our Ideas of the Sublime and Beautiful*, J. T. Boulton, ed. (1757; reprint London, 1958), 4.4.132–3. It was enshrined as yet another example of the "James–Lange" theory of emotions in William James, *The Principles of Psychology*, 2 vols. (1890; reprint New York, 1950), 2:464.

   See also Kurt Seligman, *The History of Magic* (New York, 1948), 27, 223, 247–8, 298; Lynn Thorndike, *A History of Magic and Experimental Science*, 7 vols. (New York, 1923–58), 7:291–301, 304–9; Robert L. Ellis, Preface to Bacon, *Works*, 1:107–8. For information on Gaffarel, see notices in *Biographie Universelle* (Paris, n.d.), 15:347–8, and in *Nouvelle Biographie Générale* (Paris, 1858), 19:146–7.

124 James George Frazer, *The New Golden Bough*, Theodor H. Gaster, ed. (New York, 1959), 35; cf. Bacon, *Advancement of Learning*, in *Works*, 3:381.

125 Campanella defended Telesio in *F. Thomae Campanellae Philosophia Sensibus Demonstrata* (Naples, 1591) and Galileo in *Apologia pro Galileo* (Frankfurt, 1622). See Neil C. Van Deusen, *Telesio: The First of the Moderns* (New York, 1932), 8 n. 14; Thorndike, *History of Magic*, 7:299–300; Grillo, *Campanella*, 33–4; Bonansea, *Campanella*, 25–7, 49–56, 61–70, 96, 106–15.

126 Bonansea, *Campanella*, 52; the quotation is Bonansea's paraphrase.

127 Bulwer, *Chironomia*, 143.

128 Bulwer, *Anthropometamorphosis*, sigs. ***3ᵛ–***4.

129 Ibid., sig. B3ᵛ. See Margaret T. Hogden, *Early Anthropology in the Sixteenth and Seventeenth Centuries* (Philadelphia, 1964), 128–9; H. J. Norman, "John Bulwer and his *Anthropometamorphosis*," in *Science, Medicine and History: Essays on the Evolution of Scientific Thought and Practice Written in Honour*

of Charles Singer, E. Ashworth Underwood, ed., 2 vols. (London, 1953), 2:81–99.

130 Campanella had actually attacked Machiavelli in print; see Bonansea, *Campanella,* 20, 265. It was Prynne who "in 1659 substituted a slanderous frontispiece and added an equally malicious preface to the reissue of [Campanella's] *De Monarchia Hispanica Discursus,"* written in 1601 and translated, again, by Edmund Chilmead, chaplain of Christ Church. Prynne's title read in part *Thomas Campanella an Italian friar and second Machiavel. His advice to the King of Spain for attaining the universal monarchy of the World. Particularly concerning England, Scotland and Ireland, how to raise division between King and Parliament, to alter the government from a Kingdome to a commonwealth;* Grillo, *Campanella,* 11–15; Raab, *Machiavelli,* 115–16. Chilmead differed with Prynne over Campanella; see notices on Chilmead in *Dictionary of National Biography,* 4:257–8, and on Prynne, ibid., 16:432–7; see also William M. Lamont, *Marginal Prynne 1600–1669* (London, 1963), 141–3.

131 John Hall, *The Advancement of Learning,* A. K. Croston, ed. (Liverpool, 1953), 38, 36.

132 Charles Phythian-Adams argues that part of the urban crisis of the mid-sixteenth century was owing to the rising costs of a ceremonialized marketplace, among them the costs of plays and processions; see his "Urban Decay in Late Medieval England," in *Towns in Society,* Philip Abrams and E. A. Wrigley, eds. (Cambridge, Eng., 1978), 159–85. See also Alan Everitt, "The English Urban Inn, 1560–1760," in *Perspectives in English Urban History* (London, 1973), 91–137. On privatization or "interiorization" within the English household, see Yi-Fu Tuan, "House and Household," in *Segmented Worlds and Self: Group Life and Individual Consciousness* (Minneapolis, 1982), 52–85. On the decay of hospitality, see Felicity Heal, "The Idea of Hospitality in Early Modern England," *Past and Present,* 102 (February 1984), 66–93.

133 W. J. Lawrence, *Speeding Up Shakespeare* (London, 1937), 4–14; see also Andrew Gurr, *The Shakespearean Stage, 1574–1642* (Cambridge, Eng., 1970), 73–4.

134 See listings under "actor" in the *Oxford English Dictionary.*

135 Hobbes, *Leviathan,* ch. 16. On the usage of "personation," see Gurr, *Shakespearean Stage,* 73–4. On Hall's Hobbesianism, see Quentin Skinner, "The Context of Hobbes's Theory of Political Obligation," in *Hobbes and Rousseau,* Richard S. Peters, ed. (Garden City, N.Y., 1972), 127. For a full discussion of Hobbes's analogy between the actor and the political and commercial representative, see Hanna Fenichel Pitkin, *The Concept of Representation* (Berkeley and Los Angeles, 1967), 17–28, 121–2. J. Leeds Barroll makes no reference to Hobbes's usage in his *Artificial Persons: The Formation of Character in the Tragedies of Shakespeare* (Columbia, S.C., 1974), but Jonas Barish does in his perceptive analysis of Puritan antistage polemic; see *The Antitheatrical Prejudice* (Berkeley and Los Angeles, 1981), 155–8.

136 McAlindon, *Shakespeare and Decorum,* 6; see also Frances A. Shirley, *Swearing and Perjury in Shakespeare's Plays* (London, 1979).

137 William Prynne, *Histrio-Mastix, The Players Scovrge, or, Actors Tragedie* (London, 1633), 87.

138 This line of thought is developed in different ways by Barish, *Antitheatrical Prejudice,* by Russell Fraser, *The War Against Poetry* (Princeton, N.J., 1970), and by David Leverenz, *The Language of Puritan Feeling: An Exploration in Literature, Psychology, and Social History* (New Brunswick, N.J., 1980), esp. ch. 1. For a general overview of the Puritan opposition to the stage, see Elbert N. S. Thompson, *The Controversy between the Puritans and the Stage* (New York, 1903); William Ringler, "The First Phase of the Elizabethan Attack on the Stage, 1558–1579," *Huntington Library Quarterly,* 5 (1941–2), 391–418; Edmund S. Morgan, "Puritan Hostility to the Theatre," *Proceedings of the American Philosophical Society,* 110 (October 1966), 340–7.

3. ARTIFICIAL PERSONS

1 Thomas Hobbes, *Leviathan,* Michael Oakeshott, ed. (New York, 1962), 19–20, 125–8. My discussion of Hobbes's views on representation and of the etymology of the word itself draws heavily on Hanna Fenichel Pitkin, *The Concept of Representation* (Berkeley and Los Angeles, 1972), 14–37, 241–52; see also listings under "representation" and "representative" in the *Oxford English Dictionary.* On the concept of the player-king, see James Winny, *The Player King: A Theme of Shakespeare's Histories* (London, 1968).

2 Pitkin, *Concept of Representation,* 23–6; M. C. Bradbrook, *The Rise of the Common Player* (Cambridge, Mass., 1962), 123. Accused of interpolating political statements into his plays, the playwright George Chapman replied, "I see not myne owne Plaies; nor carrie the Actors Tongue in my mouthe"; quoted in Virginia Crocheron Gildersleeve, *Government Regulation of the Elizabethan Drama* (1908; reprint New York, 1961), 106.

3 On the distinction between representation in rituals and presentation in drama, see Mary Gluckman and Max Gluckman, "On Drama, and Games and Athletic Contests," in *Secular Ritual,* Sally F. Moore and Barbara G. Meyerhoff, eds. (Assen/Amsterdam, 1977), 235–7; Northrup Frye, *A Natural Perspective: The Development of Shakespearean Comedy and Romance* (Princeton, N.J., 1965), 59 and passim. On the survival of ritual elements in Elizabethan drama, see Francis Fergusson, *The Idea of a Theatre* (Princeton, N.J., 1949), esp. 116–19; C. L. Barber, *Shakespeare's Festive Comedy: A Study of Dramatic Form and Its Relation to Social Custom* (Princeton, N.J., 1959). Both the Gluckmans (p. 236) and Barber (p. 220) consider later melodrama a more proximate substitute for ritual than Elizabethan comedy.

4 Rhetorical devices are conventions that persuade spectators "to accept characters and situations whose validity is ephemeral and bound to the theatre." Authenticating devices are conventions that actors observe as characters in a play in order to suggest "a total and external code of values and norms of conduct from which the speech and action of the play are drawn" (Elizabeth Burns, *Theatricality: A Study in the Theatre and in Social Life* [New York, 1972], 31–2).

5 V. A. Kolve, *The Play Called Corpus Christi* (Stanford, Calif., 1966), 32; Richard Southern, *The Medieval Theatre in the Round*, 2nd ed. (London, 1975), 80; Richard Axton, "Folk Play in Tudor Interludes," in *English Drama: Forms and Development*, Maria Axton and Raymond Williams, eds. (Cambridge, 1977), 19; Glynne Wickham, *Early English Stages*, 3 vols. (London, 1959–81), 1:272.

6 R. T. Davies, ed., *The Corpus Christi Play of the Middle Ages* (London, 1972), 3–6; David M. Bevington, *From "Mankind" to Marlowe: Growth of Structure in the Popular Drama of Tudor England* (Cambridge, Mass., 1962), 49; William Tydeman, *The Theatre in the Middle Ages* (Cambridge, Eng., 1978), 204.

7 Anne Righter, *Shakespeare and the Idea of the Play* (London, 1962), 20.

8 Bruce Wilshire, *Role Playing and Identity: The Limits of Theatre as Metaphor* (Bloomington, Ind., 1982), 240.

9 Righter, *Idea of the Play*, 28. For a brief overview of the changing spatial arrangements within the theater and of their relation to concepts of self and society, see Yi-Fu Tuan, "Theater and Society," in *Segmented Worlds and Self: Group Life and Individual Consciousness* (Minneapolis, 1982), 86–113.

10 Righter, *Idea of the Play*, 15–29; see also Bradbrook, *Common Player*, ch. 1.

11 Righter, *Idea of the Play*, 29–32; Bradbrook, *Common Player*, 18, 23–32; E. K. Chambers, *The Medieval Stage*, rev. ed., 2 vols. (Oxford, 1943), 2:180–7; Chambers, *The Elizabethan Stage*, 4 vols. (Oxford, 1923), 1:3; Tydeman, *Theatre*, 221.

12 Righter, *Idea of the Play*, 32–42; Bradbrook, *Common Player*, 128–9; Bradbrook, *The Growth and Structure of Elizabethan Comedy* (London, 1955), 14–15.

13 Jackson I. Cope, *The Theater and the Dream: From Metaphor to Form in Renaissance Drama* (Baltimore, 1973), 101–7.

14 T. W. Craik, *The Tudor Interlude* (Leicester, 1958), 3.

15 Stephen Greenblatt, *Renaissance Self-Fashioning: From More to Shakespeare* (Chicago, 1980), 31.

16 Chambers, *Elizabethan Stage*, 1:106–7; Bradbrook, *Common Player*, ch. 2; David M. Bergeron, *English Civic Pageantry, 1588–1642* (London, 1971), ch. 1.

17 Bradbrook, *Common Player*, 282–3; Gildersleeve, *Government Regulation*, 31–2.

18 See, for example, Thomas Lodge, *An Alarum Against Usurers* (London, 1584), 11; see also Lewis Einstein, *The Italian Renaissance in England* (New York, 1902), 60, 75; William Creizenach, *The English Drama in the Age of Shakespeare* (1916; reprint New York, 1964), 64, 91, 144–9; Celeste Turner Wright, "Some Conventions Regarding the Usurer in Elizabethan Literature," *Studies in Philology*, 31 (April 1934), 187–9; Louis B. Wright, *Middle-Class Culture in Elizabethan England* (Chapel Hill, N.C., 1935), 614–28; L. C. Knights, *Drama and Society in the Age of Jonson* (London, 1937), 173–4;

Robert Ashton, "Usury and High Finance in the Age of Shakespeare and Jonson," *Renaissance and Modern Studies*, 4 (1960), 14–53.

19 Bradbrook, *Common Player*, 39–40; see also Chambers, *Elizabethan Stage*, 1:271. John Earle wrote in his "character" of the player: "Hee do's not only personate on the stage, but sometime in the Street, for he is mask'd still in the habit of a Gentleman" (*Micro-cosmographie. Or, A Peece of the World Discovered*, 2nd ed. [London, 1628], sig. E3ᵛ).

20 The construction of the London theaters, Bradbrook suggests, "was almost a form of Enclosure, comparable to the enclosure of the common fields, and even more profitable" (*Common Player*, 41).

21 Ibid., 122–3; Bradbrook, *Themes and Conventions of Elizabethan Tragedy* (1935; reprint Cambridge, Eng., 1974), 24; Righter, *Idea of the Play*, 60–2.

22 Glynne Wickham, *The Medieval Theatre* (London, 1974), 111; Bevington, *Mankind to Marlowe*, 71–3, 114–15, 120–3; Righter, *Idea of the Play*, 36; Victor Oscar Freeburg, *Disguise Plots in Elizabethan Drama: A Study in Stage Tradition* (New York, 1915), 121–37; Robert Potter, *The English Morality Play: Origins, History and Influence of a Dramatic Tradition* (London, 1975), 105–22; Craik, *Tudor Interlude*, 73, 90; Bernard Spivack, *Shakespeare and the Allegory of Evil: The History of a Metaphor in Relation to His Major Villains* (New York, 1958), 213. For an alternative view of the characters of the morality, see Natalie Crohn Schmitt, "The Idea of a Person in Medieval Morality Plays," *Comparative Drama*, 12 (Spring 1978), 22–34.

23 Bevington, *Mankind to Marlowe*, 116–19, 136; R. Axton, "Folk Play," 23.

24 Righter, *Idea of the Play*, 56, 60–2; Bradbrook, *Themes and Conventions*, 124–36; Morris LeRoy Arnold, *The Soliloquies of Shakespeare: A Study in Technic* (New York, 1911), 56–60, 90–7; Doris Fenton, *The Extra-Dramatic Moment in Elizabethan Plays Before 1616* (Philadelphia, 1930).

25 Bradbrook, *Themes and Conventions*, 121–4; David Bain, *Actors and Audience: A Study of Asides and Related Conventions in Greek Drama* (Oxford, 1977). Though Spivack acknowledges the increasing exploitation of these devices, he does not see these uses as substantially altering the older homiletic function of extradramatic address (*Allegory of Evil*, 119, 176–93).

26 See, in this connection, Robert J. Nelson, *Play within a Play, The Dramatist's Conception of His Art: Shakespeare to Anouilh* (New Haven, Conn., 1958), 2–10; Wilshire, *Role Playing*, 61–9; cf. Cope, *Theater and Dream*, 170–2.

27 Victor Turner, "Liminal to Liminoid, in Play, Flow, and Ritual: An Essay in Comparative Symbology," *Rice University Studies*, 60 (Summer 1974), 53–92; Wilshire, *Role Playing*, 6; A. W. Ward, *Shakespeare and the Makers of Virginia* (London, 1919), 10–12; cf. Michael D. Bristol, "Carnival and the Institutions of Theater in Elizabethan England," *ELH*, 50 (Winter 1983), 637–54.

28 Raymond Williams, *The Sociology of Culture* (New York, 1981), 142.

29 Chambers, *Medieval Stage*, 1:63; Chambers, *Elizabethan Stage*, 2:78–83; Bevington, *Mankind to Marlowe*, 13.

30 Wilshire, *Role Playing*, 16, 69–75; Nelson, *Play within a Play*, 17–30; gen-

erally, Thomas F. Van Laan, *Role-playing in Shakespeare* (Toronto, 1978), esp. ch. 9.

31 Jonas Barish, "The Antitheatrical Prejudice," *Critical Inquiry*, 8 (Winter 1960), 331–2; Louis Adrian Montrose, "The Purpose of Playing: Reflections on a Shakespearean Anthropology," *Helios*, 7 (1980), 57, 66; cf. Willard Thorp, *The Triumph of Realism in Elizabethan Drama 1558–1612* (Princeton, N.J., 1938).

32 *Richard II*, act 5, sc. 5, lines 31–2. See Leonard F. Dean, *"Richard II: The State and the Image of the Theater,"* *PMLA*, 67 (March 1952), 211–18; Winny, *Player King*, ch. 2; Stephen J. Greenblatt, *Sir Walter Ralegh: The Renaissance Man and His Roles* (New Haven, Conn., 1973), ch. 2; Righter, *Idea of the Play*, 116–21.

33 Cope, *Theater and Dream*, 107–10. See also Righter, *Idea of the Play*, 51; Chambers, *Elizabethan Stage*, 3:27, 4:30. Chambers dates the interlude to 1562–3.

34 Creizenach, *English Drama*, 221; Chambers, *Elizabethan Stage*, 3:446, 4:32–3.

35 Bradbrook, *Common Player*, 123. See also Harry Berger, Jr.'s discussion of the "second world" in "Theater, Drama, and the Second World," *Comparative Drama*, 2 (Spring 1968), 3–20.

36 Bradbrook, *Themes and Conventions*, 122; Clarence Valentine Boyer, *The Villain as Hero in Elizabethan Tragedy* (London, 1914), 53–7.

37 Erving Goffman, "Role Distance," in *Encounters: Two Studies in the Sociology of Interaction* (Indianapolis, Ind., 1961), 85–152; Alfred B. Harbage, *Shakespeare's Audience* (New York, 1941), 109–12. Harbage downplays the boisterousness of the Elizabethan audience, but William Empson sees the overt theatricality of *Hamlet* as a deliberate strategy to avoid the ridicule his audience would have voiced over the prospect of another stale avenger plot (*"Hamlet* When New," *Sewanee Review*, 61 [1953], 15–42, 185–205).

38 Righter, *Idea of the Play*, 67–70; Bradbrook, *Common Player*, 130.

39 Arnold Williams, *The Characterization of Pilate in the Towneley Plays* (East Lansing, Mich., 1950), 14–16; but cf. Kolve, *Play Called Corpus Christi*, 232–3. See also L. W. Cushman, *The Devil and the Vice in English Dramatic Literature Before Shakespeare* (Halle, 1900), 52–4; Chambers, *Medieval Stage*, 1:203–4; Olive Mary Busby, *Studies in the Development of the Fool in Elizabethan Drama* (1923; reprint, New York, 1973); Robert Withington, "The Ancestry of the 'Vice,' " *Speculum*, 7 (October 1932), 525–9; Withington, "Braggart, Devil, and 'Vice': A Note on the Development of Comic Figures in the Early Elizabethan Drama," ibid., 11 (April 1936), 124–9; Frances H. Mares, "The Origin of the Figure Called 'the Vice' in Tudor Drama," *Huntington Library Quarterly*, 22 (November 1958), 11–29; Spivack, *Allegory of Evil*, 60–205; Peter Happé, "The Vice and the Folk-Drama," *Folklore*, 75 (Autumn 1964), 161–93; Ann Wierum, "'Actors' and 'Play Acting' in the Morality Tradition," *Renaissance Drama*, new ser., 3 (1970), 189–214.

40 Bevington, *Mankind to Marlowe*, 50, 175; Cushman, *Devil and Vice*, 72–3.

41 Bradbrook, *Common Player*, 129; Righter, *Idea of the Play*, 55; Bevington, *Mankind to Marlowe*, 122–3.

42 See, generally, Gildersleeve, *Government Regulation*; William J. Griffin, "Notes on Early Tudor Control of the Stage," *Modern Language Notes*, 58 (January 1943), 50–4.

43 Bradbrook, *Common Player*, 32–46; Chambers, *Elizabethan Stage*, 1:279–91.

44 William Prynne, *Histrio-Mastix, The Players Scovrge, or, Actors Tragedie* (London, 1633), 97.

45 Normand Berlin, *The Base String: The Underworld in Elizabethan Drama* (Rutherford, N.J., 1968), 84; Boyer, *Villain as Hero*, passim; Felix Raab, *The English Face of Machiavelli* (London, 1965), 57–8; Potter, *English Morality Play*, 146–52; Spivack, *Allegory of Evil*, chs. 1, 2, and 12; Stanley Edgar Hyman, *Iago: Some Approaches to the Illusion of His Motivation* (New York, 1970), 27–8; Rainer Pineas, "The Morality Vice in *Volpone*," *Discourse*, 5 (1962), 451–9.

46 *Richard III*, act 3, sc. 1, lines 82–3.

47 For a discussion of the influence of popular preaching on English drama, see G. R. Owst, *Literature and Pulpit in Medieval England*, 2nd ed. (Oxford, 1961), 55n, 478, 523–36. Benjamin Boyce sees the "characters" of Thomas Overbury as owing inspiration in part to his friend Jonson's "humors" (*The Theophrastan Character in England to 1642* [Cambridge, Mass., 1947], 104–5, 138). See also Wendell Clausen, "The Beginning of English Character Writing in the Early Seventeenth Century," *Philological Quarterly*, 25 (May 1946), 32–45. The presence of character types is less visible in Shakespeare, but S. L. Bethell finds some Theophrastan resemblances in *Shakespeare and the Popular Dramatic Tradition* (London, 1949), 78–80.

48 Captain Gainsford, *The Rich Cabnit Furnished with a Variety of Descriptions* (1616), quoted in Elbert N. S. Thompson, *The Controversy Between the Puritans and the Stage*, Yale Studies in English, vol. 20 (New York, 1903), 142, 143.

49 Sir Thomas Overbury, *The Overburian Collection*, W. J. Paylor, ed. (Oxford, 1936), 77. The playwright John Webster is believed (p. xx) to have written the character of "An Excellent Actor" for Overbury in reply to John Stephens's attack on "A Common Player." John Earle's *Micro-cosmographie* also contains a "character" of the actor (sigs. E3–E4ᵛ).

50 On equivocation and the dramatist, see Harriett Hawkins, *Likenesses of Truth in Elizabethan and Restoration Drama* (London, 1972), 159–60. On Jesuit and Puritan associations with equivocation, see George L. Mosse, *The Holy Pretence: A Study of Christianity and Reason of State from William Perkins to John Winthrop* (Oxford, 1957), 45–6; Christopher Hill, *Society and Puritanism in Pre-Revolutionary England* (New York, 1964), 395–6. On the peculiar estatelessness of the player, see Bradbrook, *Common Player*, 40, 188; Montrose, "Purpose of Playing," 55–7.

51 *The Revenge of Bussy D'Ambois*, act 1, sc. 1, lines 342–51, in *Plays and Poems of George Chapman*, Thomas N. Parrott, ed., 4 vols. (London, 1910–14), 1:90. For Chrysostom's views, see *The Homilies of St. John Chrysostom on the Epistle of St. Paul the Apostle to the Romans* (Oxford, 1841), homily

4; *The Homilies of St. John Chrysostom on the Statues, or To the People of Antioch* (Oxford, 1842), homilies 3:11; 15:1, 11; 17:9.

52 Scholars still use John Bulwer's *Chirologia ... Chironomia* (1644) as a guide to Elizabethan acting techniques; see B. L. Josephs, *Elizabethan Acting*, rev. ed. (London, 1964), 6–9 and passim.

53 Jean Jacquot, " 'Le Théâtre du monde'de Shakespear à Calderon," *Revue de littérature comparée*, 31 (July–September 1957), 342–8; Thomas B. Stroup, *Microcosmos: The Shape of the Elizabethan Play* (Lexington, Ky., 1965), 17–18; Harold Fisch, *Hamlet and the Word* (New York, 1971), ch. 9; Greenblatt, *Sir Walter Ralegh*, 44; Willard Farnham, *The Medieval Heritage of Elizabethan Tragedy* (1936; reprint Oxford, 1956), 54–60 and passim; Bridget Gellert Lyons, *Voices of Melancholy* (London, 1971), chs. 3 and 4; Charles K. Cannon, " 'As in a Theater': *Hamlet* in the Light of Calvin's Doctrine of Predestination," *Studies in English Literature*, 11 (Spring 1971), 203–22.

54 Earle, *Micro-cosmographie*, sig. E3^v; see also Bradbrook, *Common Player*, 76.

55 Prynne, *Histrio-Mastix*, 157, 337; Stephen Gosson, *Playes Confuted in Fiue Actions* (London, 1582), sig. G5^v.

56 Prynne, *Histrio-Mastix*, 160.

57 Henry Chettle, *Kind-Hartes Dream* (1592; reprint London, 1923), 55; see also Bradbrook, *Common Player*, ch. 7, esp. 170–1.

58 From the preface to the first edition of *Troilus and Cressida*, quoted in Thompson, *Puritans and Stage*, 229.

59 Thomas Dekker, *The Gulls Horn-Book*, in *The Non-Dramatic Works of Thomas Dekker*, Alexander B. Grosart, ed., 5 vols. (1885; reprint New York, 1963), 2:246–7.

60 *Bartholomew Fair*, in *Ben Jonson*, C. H. Herford and Percy Simpson, eds., 11 vols. (Oxford, 1925–52), 6:15–16. On the individuating effects of Jonson's framing devices on his audience, see Jonathan Haynes, "Festivity and the Dramatic Economy of Jonson's *Bartholomew Fair*," *ELH*, 51 (Winter 1984), 659–62. On the escape clauses that Jonson inserted for himself within the agreement, see Joel H. Kaplan, "Dramatic and Moral Energy in Ben Jonson's *Bartholomew Fair*," *Renaissance Drama*, new ser., 3 (1970), 155–6.

61 Ian Donaldson, *The World Turned Upside Down: Comedy from Jonson to Fielding* (Oxford, 1970), 58–60.

62 Richard Levin, "The Structure of *Bartholomew Fair*," *PMLA*, 80 (June 1965), 176. Kaplan describes Jonson's Smithfield "as something of an ecological unit that thrives only when its visitors arrive to complete a natural cycle of predator and prey" ("Dramatic and Moral Energy," 143); see also Brian Gibbons, *Jacobean City Comedy*, 2nd ed. (London, 1980), 148.

63 On Jonson's anti-Puritan and antiacquisitive ethos, see Knights, *Drama and Society*, 190.

64 See E. A. J. Johnson, *Predecessors of Adam Smith: The Growth of British Economic Thought* (New York, 1937), esp. chs. 3–5; Joyce Oldham Appleby, *Economic Thought and Ideology in Seventeenth-Century England* (Princeton, N.J., 1978), passim.

65 This dimension of Jonson (and his fellow playwrights) is most effectively discussed by Donaldson, *World Upside Down*, ch. 3, and by Susan Wells, "Jacobean City Comedy and the Ideology of the City," *ELH*, 48 (Spring 1981), 37–80.

66 See Henry Farnam, *Shakespeare's Economics* (New Haven, Conn., 1931), 105–7; Knights, *Drama and Society*, 127–30; Wright, "Usurer in Elizabethan Literature"; R. H. Tawney, Introduction to Thomas Wilson, *A Discourse Upon Usury* (1572; reprint London, 1925), 87; cf. Fernand Braudel, *The Wheels of Commerce*, Siân Reynolds, tr. (New York, 1982), ch. 4.

67 *The Merchant of Venice*, act 2, sc. 5, line 37.

68 Lodge, *Alarum Against Usurers*, sig. B3ᵛ. Dekker, in a passage borrowed from Thomas Nashe, pictured Envy as a "long tongue and tooth'd *malevole* (that lookes as desperately on the prosperity of any as your vsurer on a young heire, greedy to deuoure him) . . . but he hath as many shapes besides, as *Proteus* . . . so will hee shift himselfe into severall suites of Apparell" (*Iests to Make You Merrie*, in *Non-Dramatic Works*, 2:304); cf. *Pierce Penilesse His Svpplication to the Diuell*, in *The Works of Thomas Nashe*, Ronald B. McKerrow, ed., 5 vols. (1904–10), 1:183, 186.

69 Quoted from a sermon of 1589 in M. M. Knappen, *Tudor Puritanism* (Chicago, 1939), 419–20.

70 Raab, *English Face of Machiavelli*, 217; see also Ashton, "Usury and High Finance."

71 Georg Simmel, *The Philosophy of Money*, Tom Bottomore and David Frisby, trs. (Boston, 1978), 213, 216, 432.

72 *The Merchant of Venice*, act 3, sc. 1, line 67.

73 See, for example, the induction to Jonson's *The Magnetick Lady: or, Humors Reconcil'd* (1632), which pictured the playhouse as a staple of characters, a "Poetique shop" (line 6) where the audience could purchase any type they wished (*Ben Jonson*, 6:508). Support for this point can also be found in Jonas Barish, *The Antitheatrical Prejudice* (Berkeley and Los Angeles, 1981), 105, 112, 192, and in Wendy Griswold, "The Devil's Techniques: Cultural Legitimation and Social Change," *American Sociological Review*, 48 (October 1983), 668–80.

74 Anthony Munday, *A Second and Third Blast of Retrait from Plaies and Theaters* (1580; facs. reprint New York, 1973), 3; T. McAlindon, *Shakespeare and Decorum* (London, 1973), 17; Robert C. Jones, "Dangerous Sport: The Audience's Engagement with Vice in the Moral Interludes," *Renaissance Drama*, new ser., 6 (1973), 61–4; Barish, *Antitheatrical Prejudice*, 81. After 1580 Munday "changed his copy," according to one contemporary observer, and returned to the writing of plays (Thorp, *Triumph of Realism*, 39n).

75 *Bartholomew Fair*, Induction, 146–7; see also, Montrose, "Purpose of Playing," 62–3. On the triumph of an "actor's theater," see Wickham, *Medieval Theatre*, 192.

76 Knappen, *Tudor Puritanism*, 440; David Leverenz, *The Language of Puritan Feeling: An Exploration in Literature, Psychology, and Social History* (New Brunswick, N.J., 1980), 27.

77 Bevington, *Mankind to Marlowe*, 56; Potter, *English Morality Play*, 94–104.

78 Chambers, *Elizabethan Stage*, 1:242–4; Thompson, *Puritans and Stage*, 48–53, 196; Knappen, *Tudor Puritanism*, 439–440; Harold C. Gardiner, *Mysteries' End: An Investigation of the Medieval Religious Stage* (New Haven, Conn., 1946), chs. 4 and 5.

79 Gosson himself was not a Puritan but a player-playwright turned Anglican divine. See William Ringler, *Stephen Gosson: A Biographical and Critical Study*, Princeton Studies in English, vol. 25 (Princeton, N.J., 1942), 26–8, 80–1; Arthur F. Kinney, *Markets of Bawdrie: The Dramatic Criticism of Stephen Gosson*, Salzburg Studies in English Literature, no. 4 (Salzburg, 1974), 8–9, 151.

80 Bacon quoted in Patrick Collinson, *The Elizabethan Puritan Movement* (London, 1967), 393.

81 Lodge quoted in Edward Meyer, *Machiavelli and the Elizabethan Drama* (Weimar, 1897), 25.

82 Stephen Gosson, *The School of Abuse, Containing a Pleasant Invective Against Poets, Pipers, Players, Jesters &c* (1579; reprint London, 1841), 40, 41.

83 Philip Edwards, *Threshold of a Nation: A Study in English and Irish Drama* (Cambridge, Eng., 1979), 18–25, esp. 24; Charles A. Camp, *The Artisan in Elizabethan Literature* (New York, 1923), 141; Chambers, *Medieval Stage*, 1:381–2; 4:17–19; Alvin Kernan, "John Marston's Play *Histriomastix*," *Modern Language Quarterly*, 19 (June 1958), 134–40.

84 Russell Fraser, *The War Against Poetry* (Princeton, N.J., 1970), 28, 41, 46; Barish, *Antitheatrical Prejudice*, 164.

85 *Richard III*, act 3, sc. 7, lines 133–4; *3 Henry VI*, act 3, sc. 2, lines 184–5; see also Meyer, *Machiavelli*, 58–9.

86 Quoted in Meyer, *Machiavelli*, 44.

87 Philip Stubbes, *The Anatomie of Abuses* (1583; facs. reprint New York, 1973), sig. L4^v.

88 Gosson, *Playes Confuted*, sig. G5^v.

89 Dekker, *Non-Dramatic Works*, 2:247. See also Harbage, *Shakespeare's Audience*, ch. 3; John V. Curry, *Deception in Elizabethan Comedy* (Chicago, 1955), 1, 164.

90 Gosson, *Playes Confuted*, sig. C5. The final portion of this passage was appropriated by the Puritan critic William Rankins in his *Mirrour of Monsters* (1587); see Cope, *Theater and Dream*, 124; Bradbrook, *Common Player*, 72–3; Chambers, *Elizabethan Stage*, 1:254.

91 See, for example, Alice Clark, *The Working Life of Women in the Seventeenth Century* (New York, 1920), 28–9, 51–2, 197–234; Roger Thompson, *Women in Stuart England and America* (London, 1974), 240–4; R. H. Hilton, "Lords, Burgesses and Hucksters," *Past and Present*, 97 (November 1982), 3–15.

92 See, in this connection, Gayle Rubin, "The Traffic in Women: Notes on the 'Political Economy of Sex,' " in *Toward an Anthropology of Women*, Rayna R. Reiter, ed. (New York, 1975), 157–210.

93 Perez Zagorin, *The Court and the Country: The Beginning of the English Revolution* (New York, 1970), 29, 49; Harbage, *Shakespeare's Audience*, 76;

W. T. MacCaffery, "Place and Patronage in Elizabethan Politics," in *Elizabethan Government and Society: Essays Presented to Sir John Neale*, S. T. Bindoff, J. Hurstfield, and C. H. Williams, eds. (London, 1961), 95–126; David Mathew, *The Social Structure of Caroline England* (Oxford, 1948), 6. See also Lawrence Stone, *The Crisis of the Aristocracy, 1558–1641* (Oxford, 1965), esp. 36–9, 57–61, 65–128, 666, 743; Stone, "Social Mobility in England, 1500–1700," in *Society in an Age of Revolution*, Paul S. Seaver, ed. (New York, 1976), 33–4; Thomas Henry Hollingworth, *The Demography of the British Peerage* (London, 1965), 33. The sexual dimensions of social courtship are brilliantly treated in Kenneth Burke, *A Rhetoric of Motives* (1950; reprint Berkeley and Los Angeles, 1969), 115–18.

94 Zagorin, *Court and Country*, 71.
95 On the relation of boundary loss to purificatory social movements, see Mary Douglas, *Purity and Danger: An Analysis of the Concepts of Pollution and Taboo* (London, 1966), esp. chs. 6–8.
96 Stubbes, *Anatomie of Abuses*, sig. F5ᵛ.
97 Edwards, *Threshold of a Nation*, 29; L. B. Wright, *Middle-Class Culture*, 494, 495; *Hic Mulier: Or, The Man-Woman: Being a Medicine to cure the Coltish Disease of the Staggers in the Masculine-Feminines of Our Times* and *Haec-Vir: Or The Womanish-Man: Being an Answere to a late Booke intituled Hic-Mulier* (1620; facs. reprint Exeter, Mass., 1973). See also Leverenz, *Language of Puritan Feeling*, 12, 23–40; Zevedei Barbu, *Problems of Historical Psychology* (London, 1960), 166–8. Michael Walzer (*Revolution of the Saints* [Cambridge, Mass., 1965]) shares with Barbu and Leverenz the view of English Puritanism as a reaction formation, simply put, against social and personal upheavals; though it differs in important respects, my argument is deeply indebted to Walzer's work.
98 *Bartholomew Fair*, act 5, sc. 5, lines 51–105.
99 See, for example, John Rainoldes, William Gager, and Alberico Gentili, *Th'overthrow of Stage Playes* (1599; facs. reprint New York, 1974), 15–18, 33–45, and passim.
100 Leverenz, *Language of Puritan Feeling*, 3, 12, 34–6. There is a striking resemblance between Leverenz's view of the Puritan male and the "symbolic fatherlessness" that Robert Jay Lifton has imputed to his "Protean Man" (*Partisan Review*, 35 [Winter 1968], 18–19).
101 Stubbes complained that the refusal to swear earned a man the suspicion of effeminacy; see discussion in Frances A. Shirley, *Swearing and Perjury in Shakespeare's Plays* (London, 1979), ch. 3.
102 Leverenz, *Language of Puritan Feeling*, 24.
103 Perkins quoted in Barish, *Antitheatrical Prejudice*, 92.
104 See, for example, *Bartholomew Fair*, act 5, sc. 5, lines 84–7.
105 Chettle, *Kind-Hartes Dream*, 42.
106 William Holden, *Anti-Puritan Satire, 1572–1642* (New Haven, Conn., 1954), 41.
107 Thompson, *Puritanism and Stage*, 238; Aaron Michael Myers, *Representation and Misrepresentation of the Puritan in Elizabethan Drama* (Philadelphia, 1931), 92–5, 111–14, 131–2.

108 Gosson, *Playes Confuted*, sig. A8^v.

109 William M. Lamont, *Marginal Prynne, 1600–1669* (London, 1963), 30.

110 Prynne, *Histrio-Mastix*, 816.

111 Ibid., 133.

112 Ibid., 158, 156.

113 See, for example, Earle, *Micro-cosmographie*, sig. E3; Samuel Butler, *Characters*, Charles W. Daves, ed. (Cleveland, 1970), 300; see also listings under "prestige" in the *Oxford English Dictionary*.

114 A. G. H. Bachrach, "The Great Chain of Acting," *Neophilogus*, 33 (April 1949), 166. See also Josephs, *Elizabethan Acting*, v–vii, 17. On rhetorical culture in general, see Walter J. Ong, *The Presence of the Word: Some Prolegomena for Cultural and Religious History* (New Haven, Conn., 1967); Ong, *Orality and Literacy: The Technologizing of the Word* (London, 1982).

115 Thomas Heywood, *An Apology for Actors* (1612; reprint London, 1841), 29.

116 Ibid., 12, 57–60; A. D. J. Macfarlane, *Witchcraft in Tudor and Stuart England* (New York, 1970), 122, 124–6; Keith Thomas, *Religion and the Decline of Magic* (New York, 1971), 117, 212–18; Lynn Thorndike, *A History of Magic and Experimental Science*, 7 vols. (New York, 1923–58), 6:502. For an insightful discussion of the way in which Puritan theology assimilated older notions of magical possession and divination into its own vision of divine and patriarchal power (thus sensitizing it to putatively rival claims), see Ann Kibbey, "Mutations of the Supernatural: Witchcraft, Remarkable Providences, and the Power of Puritan Men," *American Quarterly*, 34 (Summer 1982), 125–48.

117 Munday was renamed Antonio Balladino in *The Case is Altered* (ca. 1599); Jones was called Iniquo Vitruvious in *Love's Welcome at Bolsover* (1634). See Frances Yates, *The Theatre of the World* (Chicago, 1969), 88. Jonson's own sensitivity to drama à clef occasioned the famous "War of the Theaters" of 1599–1601. See also Una Ellis-Fermor, *The Jacobean Drama: An Interpretation*, rev. ed. (New York, 1964), 313–15; Nashe, *Works*, 5:34–65, 184–92.

118 Frank Aydelotte, *Elizabethan Rogues and Vagabonds* (1913; reprint New York, 1967), 74.

119 Chambers, *Elizabethan Stage*, 1:292; Bethell, *Shakespeare*, 132.

120 William Haller, *The Rise of Puritanism* (New York, 1938), 31–3; see also Edmund S. Morgan, "Puritan Hostility to the Theatre," *Proceedings of the American Philosophical Society*, 110 (October 1966), 340–7.

121 Prynne, *Histrio-Mastix*, 39; Richard Sibbes quoted in Haller, *Rise of Puritanism*, 125.

122 Macfarlane, *Witchcraft*, 106.

123 Gosson, *Playes Confuted*, sigs. G6^v–G7^v; cf. William Perkins, "A Treatise of the Vocations or Callings of Men," in *The Work of William Perkins*, Ian Breward, ed. (Appleford, Eng., 1970), 446–76.

124 Gosson, *Playes Confuted*, sig. G7^v.

125 Perkins, "Treatise of Vocations," 455–6.

126 Gosson, *Playes Confuted*, sig. F8; cf. Thomas Wright, *The Passions of the Minde in Generall* (1604; facs. reprint Urbana, Ill., 1971), 17, 86, where he opposes the mortification of the passions.

127 Carl D. Schneider, *Shame, Exposure and Privacy* (Boston, 1977), 16, 24–6, 38; Helen Merrell Lynd, *On Shame and the Search for Identity* (New York, 1958), 21, 31, 35–6, 47.

128 Hill, *Society and Puritanism*, 510. C. L. Barber found a similar degeneration in the aristocratic counterideal of honor during the Restoration (*The Idea of Honour in the English Drama, 1591–1700*, Gothenburg Studies in English, vol. 6 [Göteburg, 1957], 136 and passim). But cf. Curtis Brown Watson, *Shakespeare and the Renaissance Concept of Honor* (Princeton, N.J., 1960); Henri Peyre, *Literature and Sincerity* (New Haven, Conn., 1963), ch. 1; Lionel Trilling, *Sincerity and Authenticity* (Cambridge, Mass., 1972), 12–25; Leon Guilhamet, *The Sincere Ideal: Studies on Sincerity in Eighteenth-Century Literature* (Montreal, 1974), 1–9, 27.

129 Douglas, *Purity and Danger*, 162, 136; see also Kenneth Burke's discussion of the paradox of purity in *A Grammar of Motives* (1945; reprint Berkeley and Los Angeles, 1969), 35–8.

130 Perkins, *Work*, 382–3.

131 Quoted in Mosse, *Holy Pretence*, 61.

132 Perkins, *Work*, 405; Perry Miller, *The New England Mind: From Colony to Province*, (Cambridge, Mass., 1953), 69.

133 Christopher Hill, "Protestantism and the Rise of Capitalism," in *Change and Continuity in Seventeenth-Century England* (London, 1974), 86–7; Barish, *Antitheatrical Prejudice*, 95–6.

134 Miller, *New England Mind: Colony to Province*, 69; Miller, *The New England Mind: The Seventeenth Century* (1939; reprint Cambridge, Mass., 1954), 375. For a revision of Miller's views on covenant theology, see Norman Petit, *The Heart Prepared: Grace and Conversion in Puritan Spiritual Life* (New Haven, Conn., 1966). For a discussion of the problems and chronology of the doctrine of visible sainthood, see Edmund S. Morgan, *Visible Saints: The History of a Puritan Idea* (Ithaca, N.Y., 1963).

135 Bernard Williams, "Deciding to Believe," in *Problems of the Self: Philosophical Papers 1956–1972* (Cambridge, Eng., 1973), 147.

136 Butler, *Characters*, 51–2.

137 Miller, *New England Mind: Colony to Province*, 69.

138 Perkins, *Work*, 347; Cicero, *De Oratore*, 3.57; cf. John Bulwer, *Chirologia: or the Naturall Language of the Hand* ... (London, 1644), 23.

139 Perkins, *Work*, 348; Nashe quoted in Holden, *Anti-Puritan Satire*, 55.

140 Bishop John Jewell quoted in Collinson, *Elizabethan Puritan Movement*, 34.

141 Hill, *Society and Puritanism*, 61–2, 98–9; Collinson, *Elizabethan Puritan Movement*, 275, 320; Cornelius Walford, *Fairs, Past and Present* (London, 1883), 200–1.

142 Haller, *Rise of Puritanism*, 128.

143 Hill, *Society and Puritanism*, 45–6.

144 Perkins, "A Faithful and Plain Exposition upon Zephaniah 2.1–2," in *Work*, 300.

145 Butler, *Characters*, 53. On the image of the Puritan as usurer, see Paul N. Siegel, "Shylock and the Puritan Usurers," in *Studies in Shakespeare*, A. D. Mathews and C. M. Emery, eds. (Coral Gables, Fla., 1953), 187–9; cf. Charles H. George, "English Calvinist Opinion on Usury, 1600–1640," *Journal of the History of Ideas*, 18 (1957), 462–71.

146 James I quoted in Donaldson, *World Upside Down*, 75.

147 Butler, *Characters*, 45; see also Butler's "characters" of a Fifth Monarchy Man and A Silenc'd Presbyterian, 79–81, 312–13.

148 Barish, *Antitheatrical Prejudice*, 85; see the third listing under "solstice" in the *Oxford English Dictionary*.

149 On pilgrimages as liminal experiences, see Victor Turner, "Pilgrimages as Social Processes," in *Dramas, Fields, and Metaphors: Symbolic Action in Human Society* (Ithaca, N.Y., 1974), 166–230. On the Presbyterian baptism, see H. Clay Trumbull, *The Threshold Covenant* (New York, 1896), 137.

150 Victor Turner describes the status of participants in liminal rituals as that of androgynous beings who are "dead to the world"; see his "Variations on a Theme of Liminality," in *Secular Ritual*, Moore and Meyerhoff, eds., 37. For some examples of the carnivalesque aspects of the Reformation, see Bob Scribner, "Reformation, Carnival and the World Turned Upside Down," *Social History*, 3 (October 1978), 303–29; generally, Christopher Hill, *The World Turned Upside Down: Radical Ideas During the Revolution* (New York, 1972).

151 Hill, *Society and Puritanism*, 257; Miller, *New England Mind: Seventeenth Century*, 68–81.

152 Perkins, *Work*, 447; Cotton quoted in Miller, *New England Mind: Seventeenth Century*, 79; see Walzer, *Revolution of Saints*, ch. 6.

153 Walter J. Ong, "Ramist Method and the Commercial Mind," in *Rhetoric, Romance, and Technology: Studies in the Interaction of Expression and Culture* (Ithaca, N.Y., 1971), 189.

154 See listings under "purchase" and "factory" in the *Oxford English Dictionary*.

155 Gildersleeve, *Government Regulation*, 222–3; Leslie Hotson, *The Commonwealth and Restoration Stage* (Cambridge, Mass., 1928), chs. 1 and 2.

156 Stroup, *Microcosmos*, 21–2; Prynne, *Histrio-Mastix*, 31.

157 Joseph De La Vega, *Confusion De Confusiones* (1688; reprint Boston, 1957), 14, 16. See Fernand Braudel, *The Wheels of Commerce*, Siân Reynolds, tr. (New York, 1982), 395; Violet Barbour, *Capitalism in Amsterdam in the Seventeenth Century*, Johns Hopkins University Studies in Historical and Political Science, vol. 67 (Baltimore, 1949), 78–9.

158 Michael Long, *The Unnatural Scene: A Study of Shakespearean Tragedy* (London, 1976), 51; Righter, *Idea of the Play*, 171 (emphasis added); but cf. Robert Egan, *Drama within Drama: Shakespeare's Sense of His Art* (New York, 1975), 14, 112–18.

159 Righter, *Idea of the Play*, 181, 203–5.

160 Frances Yates, *Shakespeare's Last Plays: A New Approach* (London, 1975), ch. 4. See also Arthur O. Lovejoy, *The Great Chain of Being: A Study of the History of an Idea* (Cambridge, Mass., 1936), 101–2; Richard Southern, *The Open Stage* (London, 1953).

161 Gildersleeve, *Government Regulation*, 217–18; Harbage, *Shakespeare's Audience*, 60, 81–2, 107; Hotson, *Commonwealth Stage*, 90.

162 Wickham, *Early English Stages*, 2:93–5. On the dominating presence of the Elizabethan gentry at both public and private theaters, see Ann Jennalie Cook, *The Privileged Playgoers of Shakespeare's London* (Princeton, N.J., 1981).

163 Wickham, *Early English Stages*, 2:237; Bergeron, *English Civic Pageantry*, ch. 2; Sheila Williams, "The Lord Mayor's Show in Tudor and Stuart Times," *Guildhall Miscellany*, 10 (September 1959), 3–18; Theodore B. Leinwand, "London Triumphing: The Jacobean Lord Mayor's Show," *Clio*, 2 (Winter 1982), 137–53. On the relation of the merchant magistrates to the crown, see Valerie Pearl, *London and the Outbreak of the Puritan Revolution: City Government and National Politics 1625–1641* (Oxford, 1961); Robert Brenner, "The Civil War Politics of London's Merchant Community," *Past and Present*, 58 (February 1973), 53–107; Robert Ashton, *The City and the Court 1603–1643* (Cambridge, Eng., 1979), esp. chs. 3 and 4.

164 Pamphlet quoted in Hotson, *Commonwealth Stage*, 42. Thomas Rymer (1641–1713) was the first to have used the phrase "poetic justice," though the concept dates to Plato; see M. A. Quinlan, *Poetic Justice in the Drama* (Notre Dame, Ind., 1912).

165 For the promissory or negotiable perspective on role behavior, see Erving Goffman, *The Presentation of Self in Everyday Life* (Garden City, N.Y., 1959), 1–16; David J. De Levita, *The Concept of Identity*, Ian Finlay, tr. (Paris, 1965), 98, 131–2. On the shift from honor-based to credit-based ideas of identity, see Peter L. Berger, Brigitte Berger, and Hansfried Kellner, "On the Obsolescence of the Concept of Honor," in *The Homeless Mind: Modernization and Consciousness* (Garden City, N.Y., 1973), 83–96; Pat O'Malley, "From Feudal Honour to Bourgeois Reputation: Ideology, Law and the Rise of Industrial Capitalism," *Sociology*, 15 (February 1981), 79–93.

166 Yates, *Theatre of the World*, 27–32, 86; Stephen Orgel, *The Illusion of Power: Political Theater in the English Renaissance* (Berkeley and Los Angeles, 1975), 55–6; Chambers, *Elizabethan Stage*, 1:107; Jonson, "An Expostulation with Inigo Jones," in *Ben Jonson*, 7:413–14.

167 Yates, *Theatre of the World*, 78.

168 Bergeron, *English Civic Pageantry*, 5, 74–5, 105–8; Stroup, *Microcosmos*, 98; Orgel, *Illusion of Power*, 50, 53–5.

169 See Robert Weimann, "Le Declin de la scène "indivisible" Elisabethaine: Beaumont, Fletcher et Heywood," in *Dramaturgie et société: Rapports entre l'oeuvre théâtrale, son interpretation et son public aux XVIe et XVIIe siècles*, Jean Jacquot, ed., 2 vols. (Paris, 1968), 2:815–27; L. B. Wright, *Middle-*

Class Culture, 615–54; Stroup, *Microcosmos*, 78–86; Ellis-Fermor, *Jacobean Drama*, 277–80.

170 Jonson, "An Expostulation," 414.

171 A "machine" meant either a military or stage device in the early seventeenth century; see Yates, *Theatre of the World*, 85. John Bulwer uses "scenical" in this fashion in *Chironomia*, 103; Raymond Williams credits William Cowper with introducing this usage of "scenery," in *The Country and the City* (New York, 1973), 125–6. Such usage of theatrical terminology was in distinction to the meaning of "theater" as a catalogue or inventory of natural phenomena, as in John Parkinson's *Theatricum Botanicum* (1640), Elias Ashmole's *Theatricum Chemicum Britanicum* (1652), or the more well known *Theatrum-Mundi* (1566?) of Boaistuau. See L. B. Wright, *Middle-Class Culture*, 555, 577, 593, also 146n, 460–1, 319, 573n; J. B. Jackson, "Landscape as Theatre," in *The Necessity for Ruins* (Amherst, Mass., 1980), 67–75.

172 Orgel, *Illusion of Power*, 20. For a history of the evolution of these framing devices, see George B. Kernodle, *From Art to Theatre: Form and Convention in the Renaissance* (Chicago, 1944).

173 Bevington, *Mankind to Marlowe*, 112; Maria Axton, "The Tudor Mask and Elizabethan Court Drama," in *English Drama*, Axton and Williams, eds., 26.

174 Stephen Orgel, *The Jonsonian Masque* (Cambridge, Mass., 1965), 8–14; Orgel, *Illusion of Power*, 40; Bachrach, "Great Chain of Acting," 162. See, for example, Thomas Hoby, tr., *The Courtyer of Count Baldessar Castilio* (1561; reprint New York, 1967), 348–9; Lodge, *Alarum*, sig. D^v; cf. the discussion of decorum, stage-illusion, and the "speechless tradition" in late seventeenth- and eighteenth-century French theater in Frederick Brown, *Theater and Revolution: The Culture of the French Stage* (New York, 1980), ch. 2. On the antistage tradition in France, see Moses Baras, *The Stage Controversy in France from Corneille to Rousseau* (1933; reprint New York, 1973); Henry Phillips, *The Theatre and Its Critics in Seventeenth-Century France* (Oxford, 1980).

4. THE SPECTACLE OF THE MARKET

1 Elizabeth quoted in J. E. Neale, *Elizabeth I and Her Parliaments*, 2 vols. (New York, 1958), 2:119; John Winthrop, "A Modell of Christian Charity," *The Winthrop Papers*, 5 vols. (Boston, 1929–47), 2:294–5.

2 Hugh F. Rankin, *The Theater in Colonial America* (Chapel Hill, N.C., 1965), 92–6, 189–90; see also Arthur Hornblow, *A History of the Theater in America*, 2 vols. (Philadelphia, 1919), 1:21–65.

3 Royall Tyler, *The Contrast: A Comedy* (New York, 1970).

4 Bernard Bailyn, *The New England Merchants in the Seventeenth Century* (New York, 1955), 13, 20, 134–42, 168–92; Darrett B. Rutman, *Winthrop's Boston* (Chapel Hill, N.C., 1965), 180–90; G. B. Warden, *Boston 1689–1776* (Boston, 1970), 48–57, 76–7, 106–7; E. A. J. Johnson, *American Economic Thought in the Seventeenth Century* (London, 1932), 7–9, 14–19, 121–36, 143–4.

5 Jon C. Teaford, *The Municipal Revolution in America: Origins of Modern Urban Government 1650–1825* (Chicago, 1975), 16–44; Gary B. Nash, *The Urban Crucible: Social Change, Political Consciousness, and the Origins of the American Revolution* (Cambridge, Mass., 1979), 32, 129–36. For a useful history of early public markets, see Thomas F. De Voe, *The Market Book*, 2 vols. (1862; reprint New York, 1969). Barbara Clark Smith sees the eighteenth-century campaign to establish a public regulated market in Boston as an effort to remove exchange relations from the "moral economy" that the city's hucksters and their customers had developed in the streets and squares. In this light, the city itself appears to be a traditional open (but not free) market and the public market proposal an extension of the concept of the private shop or store, very much like what is found today in Boston's Quincy Market ("Markets, Streets, and Stores: Contested Terrain in Eighteenth Century Boston," unpublished paper, 1984).

6 J. E. Crowley draws the connection between religious and secular awakenings as responses to the threat of commercialization in *This Sheba, Self: The Conceptualization of Economic Life in Eighteenth-Century America* (Baltimore, 1974), ch. 5. Case studies supporting this view included Richard L. Bushman, *From Puritan to Yankee: Character and the Social Order in Connecticut, 1690–1765* (Cambridge, Mass., 1967); Stephen Nissenbaum and Paul Boyer, *Salem Possessed* (Cambridge, Mass., 1975); but cf. Stephen Innes, *Labor in a New Land: Economy and Society in Seventeenth-Century Springfield* (Princeton, N.J., 1983), xviii–ix, 137–8, and passim.

7 See Michael Zuckerman, "The Fabrication of Identity in Early America," *William & Mary Quarterly*, 3rd ser., 34 (April 1977), 183–214.

8 Teaford, *Municipal Revolution*, 47–78; Eric Foner, *Tom Paine and Revolutionary America* (New York, 1976), 145–82; James A. Henretta, *The Evolution of American Society, 1700–1815* (Lexington, Mass., 1973), 182–4; David Grimsted, *Melodrama Unveiled: American Theater and Culture, 1800–1850* (Chicago, 1968), ch. 3; Hornblow, *Theater in America*, 1:299–326. It is interesting that British troops turned the marketplace in Faneuil Hall into a temporary theater during the occupation.

9 Leslie Hotson, *The Commonwealth and Restoration Stage* (Cambridge, Mass., 1928), chs. 4–8; Sybil Rosenfeld, *Strolling Players and Drama in the Provinces 1660–1765* (Cambridge, Eng., 1939); Rosenfeld, *The Theater of the London Fairs in the 18th Century* (Cambridge, Eng., 1960).

10 M. C. Bradbrook, *English Dramatic Form: A History of Its Development* (New York, 1965), 16; Raymond Williams, *The Sociology of Culture* (New York, 1981), 156; Robert D. Hume, *The Development of English Drama in the Late Seventeenth Century* (Oxford, 1976), 490.

11 Dane Farnsworth Smith, *Plays About the Theatre in England from The Rehearsal in 1671 to the Licensing Act in 1737* (London, 1936), xi; Raymond Williams, *The Long Revolution*, rev. ed. (New York, 1965), 257.

12 See, in this regard, Allardyce Nicoll, *The Garrick Stage: Theatres and Audience in the Eighteenth Century*, Sybil Rosenfeld, ed. (Athens, Ga., 1980), 9–15; Ronald Paulson, "Life as Journey and as Theater: Two Eighteenth-

Century Narrative Structures," *New Literary History*, 7 (Autumn 1976), 43–58; Mary Klinger, "William Hogarth and London Theatrical Life," *Studies in Eighteenth-Century Culture*, 5 (1976), 11–27; Leo Hughes, "Theatrical Convention in Richardson: Some Observations on a Novelist's Technique," in *Restoration and Eighteenth-Century Literature: Essays in Honor of Alan Dugald McKillop*, Carroll Camden, ed. (Chicago, 1963), 239–50; Michael Fried, *Absorption and Theatricality: Painting and Beholder in the Age of Diderot* (Berkeley, 1980), chs. 2 and 3.

13 On the fundamentally conservative nature of dramatic and nondramatic satire, see John Loftis, *The Politics of Drama in Augustan England* (Oxford, 1963), 154–61; Stuart M. Tave, *The Amiable Humorist: A Study in the Comic Theory and Criticism of the Eighteenth and Early Nineteenth Centuries* (Chicago, 1960); Jacob Viner, "Satire and Economics in the Augustan Age of Satire," in *The Augustan Milieu: Essays Presented to Louis A. Landa*, Henry Knight Miller, Eric Rothstein, and G. S. Rousseau, eds. (Oxford, 1970), 77–101. On the number of plays about theater, see Smith, *Plays About the Theatre*, 241.

14 Williams, *Sociology of Culture*, 157.

15 Jonas Barish, "The Antitheatrical Prejudice," *Critical Inquiry*, 8 (Winter 1960), 331–2.

16 Richard Sennett, *The Fall of Public Man* (New York, 1977), 39–41 and passim; see also Donald Fleming, "Attitude: the History of a Concept," *Perspectives in American History*, 1 (1967), 287–365.

17 E. P. Thompson, "Patrician Society, Plebeian Culture," *Journal of Social History*, 7 (Summer 1974), 390; J. H. Plumb, *The Growth of Political Stability in England 1675–1725* (London, 1967); W. A. Speck, *Stability and Strife: England, 1714–1760* (Cambridge, Mass., 1977), ch. 5.

18 Thompson, "Patrician Society," 389; R. W. Malcolmson, *Life and Labour in England 1700–1780* (London, 1981), 101–35, 149–52.

19 Thompson, "Patrician Society," 360; see, in this connection, the contributions of Thompson, Douglas Hay, Peter Linebaugh, John G. Rule, and Cal Winslow to *Albion's Fatal Tree: Crime and Society in Eighteenth-Century England* (New York, 1975) and to John Brewer and John Styles, eds., *An Ungovernable People: The English People and Their Law in the Seventeenth and Eighteenth Centuries* (New Brunswick, N.J., 1980).

20 Thompson dates the consolidation to the 1790s ("Patrician Society," 403); Speck, to the 1760s (*Stability and Strife*, 3, 146–7); see also E. P. Thompson, "Eighteenth-Century English Society: Class Struggle without Class?" *Social History*, 3 (May 1978), 155.

21 On agricultural developments, see Eric Kerridge, *The Agricultural Revolution* (London, 1967); E. L. Jones, "Agriculture and Economic Growth in England, 1660–1750: Agricultural Change," *Journal of Economic History*, 25 (March 1965), 1–18; A. H. John, "Agricultural Productivity and Economic Growth in England, 1700–1760," ibid., 19–34; Sidney Pollard and David W. Crossley, *The Wealth of Britain, 1085–1966* (London, 1968), 125–34, 155–63. On mercantilist policy, see Joyce Oldham Appleby, *Economic*

Thought and Ideology in Seventeenth Century England (Princeton, N.J., 1978), ch. 9.

22 T. S. Ashton, *Economic Fluctuations in England 1700–1800* (Oxford, 1959), 27–48, 106–37; D. W. Jones, "London Merchants and the Crisis of the 1690s," in *Crisis and Order in English Towns 1500–1700*, Peter Clark and Paul Slack, eds. (London, 1972), 311–55; Appleby, *Economic Thought*, 260–7.

23 Appleby, *Economic Thought*, 269–70, 276; Speck, *Stability and Strife*, 57; cf. Jacob Viner, *The Role of Providence in the Social Order* (Princeton, N.J., 1976), ch. 3.

24 P. G. M. Dickson, *The Financial Revolution in England: A Study in the Development of Public Credit, 1688–1756* (London, 1967), 32–3; J. G. A. Pocock, "The Mobility of Property and the Rise of Eighteenth-Century Sociology," in *Theories of Property: Aristotle to the Present*, Anthony Parel and Thomas Flanagan, eds. (Waterloo, Ont., 1979), 149.

25 R. D. Richards, *The Early History of Banking in England* (London, 1929), chs. 5, 6, and 8; J. G. A. Pocock, *The Machiavellian Moment: Florentine Political Thought and the Atlantic Republican Tradition* (Princeton, N.J., 1975), 425–6; Pocock, "Mobility of Property," 147–9; Dickson, *Financial Revolution*.

26 See listings under "speculation" in the *Oxford English Dictionary*.

27 J. G. A. Pocock, "Modes of Political and Historical Time in Early Eighteenth-Century England," in *Studies in Eighteenth-Century Culture*, 5 (1976), 97, 99; Pocock, "Mobility of Property," 151–2.

28 See Samuel Johnson, "Preface to Shakespeare" (1765), in *Johnson on Shakespeare*, Arthur Sherbo, ed., 2 vols. (New Haven, Conn., 1968), 1:77–8; Allardyce Nicoll, *The Theatre and Dramatic Theory* (London, 1962), 23–4; R. D. Stock, *Samuel Johnson and Neoclassical Dramatic Theory: The Intellectual Context of the Preface to Shakespeare* (Lincoln, Neb., 1973), 89–100. On the underlying bonds of Britain's Court and Country factions, see Paul Lucas, "A Note on the Comparative Study of the Structure of Politics in Mid-Eighteenth Century Britain and Its American Colonies," *William & Mary Quarterly*, 3rd ser., 28 (April 1971), 301–9.

29 Henry Fielding, *The History of Tom Jones, A Foundling* (New York, 1965), bk. 7, ch. 1, 273; see Maximillien E. Novak, introduction to *English Literature in the Age of Disguise* (Berkeley, 1977), 1–14.

30 Gordon S. Wood, "Conspiracy and the Paranoid Style: Causality and Deceit in the Eighteenth Century," *William & Mary Quarterly*, 3rd ser., 39 (July 1982), 407.

31 Susie I. Tucker, *Protean Shape: A Study in Eighteenth-Century Vocabulary and Usage* (London, 1967), 81; see also listings under "cabal" in the *Oxford English Dictionary*. The names of the councilors were Clifford, Arlington, Buckingham, Ashley, and Lauderdale.

32 Wood, "Conspiracy," 409–10; on earlier Machiavellianism, see Felix Raab, *The English Face of Machiavelli* (London, 1965); but cf. Thomas L. Haskell, "Capitalism and the Origins of the Humanitarian Sensibility," *American Historical Review*, 90 (April 1985), 339–61 and (June 1985) 547–66.

33 Wood, "Conspiracy," 411.

34 An estimated 1.7 percent of London's population attended its theaters during Garrick's time, in contrast to an estimated 13 percent during Shakespeare's epoch. See Henry William Pedicord, *The Theatrical Public in the Time of Garrick* (New York, 1954), 14–17; Alfred Harbage, *Shakespeare's Audience* (New York, 1941), 41. For the impact of the Licensing Act on drama and the novel, see Loftis, *Politics of Drama*, ch. 6. On the shift from stage to print and the growth of a reading public, see Williams, *Long Revolution*, 262–4; John Loftis, *Comedy and Society from Congreve to Fielding* (Stanford, Calif., 1959), 136–7; Ian Watt, *The Rise of the Novel: Studies in Defoe, Richardson and Fielding* (Berkeley and Los Angeles, 1957), 35–59. On Grub Street, see Pat Rogers, *Hacks and Dunces: Pope, Swift and Grub Street* (London, 1980).

35 Louis Dudek, *Literature and the Press* (Toronto, 1960), 30; Laurence Hanson, *Government and the Press 1695–1763* (London, 1936), 36–83; but on the effect of Walpole's indifference to literary patronage, see Bertrand A. Goldgar, *Walpole and the Wits: The Relation of Politics to Literature, 1722–1742* (Lincoln, Neb., 1976).

36 Anthony, Earl of Shaftesbury, "A Letter Concerning Enthusiasm" (1707), in *Characteristics of Men, Manners, Opinions, Times,* John M. Robertson, ed., 2 vols. (1711; reprint Indianapolis, 1964), 1:10, 37, 39. Shaftesbury was one of the first lay writers to give "enthusiasm" a positive and secular meaning; see Susie I. Tucker, *Enthusiasm: A Study in Semantic Change* (Cambridge, Eng., 1972), 21, 132, 162–5.

37 Shaftesbury, *"Sensus Communis;* An Essay on the Freedom of Wit and Humour" (1709), in *Characteristics,* 1:45, 85.

38 Shaftesbury, *"Soliloquy* or Advice to an Author" (1710) in *Characteristics,* 1:123.

39 Ibid., 1:105.

40 Ibid., 1:109.

41 Ibid., 1:128–9, 131.

42 Paulson, "Life as Journey," 46.

43 Shaftesbury, *"Sensus Communis,"* 1:45–6; Shaftesbury, *"Soliloquy,"* 1:122.

44 Shaftesbury, *"Soliloquy,"* 1:124.

45 Ibid., 1:206–7.

46 Ibid., 1:113–14, 183.

47 Ibid., 1:123.

48 My argument here follows closely the analysis of Shaftesbury's ambivalence toward the printed book that can be found in the first section of David Marshall's *Figure of Theater: Shaftesbury, Defoe, Adam Smith, and George Eliot* (New York, 1986). Here and throughout this chapter, I am indebted to his readings of the theatrical dimensions of eighteenth-century literature, some of which were developed and refined in an interdisciplinary seminar we taught together at Yale University in 1982.

49 Shaftesbury, "Miscellaneous Reflections on the preceding Treatises, etc." (1711), in *Characteristics,* 2:168, 163.

50 Ibid., 2:197.
51 Ibid., 2:198.
52 Ibid.
53 See A. S. Collins, *Authorship in the Days of Johnson* (London, 1927), chs. 3 and 4; Phoebe Sheavyn, *The Literary Profession in the Elizabethan Age,* 2nd ed. (Manchester, 1967), 85, 162; Marjorie Plant, *The English Book Trade: An Economic History of the Making and Sale of Books,* 2nd ed. (London, 1965), 68–9, 73–9; Elizabeth L. Eisenstein, *The Printing Press as an Agent of Change* (Cambridge, Eng., 1979), 156–9; Diane Laurenson, "The Writer and Society," in Diane Laurenson and Alan Swingewood, eds., *The Sociology of Literature* (New York, 1972), 91–140.
54 Shaftesbury, *"Soliloquy,"* 1:165.
55 Ibid., 1:131.
56 Shaftesbury, "Miscellaneous Reflections," 2:167.
57 Shaftesbury, *"Soliloquy,"* 1:131.
58 Ibid., 1:172–3.
59 Ibid., 1:109.
60 Shaftesbury, "Letter Concerning Enthusiasm," 1:9. On the importance of subscriptions to the book trade in general, see Dudek, *Literature and Press,* 32–3; Plant, *English Book Trade,* 227–32.
61 Shaftesbury, *"Soliloquy,"* 1:131.
62 Ibid., 1:132.
63 On the distinction between "audience" as a collective noun and "readership" as an abstraction and the corresponding efforts of authors to "fictionalize" their readers, see Walter J. Ong, "The Writer's Audience Is Always a Fiction," in *Interfaces of the Word: Studies in the Evolution of Consciousness and Culture* (Ithaca, N.Y., 1977), 53–81; John Preston, *The Created Self: The Reader's Role in Eighteenth-Century Fiction* (London, 1970).
64 Cecil Price, *Theatre in the Age of Garrick* (London, 1973), 84–5; Sennett, *Public Man,* 80.
65 On the theme of natural affections, see Shaftesbury, "An Inquiry Concerning Virtue or Merit" (1710), in *Characteristics,* 1:293–316.
66 J. H. Plumb, "The *Spectator,*" in *In the Light of History* (Boston, 1973), 52–6.
67 Collins, *Authorship,* 232–59; J. H. Plumb, "The Public, Literature and the Arts in the 18th Century," in *The Triumph of Culture: 18th Century Perspectives,* Paul Fritz and David Williams, eds. (Toronto, 1972), 27–48; Plumb, *The Commercialization of Leisure in Eighteenth-century England* (Reading, Eng., 1974); Dorothy Davis, *A History of Shopping* (London, 1966), chs. 8–11; Neil McKendrick, John Brewer, and J. H. Plumb, *The Birth of a Consumer Society* (Bloomington, Ind., 1982); Chandra Mukerji, *From Graven Images: Patterns of Modern Materialism* (New York, 1983), chs. 5–7.
68 Robert Donald Spector, "The *Connoisseur:* A Study of the Functions of a Persona," in *English Writers of the Eighteenth Century,* John H. Middendorf, ed. (New York, 1971), 109–21; see also listings under "connoisseur" in the *Oxford English Dictionary.*

69 See listings under "taste" in the *Oxford English Dictionary* and in Raymond Williams, *Keywords: A Vocabulary of Culture and Society* (New York, 1976), 264–6. See also Arnold Hauser, *The Social History of Art*, Stanley Codman, tr., 4 vols. (New York, 1951), 3:38–84; David Daiches, "Literature and Social Mobility," in *Aspects of History and Class Consciousness*, Istvan Meszáros, ed. (New York, 1972), 160–1; James H. Bunn, "The Aesthetics of Mercantilism," *New Literary History*, 11 (Winter 1980), 311–13. For a discussion of "taste" in the Enlightenment, see Walter Jackson Bate, *From Classic to Romantic: Premises of Taste in Eighteenth-Century England* (Cambridge, Mass., 1946); Ernst Cassirer, *The Philosophy of the Enlightenment*, Fritz C. A. Koelln and James P. Pettegrove, trs. (Princeton, N.J., 1951), 297–311; Peter Gay, *The Enlightenment: an Interpretation*, 2 vols. (New York, 1966–9), 2:290–318.

70 *The Spectator*, Donald F. Bond, ed., 5 vols. (Oxford, 1965), no. 219; all references will be to issue number.

71 Ibid.

72 Ibid., no. 10.

73 Shaftesbury, *"Sensus Communis,"* 153.

74 James Arbuckle on Shaftesbury quoted in J. T. Boulton's introduction to Edmund Burke, *A Philosophical Enquiry into the Origin of Our Ideas of the Sublime and Beautiful* (London, 1958), lxvi; *Spectator*, no. 10. On Addison and Steele and the invention of journalistic intimacy, see Ong, "Writer's Audience," 66–7.

75 Thomas Dekker, *The Gulls Horn-Book* (1609), E. D. Pendry, ed. (Cambridge, Mass., 1968), 73; *Spectator*, no. 10.

76 *Spectator*, no. 10.

77 Ibid., no. 1.

78 Ibid.

79 Ibid.

80 Ibid.

81 Ibid. On the use of literary personae in the eighteenth century, see Irwin Ehrenpreis, "Personae," in *Restoration and Eighteenth-Century Literature*, Camden, ed., 25–37; Howard D. Weinbrot, "Masked Men and Satire and Pope: Toward a Historical Basis for the Eighteenth-Century Persona," *Eighteenth-Century Studies*, 16 (Spring 1983), 265–89.

82 For an overview, see S. A. Grave, *The Scottish Philosophy of Common Sense* (Oxford, 1960). Because of Smith's stress on sentiment, he does not belong, strictly speaking, to the Common Sense school of thought; still, his affinities with the school were strong in other respects, and his economic theory formed part of its nineteenth-century bulwark.

83 Pocock, "Mobility of Property," 47.

84 On changing concepts of honor and gentility, see W. Lee Ustick, "Changing Ideals of Aristocratic Character and Conduct in Seventeenth Century England," *Modern Philology*, 30 (November 1932), 147–66; C. L. Barber, *The Idea of Honour in Restoration Drama*, Göthenburg Studies in English, vol. 6 (Göteburg, 1957); George C. Brauer, Jr., *The Education of a Gentleman*

(New York, 1959), 51–103; Lawrence Stone, *The Crisis of the Aristocracy, 1558–1641* (Oxford, 1965), 23–6, 29–30; Pocock, *Machiavellian Moment,* 439–40, 465–6; Michael Shinagel, *Daniel Defoe and Middle-Class Gentility* (Cambridge, Mass., 1968), ch. 11; Pat O'Malley, "From Feudal Honour to Bourgeois Reputation: Ideology, Law and the Rise of Industrial Capitalism," *Sociology,* 15 (February 1981), 79–93.

85 John Houghton quoted in Richards, *Banking in England,* 206; see H. J. Habakkuk, "English Landownership 1650–1740," *Economic History Review,* 10 (1940), 1–17; cf. Jones, "London Merchants," 334–6; B. A. Holderness, *Pre-Industrial England: Economy and Society 1500–1750* (London, 1976), 42–3.

86 *Spectator,* no. 69. On the eighteenth-century view of "le doux commerce," see Edward A. Bloom and Lillian D. Bloom, *Joseph Addison's Sociable Animal* (Providence, R.I., 1971), 65; Albert O. Hirschman, *The Passions and the Interests: Political Arguments for Capitalism before Its Triumph* (Princeton, N.J., 1977), 56–66; J. Moore, "Comment on Pocock," in *Theories of Property,* Parel and Flanagan, eds., 67–77.

87 Adam Smith, *An Inquiry into the Nature and Causes of the Wealth of Nations,* Edwin Cannan, ed. (New York, 1937), bk. 1, ch. 2, 14.

88 Ibid., bk. 4, ch. 2, 423.

89 On the emergence of the idea of a separate "economic" or market sphere, see Karl Polanyi, *The Great Transformation* (1944; reprint Boston, 1957), ch. 10; Louis Dumont, *From Mandeville to Marx: The Genesis and Triumph of Economic Ideology* (Chicago, 1977).

90 On Smith's narrowing of the scope of human motivation, see Hirschman, *Passions and Interests,* 107–13.

91 The debate on the "Adam Smith Problem" is briefly recapitulated in the editorial introduction to *The Theory of Moral Sentiments,* D. D. Raphael and A. L. Macfie, eds. (Oxford, 1976), 20–25; all further references to this work are from this edition.

92 Ibid., 9.

93 Ibid., 10.

94 Ibid.

95 Ibid., 116.

96 Ibid., 320; see also 159.

97 For helpful surveys on the "sentimentalist" tradition, see Louis I. Bredvold, *The Natural History of Sensibility* (Detroit, 1962), esp. 11–19; R. S. Crane, "Suggestions Toward a Genealogy of the 'Man of Feeling,' " in *Backgrounds to Eighteenth-Century Literature,* Kathleen Williams, ed. (Scranton, Pa., 1971), 322–49; Norman S. Fiering, "Irresistible Compassion: An Aspect of Eighteenth-Century Sympathy and Humanitarianism," *Journal of the History of Ideas,* 36 (April – June 1976), 195–218; John B. Radner, "The Art of Sympathy in Eighteenth-Century British Moral Thought," *Studies in Eighteenth-Century Culture,* 9 (1979), 189–210. See also W. L. Taylor, *Francis Hutcheson and David Hume as Predecessors of Adam Smith* (Durham, N.C., 1965); Robert Boyden Lamb, "Adam Smith's System: Sympathy not Self-Interest," *Jour-*

nal of the History of Ideas, 35 (October – December 1974), 671–82; A. W. Coats, "Adam Smith's Conception of Self-Interest in Economic and Political Affairs," *History of Political Economy*, 7 (Spring 1975), 132–6; R. H. Coase, "Adam Smith's Views of Man," *Journal of Law and Economics*, 19 (October 1976), 529–46.

98 Smith, *Theory of Moral Sentiments*, 9; see T. D. Campbell, *Adam Smith's Science of Morals* (London, 1971), 94–6; Philip Mercer, *Sympathy and Ethics* (Oxford, 1972), 85–97; Patricia Spence, "Sympathy and Propriety in Adam Smith's Rhetoric," *Quarterly Journal of Speech*, 60 (February 1974), 94; Thomas Wilson, "Sympathy and Self-Interest," in *The Market and the State: Essays in Honour of Adam Smith*, Thomas Wilson and Andrew Skinner, eds. (Oxford, 1976), 73–99; Fiering, "Irresistible Compassion," 210–12.

99 Smith, *Theory of Moral Sentiments*, 9. For useful treatments of the concepts of sympathy, see Mercer, *Sympathy and Ethics*; Max Scheler, *The Nature of Sympathy*, Peter Heath, tr. (New Haven, Conn., 1954), esp. pt. I.

100 Smith, *Theory of Moral Sentiments*, 222.

101 Ibid., 205.

102 Ibid., 183.

103 See, in this connection, Nathan Rosenberg, "Adam Smith, Consumer Tastes, and Economic Growth," *Journal of Political Economy*, 77 (May – June 1968), 361–74; but see also J. Ralph Lindgren, *The Social Philosophy of Adam Smith* (The Hague, 1973), 79–84; Robert L. Heilbroner, "The Paradox of Progress: Decline and Decay in *The Wealth of Nations*," in *Essays on Adam Smith*, Andrew S. Skinner and Thomas Wilson, eds. (Oxford, 1975), 524–39.

104 See Hiroshi Mizuta, "Moral Philosophy and Civil Society," in *Essays on Adam Smith*, Skinner and Wilson, eds., 122. Images of pillories and scaffolds abound in the *Theory* as examples of isolation and mortification; there is little sense of the occasional bond felt between crowds and criminals as occurred, for example, when Defoe was pilloried for one of his satires; see John Robert Moore, *Defoe in the Pillory and Other Studies* (Bloomington, Ind., 1939), 5–6; Shinagel, *Defoe and Gentility*, 58–69.

105 Smith, *Theory of Moral Sentiments*, 21–2.

106 Ibid., 405. "The consideration of fortune has taken up all our minds and, as I have often complained, poverty and riches stand in our imaginations in the places of guilt and innocence" (*Spectator*, no. 294).

107 Smith, *Theory of Moral Sentiments*, 5.

108 Ibid., 13.

109 Ibid., 50. Lindgren sees Smith's theory as anticipating Thorstein Veblen's concept of "pecuniary emulation" (*Social Philosophy*, 103). A more direct instance of Smith's influence on American social thought is Albion W. Small's *Adam Smith and Modern Sociology* (Chicago, 1907); see also Walter Nord, "Adam Smith and Contemporary Social Exchange Theory," *American Journal of Economics and Sociology*, 32 (October 1973), 421–36.

110 On the aspects of Hobbesianism in Smith, see Hirschman, *Passions and Interests*, 108–9, and Joseph Cropsey, *Polity and Economy: An Interpretation*

of the Principles of Adam Smith (The Hague, 1957), 27–30, 72, though Hirschman and Cropsey differ in their conclusions.

111 The most recent formulation of this perspective on social relations, though it makes no mention of Smith, is Charles Derber's *The Pursuit of Attention: Power and Individualism in Everyday Life* (New York, 1979). The same notion of attention (or access to it) as a commodity can be found in current mass-marketing theory; see, for example, Dallas W. Smythe, "Communications: Blindspot of Western Marxism," *Canadian Journal of Political and Social Theory*, 1 (Fall 1977), 1–27; Bill Livant, "The Audience Commodity: On the 'Blindspot' Debate," in ibid., 3 (Winter 1979), 91–105.

112 Credit, Charles Davenant wrote in 1698, "very much resembles, and, in many instances, is near akin to that fame or reputation which men obtain by wisdom in governing state affairs, or by valour and conduct in the field"; quoted in Pocock, *Machiavellian Moment*, 440.

113 See, for example, Thomas Hobbes, *Leviathan*, Michael Oakeshott, ed. (New York, 1962), ch. 10.

114 Smith, *Theory of Moral Sentiments*, 317.

115 Ibid., 22.

116 Smith's theory thus mimicked the move toward "natural" (i.e., less declamatory) acting within the theater of his time. See Price, *Age of Garrick*, 6–42, esp. 27; Alan S. Downer, "Nature to Advantage Dressed: Eighteenth-Century Acting," *PMLA*, 58 (December 1943), 1002–37; Walter Jackson Bate, "The Sympathetic Imagination in Eighteenth-Century English Criticism," *ELH*, 12 (March 1945), 144–64; Earl R. Wasserman, "The Sympathetic Imagination in Eighteenth-Century Theories of Acting," *Journal of English and Germanic Philology*, 46 (July 1947), 264–72; George Taylor, " 'The Just Deliberation of the Passions': Theories of Acting in the Age of Garrick," in *Essays on the Eighteenth-Century English Stage*, Kenneth Richards and Peter Thomson, eds. (London, 1972), 51–72.

117 The theatrical doubling of the self in Smith is set forth in detail in David Marshall, "Adam Smith and the Theatricality of Moral Sentiments," *Critical Inquiry*, 10 (June 1984), 592–613. As noted above, I am indebted to his insights into the subtleties of textual theatricality.

118 Smith, *Theory of Moral Sentiments*, 159; David A. Riesman, *Adam Smith's Sociological Economics* (London, 1976), 115; see also Dorothy Emmett, *Rules, Roles and Relations* (Boston, 1975), ch. 7.

119 Smith, *Theory of Moral Sentiments*, 113–34. Most of Smith's additions to later editions of the *Theory* focused on praiseworthiness and the impartial spectator – a response to those critics who felt too much weight had been placed on the quest for praise alone, apart from merit. For the genealogy and character of Smith's "impartial spectator," see A. L. Macfie, *The Individual and Society: Papers on Adam Smith* (London, 1967), 42–105; D. D. Raphael, "The Impartial Spectator," in *Essays on Adam Smith*, Skinner and Wilson, eds., 83–99.

120 Smith, *Theory of Moral Sentiments*, 153–4.

121 The "invisible hand" does occur in the *Theory* (pp. 183–5), but, as Macfie notes, "the impartial spectator in fact makes no appearance in the *Wealth of Nations*. He there becomes the impersonal market" (*Individual and Society*, 104). On Smith's functionalism, see Louis Schneider, "Adam Smith on Human Nature and Social Circumstance," in *Adam Smith and Modern Political Economy*, Gerald P. O'Driscoll, Jr., ed. (Ames, Iowa, 1979), 44–67. See also R. Anspach, "The Implications of *The Theory of Moral Sentiments* for Adam Smith's Economic Thought," *History of Political Economy*, 4 (Spring 1972), 176–206.

122 Smith, *Theory of Moral Sentiments*, 86; see William D. Grampp, "Adam Smith and Economic Man," *Journal of Political Economy*, 56 (August 1948), 315–36.

123 William Rose and Edmund Burke quoted by D. D. Raphael and A. L. Macfie in their introduction to *The Theory of Moral Sentiments*, 27, 28.

124 R. F. Brissenden, "Authority, Guilt, and Anxiety in *The Theory of Moral Sentiments*," *Texas Studies in Literature and Language*, 11 (Summer 1969), 945–62.

125 Raphael and Macfie, Introduction to *Theory of Moral Sentiments*, 25–32; Plumb, "Public, Literature and Arts," 32; Robert E. Spiller et al., *Literary History of the United States*, 3rd ed. (New York, 1963), 19.

126 *The Political Writings of John Adams*, George A. Peek, Jr., ed. (Indianapolis, Ind., 1954), 175–94.

127 Though *The Theory of Moral Sentiments* was a deliberate ideological creation, it displays some of the unconscious elements that Fredric Jameson attributes to the "ideologeme" – an "amphibious formation" that poses "an imaginary resolution of the objective contradictions to which it thus constitutes an active response" (*The Political Unconscious: Narrative as a Socially Symbolic Act* [Ithaca, N.Y., 1981], 87, 118).

128 Smith, *Theory of Moral Sentiments*, 47, 140. Smith used the words "affected" and "sentimental" in the second through fifth editions, "hypocritical" in the first and last editions.

129 Ann Douglas, *The Feminization of American Culture* (New York, 1977), 307; see also Paul E. Parnell, "The Sentimental Mask," *PMLA*, 77 (December 1963), 529–35.

130 J. H. Plumb, "Henry Fielding and the Rise of the Novel," in *Light of History*, 37–51; Loftis, *Comedy and Society*, 136–7; Lennard J. Davis, *Factual Fictions: The Origins of the English Novel* (New York, 1983), ch. 3. See also Marshall, *Figure of Theater*; Robert Alter, *Partial Magic: The Novel as a Self-Conscious Genre* (Berkeley, 1975).

131 Daniel Defoe, *The Fortunes and Misfortunes of the Famous Moll Flanders*, Juliet Mitchell, ed. (Harmondsworth, Eng., 1978), 28.

132 Ibid., 28–9. On the market in Defoe's work, see Hans H. Andersen, "The Paradox of Trade and Morality in Defoe," *Modern Philology*, 39 (August

1941), 23–46; Maximillien E. Novak, *Economics and the Fiction of Daniel Defoe* (Berkeley, 1962), ch. 3; Lois A. Chaber, "Matriarchal Mirror: Women and Capitalism in Moll Flanders," *PMLA*, 97 (March 1982), 212–26. The absence of sentiment in Defoe is treated in Benjamin Boyce, "The Question of Emotion in Defoe," *Studies in Philology*, 50 (January 1953), 45–58; Theodore Baird, "The World Turned Upside Down," *American Scholar*, 27 (Spring 1958), 215–33. On Defoe's own literary and biographical impostures, see E. Anthony James, *Daniel Defoe's Many Voices: A Rhetorical Study of Prose Style and Literary Method* (Amsterdam, 1972). On the implication of the reader in the intimacies of the text, see Preston, *Created Self*, 8–37; John J. Richetti, *Defoe's Narratives: Situations and Structures* (Oxford, 1975), 105.

133 See Barbara Babcocki-Adams, "The Novel and the Carnival World," *MLN*, 89 (December 1974), 911–37; Terry Castle, "The Carnivalization of Eighteenth-Century Narrative," *PMLA*, 99 (October 1984), 903–16.

134 Defoe, *Moll Flanders*, 30.

135 Pedicord, *Theatrical Public*, 40–1.

136 Jean-Jacques Rousseau, *Politics and the Arts: Letter to M. D'Alembert*, Allan Bloom, tr. (Ithaca, N.Y., 1968), 79.

137 See the discussion of Rousseau in Jonas Barish, *The Antitheatrical Prejudice* (Berkeley and Los Angeles, 1981), ch. 9.

138 Rousseau, *Letter to D'Alembert*, 16–17, 21, 47–9, 57; John Witherspoon, *A Serious Enquiry into the Nature and Effects of the Stage* (Glasgow, 1757), 18–19, 24, 43, 45.

139 Ibid., 53–4.

140 Rousseau, *Letter to D'Alembert*, 16–17, 98, 126–9.

141 Witherspoon, *Serious Enquiry*, 15.

142 Terence Martin, *The Instructed Vision: Scottish Common Sense Philosophy and the Origins of American Fiction* (Bloomington, Ind., 1961), 5–6. According to Martin, Witherspoon's students included 13 eventual college presidents, 114 clergymen, 6 members of the Continental Congress, 20 U.S. Senators, 24 Representatives, 13 governors, 3 Supreme Court justices, and, it may be added, 1 president – Madison. See also William Charvat, *The Origins of American Critical Thought, 1810–1835* (Philadelphia, 1936), chs. 2 and 3; John Clive and Bernard Bailyn, "England's Cultural Provinces: Scotland and America," *William & Mary Quarterly*, 3rd ser., 11 (April 1954), 200–13; Richard J. Petersen, "Scottish Common Sense in America, 1768–1850: An Evaluation of Its Influence" (Ph.D. diss. American University, 1964); D. H. Meyer, *The Instructed Conscience: The Shaping of the American National Ethic* (Philadelphia, 1972); Douglas Sloan, *The Scottish Enlightenment and the American College Ideal* (New York, 1971); Henry F. May, *The Enlightenment in America* (New York, 1976), 341–50; Garry Wills, *Inventing America: Jefferson's Declaration of Independence* (New York, 1978); Wills, *Explaining America: The Federalist* (Garden City, N.Y., 1981); but cf. Ronald Hamony, "Jefferson and the Scottish Enlightenment: A Critique of Garry Wills' *Inventing America*," *William & Mary Quarterly*, 3rd ser., 36 (October 1979), 503–23.

143 On Puritanism and Ramism, see Walter J. Ong, *Ramus: Method and the Decay of Dialogue* (Cambridge, Mass., 1958).

144 See Michael Merrill, "Cash is Good to Eat: Self-Sufficiency and Exchange in the Rural Economy of the United States," *Radical History Review*, 3 (Winter 1977), 42–71; James A. Henretta, "Families and Farms: Mentalité in Pre-Industrial America," *William & Mary Quarterly*, 3rd ser., 35 (January 1978), 3–32; Christopher Clark, "Household Economy, Market Exchange and the Rise of Capitalism in the Connecticut Valley, 1800–1860," *Journal of Social History*, 13 (Winter 1979), 169–89; Smith, "Markets, Streets, and Stores"; Rona S. Weiss, "Primitive Accumulation in the United States: The Interaction Between Capitalist and Non-Capitalist Class Relations in Seventeenth-Century Massachusetts," *Journal of Economic History*, 42 (March 1982), 77–82; but cf. Winifred B. Rothenberg, "The Market and Massachusetts Farmers, 1750–1855," ibid., 41 (June 1981), 288–314; comment by Weiss, ibid., 43 (June 1983), 473–8.

145 For example, see Ralph Lerner, "Commerce and Character: The Anglo-American as New-Model Man," *William & Mary Quarterly*, 3rd ser., 36 (January 1979), 3–26; Sean Wilentz, *Chants Democratic: New York City and the Rise of the American Working Class, 1788–1850* (New York, 1984).

146 *The Autobiography of Benjamin Franklin*, Leonard W. Labaree, ed. (New Haven, Conn., 1964), 58, 61–3, 70.

147 Max Weber, *The Protestant Ethic and the Spirit of Capitalism*, Talcott Parsons, tr. (1930; reprint New York, 1958); R. H. Tawney, *Religion and the Rise of Capitalism* (New York, 1926); Barish, *Antitheatrical Prejudice*, 116–17.

EPILOGUE: CONFIDENCE AND CULTURE

1 Both Warwick Wadlington and Gary Lindberg discuss the liminal and trickster aspects of *The Confidence-Man*, though their conclusions differ from one another and from those of this study; see Wadlington, *The Confidence Game in American Literature* (Princeton, N.J., 1975), ix–x, 5–23; Lindberg, *The Confidence Man in American Literature* (New York, 1982), 3–11. See also Karen Halttunen, *Confidence Men and Painted Women: A Study of Middle-Class Culture in America, 1830–1870* (New Haven, Conn., 1982).

2 Ralph Waldo Emerson to Lidian Emerson, June 16, 1850, *Selections from Ralph Waldo Emerson*, Stephen E. Whicher, ed. (Boston, 1957), 321–2.

3 Herman Melville, *The Confidence-Man: His Masquerade*, Elizabeth S. Foster, ed. (New York, 1954), 1, 7, 15.

4 Michael Paul Rogin, *Subversive Genealogy: The Politics and Art of Herman Melville* (New York, 1983), 241–3.

5 Melville, *The Confidence-Man*, 3, 86, 76, 206.

6 Ibid., 35.

7 See Wai-chee Sung Dimock, "Herman Melville: Authorship and Audience" (Ph.D. diss. Yale University, 1982), ch. 6.

8 See Neil Harris's discussion of the "operational aesthetic" in *Humbug: The*

Art of P.T. Barnum (Boston, 1973), ch. 3. Merlin Bowen, "Tactics of Indirection in Melville's *The Confidence-Man*," *Studies in the Novel*, 1 (Winter 1969), 401–20.

9 At one point the confidence man is accused of punning "with ideas as another man might pun with words" (Melville, *Confidence-Man*, 141).

10 Ibid., 227–8.

11 Ibid., 8. On the historical and literary sources of Melville's characters, see Edward H. Rosenberry, "Melville's Ship of Fools," *PMLA,*75 (1960), 604–8; Paul Smith, *"The Confidence-Man* and the Literary World of New York," *Nineteenth-Century Fiction*, 16 (March 1962), 329–37; Johannes Dietrich-Bergmann, "The Original Confidence Man," *American Quarterly*, 21 (Fall 1969), 561–77; Tom Quirk, *Melville's Confidence Man: From Knave to Knight* (Columbia, Mo., 1982).

12 Melville, *The Confidence-Man*, 148. One contemporary reviewer referred to the novel as a "Rabelesian piece of patchwork without any of the Rabelesian indecency"; quoted in Hugh W. Hetherington, *Melville's Reviewers, British and American, 1846–1891* (Chapel Hill, N.C., 1961), 256.

13 Dimock, "Herman Melville," 261. See also R. W. B. Lewis's afterword to the Signet edition of *The Confidence-Man* (New York, 1968), 264–5; Cecilia Tichi, "Melville's Craft and Theme of Language Debased in *The Confidence-Man*," *ELH*, 39 (December 1972), 639–58; Henry Sussman, "The Deconstructor as Politician: Melville's *Confidence-Man*," *Glyph*, 4 (1978), 32–56; Marc Shell, *Money, Language, and Thought: Literary and Philosophical Economics from the Medieval to the Modern Era* (Berkeley, 1982), 181, 187. On language as a "salable commodity" in the antebellum era, see Suzan Kuhlman, *Knave, Fool, and Genius: The Confidence Man as He Appears in Nineteenth-Century American Fiction* (Chapel Hill, N.C., 1973), 50–7.

14 Melville, *The Confidence-Man*, 122.

15 Karl Marx, *Capital: A Critique of Political Economy*, Samuel Moore and Edward Aveling, trs., Frederick Engels, ed., 3 vols. (1867–1894; reprint New York, 1967), 1:52, 74. "The possibility . . . of quantitative incongruity between price and magnitude of value," Marx wrote in 1867, "is inherent in the price-form itself. This is no defect," he added, " . . . but, on the contrary, admirably adapts the price-form to a mode of production whose inherent laws impose themselves only as the mean of apparently lawless irregularities that compensate one another" (ibid., 1:102).

16 Melville, *The Confidence-Man*, 286.

17 Hume quoted in Ernest C. Mossner, *The Forgotten Hume* (New York, 1947), 4; unsigned critic in the *New York Dispatch*, April 15, 1857, quoted in *Melville: The Critical Heritage*, Watson G. Branch, ed. (London, 1974), 369; see also pp. 36–8.

Index

"act," changing definition of, 98
Act for the Advancement of true Religion
    (Bale), 125
"actor," changing definition of, 98
actors, 99, 103, 105–6, 117–18, 122, 124,
    144; adaptations by, to new social con-
    ditions of Renaissance England, 104–5,
    106–11, 112, 114; attacks on, by Puri-
    tans, 100, 116–17, 118, 124–6, 127–8,
    130, 133, 134, 135–6, 142; in court
    masques, 146–48; debates of, with Pu-
    ritans, 125–8, 130–3, 135–6; as objects
    of suspicion, 13, 66, 96, 128–9, 194;
    social status of, 103–4, 106–8, 133–4,
    147–8
Adams, John, 186
Addison, Joseph, 169–74, 175–6, 182,
    184, 193
Advancement of Learning, The (Bacon), 84
advice manuals, 82, 83, 93; *see* self-help
    manuals
Albumazar (Tomkis), 72
All for Money, 108
Alleyn, Edward, 55
Anatomie of Abuses, The (Stubbes), 74
Anthropometamorphosis (Bulwer), 92–3,
    96, 130, 145
Apology for Actors, An (Heywood), 134
Appleby, Joyce, 2, 156, 176
Aristotle, 4, 21, 22, 25, 42, 44, 55, 84
Astrologo (Della Porta), 72
Augustine, Saint, 15
Autolycus, 21
Awdeley, John, 64, 199

Bachrach, A. G. H., 134
Bacon, Francis, 41, 79, 80, 81, 83, 84–5,
    89, 91, 93, 94, 95, 126
Bakhtin, Mikhail, 36, 59–60, 67, 200
Bale, John, 125
Ball, John, 32
Barber, Bernard, 1–2
Barclay, Alexander, 62–3

Barish, Jonas, 111, 154
Bartholomew Fair, 47, 88, 139, 200
Bartholomew Fair (Jonson), 119–21, 130,
    189
Basilikon Doron (James I), 140
Bentham, Jeremy, 3
Bevington, David, 109
Blunt, Nicholas, 65
Bolton, J. L., 28
Book of the Courtyer, The (trans. of *Il libro
    del Cortegiano*), 75–6, 77
Bosch, Hieronymous, 61–2
Boston, 149–50
Bradbrook, Muriel C., 115, 153
Brandt, Sebastian, 61
Brathwaite, Richard, 79
Braudel, Fernand, 49
Breughel, Pieter, 35–6
Brown, Norman O., 20
Browne, John, 81
Bulwer, John, 87–8, 89–90, 91–3, 94, 95–
    6, 100, 130, 144, 145, 199
Bunyan, John, 143, 199
Burbage, Cuthbert, 55
Burbage Theater, 115
Burke, Edmund, 186
Burton, William, 121–2
Butler, Joseph, 174, 184
Butler, Samuel, 101, 140, 141, 162

Cade, Jack, 55
Caliban, 148
Calvin, John, 118, 125
Campanella, Tomasso, 94–5
carnival, 34, 35, 36, 60, 111, 131, 136,
    200, 201
Casaubon, Isaac, 74
Castiglione, Baldesar, 75–6
Caveat for Common Cursitors (Harmon),
    64
Chandler, Frank, 64
Chapman, George, 117